MW01503122

THE DEADLY LIFE OF LOGISTICS

The Deadly Life of Logistics

MAPPING VIOLENCE IN GLOBAL TRADE

Deborah Cowen

University of Minnesota Press
Minneapolis
London

Published by the University of Minnesota Press
111 Third Avenue South, Suite 290
Minneapolis, MN 55401–2520
http://www.upress.umn.edu

Library of Congress Cataloging-in-Publication Data

Cowen, Deborah.
   The deadly life of logistics: mapping the violence of global trade / Deborah Cowen.
      Includes bibliographical references and index.
   ISBN 978-0-8166-8087-0 (hc: alk. paper)
   ISBN 978-0-8166-8088-7 (pb: alk. paper)
   1. Transportation corridors—Political aspects. 2. Business logistics—
Political aspects. 3. Trade routes—Security measures. 4. Freight and
freightage—Security measures. 5. Cargo theft. 6. Piracy. 7. International
trade—Political aspects. I. Title.

   HE323.C69 2014
   388'.044—dc23   2014002042

Printed in the United States of America on acid-free paper

The University of Minnesota is an equal-opportunity educator and employer.

20 19 18 17 16 15 14   10 9 8 7 6 5 4 3 2 1

CONTENTS

AFTA	ASEAN Free Trade Area
APEC	Asia Pacific Economic Cooperation
APGCI	Asia Pacific Gateway and Corridor Initiative
ASEAN	Association of Southeast Asian Nations
BDSM	bondage, discipline, dominance, submission, sadism, masochism
CBP	Customs and Border Protection (USA)
CGPCS	Contact Group on Piracy off the Coast of Somalia
COSCO	China Ocean Shipping Company
CSI	Container Security Initiative
CTF	Command Task Force
C-TPAT	Customs-Trade Partnership against Terrorism
DHS	Department of Homeland Security (USA)
DLC	Dubai Logistics City
DP	Dubai Ports
ERP	enterprise resource planning
EU NAVFOR	European Union Naval Force
GGLC	Global Gateway Logistics City
GVGC	Greater Vancouver Gateway Council
ICS	International Chamber of Shipping

ILWU	International Longshore and Warehouse Union
IMB	International Maritime Bureau
IMO	International Maritime Organization (UN)
IRTC	International Recommended Transit Corridor
ISPS	International Ship and Port Facility Security
ITF	International Transport Federation
JIT	just-in-time
LMI	Logistics Management Institute
LPI	Logistics Performance Index (World Bank)
MCLI	Maputo Corridor Logistics Initiative
MSIC	Marine Security Identity Card (Australia)
MTSCP	Marine Transport Security Clearance Program (Canada)
NAFTA	North American Free Trade Agreement
NASCO	North America's SuperCorridor Coalition
OECD	Organisation for Economic Co-operation and Development
PIP	Partnership in Protection
SCS	supply chain security
TC	Transport Canada
TEU	twenty-foot equivalent unit
TFN	Tsawwassen First Nation
TWIC	Transportation Workers Identification Credential
UAE	United Arab Emirates
UNEP	United Nations Environment Programme
UNSCR	United Nations Security Council Resolution
UPS	United Parcel Service
VNCI	Vietnam Competitive Initiative
WFP	World Food Programme (UN)
WTO	World Trade Organization

The Citizenship of Stuff in the Global Social Factory

Sneakers may still be easier to order online than smart bombs, but the industry that brings us both is making it increasingly difficult to discern the art of war from the science of business. Today, war and trade are both animated by the supply chain—they are organized by it and take its form. At stake is not simply the privatization of warfare or the militarization of corporate supply chains. With logistics comes new kinds of crises, new paradigms of security, new uses of law, new logics of killing, and a new map of the world. For many, *logistics* may only register as a word on the side of the trucks that magically bring online orders only hours after purchase or that circulate incessantly to and from big-box stores at local power centers. The entire network of infrastructures, technologies, spaces, workers, and violence that makes the circulation of stuff possible remains tucked out of sight for those who engage with logistics only as consumers. Yet, alongside billions of commodities, the management of global supply chains imports elaborate transactions into the socius—transactions that are political, financial, legal, and often martial.

With the rise of global supply chains, even the simplest purchase relies on the calibration of an astonishing cast of characters, multiple circulations of capital, and complex movements across great distances. Take the seeming simplicity of a child's doll purchased at a suburban shopping mall. We can trace its production to places like Guangdong, China, where dolls are packed into containers in large numbers, loaded onto trucks in the local Industrial Development Area, and transferred onto ships in the port of Zhongshan. Many of these dolls make the trek across the Pacific—6,401 nautical miles—via Hong Kong by sea to arrive at the Port of Long Beach approximately nineteen days and one hour later. Two days later the ships are unloaded, three days later they clear customs, and then our containers full of dolls are transferred to a set of trucks and delivered 50 miles east to a distribution center in Mira Loma, California. Here the containers are opened and the boxes are unloaded, sorted, and repacked before being loaded again onto any one of the 800 diesel trucks that pick up and drop off cargo every hour in that town. Some of these trucks travel as far as 800 miles or more to a regional distribution center before their cargo is unloaded, sorted, and reloaded onto a final truck and sent to one of Wal-Mart's 4,000 American outlets.

If this set of movements seems elaborate, this is in fact a heav-ily simplified and sanitized account of the circulation of stuff. First, it is misleading to think about a singular site of production. Commodities today are manufactured *across logistics space* rather than in a singular place. This point is highlighted if we account for "inbound logistics"— the production processes of component parts that make the manufacture of a commodity possible—and if we recognize transportation as an ele-ment of production rather than merely a service that follows production. The complexity would be enhanced dramatically if we took stock of all the ways that capital circulates through its different forms during this physical circulation of commodity to market. A more nuanced narrative would especially start to surface if we were to highlight the frequent dis-ruptions that characterize supply chains and the violent and contested human relations that constitute the global logistics industry. To the every-day delays of bad weather, flat tires, failed engines, missed connections, traffic jams, and road closures, we would also need to add more deliber-ate interruptions. Just-in-time transport systems can be disrupted by the labor actions of transport workers at any one of the multiple links along the way. Workers, organized or not, may interfere with the packing and repacking of cargo at any of the transshipment sites. Ships are frequently hijacked by pirates in key zones on open waters, and truck and rail routes are sometimes blockaded—in response to both long histories of colonial occupation and current practices of imperial expansion. Even national borders, with the unpredictable delays of customs and security checks, challenge the fast flow of goods. The threat of disruption to the circula-tion of stuff has become such a profound concern to governments and corporations in recent years that it has prompted the creation of an entire architecture of security that aims to govern global spaces of flow. This new framework of security—supply chain security—relies on a range of new forms of transnational regulation, border management, data collec-tion, surveillance, and labor discipline, as well as naval missions and aerial bombing. In fact, to meaningfully capture the social life of circulation, we would have to consider not only disruption to the system but the assembly of infrastructure and architecture achieved through land grabs, military actions, and dispossessions that are often the literal and figurative grounds for new logistics spaces.

Corporate and military logistics are increasingly entangled; this is a matter of not only military forces clearing the way for corporate trade but corporations actively supporting militaries as well. Logistics are one of the most heavily privatized areas of contemporary warfare. This is nowhere more the case than in the U.S. military bases in Iraq and Afghanistan, where private companies are contracted to do much of the feeding and housing of troops. "Public" military logisticians rapidly cycle into the private sector, often precisely to facilitate the shifting of logistics contracts to private military companies. The entanglement of military and corporate logistics may be deepening and changing form, but logistics was never a stranger to the world of warfare. The language of the supply chain (its recent corporate management speak) would have us believe that logistics emerged out of the brave new world of business to only recently colonize the old institution of the military. And yet, while national militaries have indeed been taken over by a new kind of corporate calculation, it was historically the military and warfare that gave the gift of logistics (De Landa 1991; Shoenberger 2008).

Logistics was dedicated to the art of war for millennia only to be adopted into the corporate world of management in the wake of World War II. For most of its martial life, logistics played a subservient role, enabling rather than defining military strategy. But things began to change with the rise of modern states and then petroleum warfare. The logistical complexity of mobilization in this context meant that the success or failure of campaigns came to rely on logistics. Over the course of the twentieth century, a reversal of sorts took place, and logistics began to lead strategy rather than serve it. This military history reminds us that logistics is not only about circulating *stuff* but about sustaining life. It is easy today to associate logistics with the myriad inanimate objects that it manages, but the very sustenance of populations is a key stake in the game. Indeed—the definitive role of the military art of logistics was in fueling the battlefield, and this entailed feeding men as well as machines. More recently, we see logistics conceptualized not only as a means to sustain life but as a lively system in itself. Contemporary efforts to protect supply chains invest logistical systems with biological imperatives to flow and prescribe "resilience" as a means of sustaining not only human life but the system itself. In this context, threats to circulation are treated not only as criminal acts but as profound threats to the *life* of trade. As I argue in the pages that follow, new boundaries of belonging are being drawn around spaces of circulation. These "pipelines" of flow are not only displacing the borders of national territoriality but also recasting the geographies of law and violence that were organized by the inside/outside of state space. Those on the outside of the system, who aim to contest its flows, face the raw force of rough trade without recourse to normal laws and protections. Logistics is no simple story of securitization or of distribution; it is an industry and assemblage that is at once bio-, necro-, and antipolitical.

The Deadly Life of Logistics is concerned with how the seemingly banal and technocratic management of the movement of stuff through space has become a driving force of war and trade. This book examines how the military art of moving stuff gradually became not only the "umbrella science" of business management but, in Nigel Thrift's (2007, 95) words, "perhaps the central discipline of the contemporary world." But this book considers logistics as a project and not an achievement. Logistics is profoundly political and so contested in all its iterations—on the oceans, in cities, on road and rail corridors, and in the visual and cartographic images that are also part of its assemblage. This book explores how the art and then the science of logistics continue to transform not only the geographies of production and distribution and of security and war but also our political relations to our world and ourselves, and thus practices of citizenship, too.

This book makes four central arguments. First, it insists on the precarity of the distinction between "civilian" and "military," even as it also attends to the political, historical, and geographical force of that distinction's effects. It asks that we at once acknowledge the work of the separation of war and trade in the world as we also interrogate their entanglement. Second, in concert with countless other contemporary works, this book elaborates on the profoundly political life of forms of knowledge and calculation that present themselves as purely technical. It tells a story of logistics that highlights rather than hides the histories and geographies of conflict and violence through which the field has emerged in its present form. This work positions logistics' claims to "technicality"—the profession's assertion of its own expertise, objectivity, and political neutrality—firmly within that trajectory of struggle. This book addresses the antipolitical assemblage of logistics primarily through its constitutive cartographies, taking up the mapping of spaces of circulation as fundamental to the profoundly political and contested production of logistics space. The third intervention is related to the first and second; it highlights questions of violence and calculation specifically by interrogating the shifting boundaries between "civilian" and "military" domains. These boundaries are not only conceptual and legal; they are also geographical

(Mbembe 2003). As many scholars have outlined, the architecture of modern war was also a map of the modern state. War "faces out" from national territory, whereas the civilian was said to occupy domestic space (Giddens 1985, 192; Foucault [1997] 2003, 49). In the context of modernity, war designated "a conflict in some sense external to the structures of sovereignty and civil war a conflict internal to them" (Evans and Hardt 2010). But these boundaries are in significant flux. If we are living in an era of "global civil war" (Hardt and Negri 2002), wherein the national territorial framework that underpinned modern war erodes, then we are also seeing a corresponding "shift from the external to the internal use of force," with armed conflicts administered not "as military campaigns but police actions" (Evans and Hardt 2010). And yet, this shift takes on a much more specific spatiality; the networked infrastructure and architecture of the supply chain animates both war and trade. This book insists that any serious engagement with contemporary political life must think through the violent economies of space. Our theory needs to engage our present as fundamentally a *time* of *logistics space*.

Finally, *The Deadly Life of Logistics* aims to open a queer engagement with logistics. This is not primarily a project of performing a "queer reading" of logistics, as J. K. Gibson-Graham (1996) aims to do of capitalism more broadly, but of highlighting the queerness that is already installed in this assemblage (cf. Puar 2005). This engagement exposes the vital role of this banal management science—a science that was born of war—in the recasting of the economies of life and death. It interrogates the uneven terrain of logistics space and how it differentiates groups' rights and rights to life on the basis of their relationship to systems of supply. A profoundly imperial cartography, while logistics space takes new shape and sets a new pace to social life, it also demonizes old enemies of empire—workers of many kinds fighting exploitation and oppression, and especially racialized peoples, differently positioned, fighting dispossession. This engagement also therefore allows for a reconsideration of the central place of geography in the constitution of our material, political, and martial infrastructures. Beyond this diagnostic dimension—a queer engagement opens up the instabilities of the "system," highlighting the "perverse installed within" (cf. Puar 2005, 126) that also incubates alternative spaces and futurities.

Markets and Militaries

While it is rarely acknowledged or interrogated, the old military art of logistics played a critical role in the making of the global social factory—not simply the globalization of production, but the invention of the contemporary supply chain and the reorganization of national economies into transnational systems. Logistics was once a military art of moving soldiers and supplies to the front. In the years after World War II, the broad managerial uses of logistics were at the fore of research and gave rise to a business science. Writing for the RAND Corporation in 1960, Murray Geisler marks this growing interest in the civilian uses of military logistics. He explained that the "management problems of large military organizations share much in common, both on the general and specific level, with those of private industrial and commercial organizations," and he argued that military logistics research should thus have relevance to civilian corporations. Geisler outlined two desires—that management sciences would learn from military logistics and that the former would assist the latter by taking up logistical challenges as central to their work. "The demands on the Air Force managers are becoming more challenging and difficult. Their need for assistance from management science is growing proportionately," he explains (1960, 453). His desires materialized in the decade that followed. Business logistics began to lead the field, though always in close conversation with martial actors and institutions. For business management, a "revolution in logistics" took shape in the 1960s that entirely transformed the ways that corporations imagine, calculate, plan, and build spaces of production and of distribution and gradually remade the global economy. The revolution in logistics gave rise to transnational circulatory systems that span sites of production and consumption. Yet despite the postwar rise of a business science of logistics out of a military art, the revolution in logistics hardly marked its "civilianization" but rather a different and deepened entanglement between the just-in-time geographies of production and destruction. The entwined military and civilian life of logistics is particularly stark in the present. The recent rise of "supply chain security," a network security that troubles borders and territory, highlights the profound entanglement of war and trade through logistics (Amoore and De Goede 2008; Bigo 2001; Bonacich 2005; Bonacich and Wilson 2008; Cooper et al. 1997; Flynn 2003; Haveman and Shatz 2006).

The idea that war and trade are intimately acquainted is hardly new. Critics have been marking the growing interlacing of the supposedly separate spheres of military and corporate life for some time. In his famous departing words, U.S. president Eisenhower warned of the "total influence" of an expanding *military-industrial complex*. Writing in 1974, Seymour Melman published a powerful analysis of the "permanent war economy," in which he argued that postwar American industry was increasingly organized around martial accumulation. More recently, a lively literature traces the rise of private military companies as a central force in contemporary war. Yet even as we are seeing the militarization of the economy and the privatization of warfare (Kinsey 2006; Chestermann and Lehnardt 2007; Leander 2010), I argue that something more significant is under way. Both war and trade are changing in an era of globalization and privatization in ways that warrant attention, but the long history and complex geography of their entanglement prompt us to investigate the very salience of the military–civilian conceptual divide. Scholars including Foucault ([1997] 2003, 2007), Barkawi (2011), De Landa (1991, 2005), Griggers (1997), Mann (1988), Jabri (2007), Mbembe (2003), Mohanty (2011), and Neocleus (2000) argue for such a profound rethinking of the ways we conceive military and civilian life. Their work is part of a tradition that reaches far back, even as it has also been recently renewed. Writing in 1938, Bertrand Russell (1938, 123) argued that all economic power, "apart from the economic power of labor . . . consists in being able to decide, by the use of armed force if necessary, who shall be allowed to stand upon a given piece of land and to put things into it and take things from it." His conception is helpful not only because it places geography at the center of the analysis but also because he theorizes law as part of the operation of this violence rather than its antithesis. After elaborating on how the most banal of legal arrangements over land ownership (a tenant farmer paying rent to the landowner) have their historical source in conquest, Russell suggests that law is the relation of force that reproduces the power relations and social ordering achieved by physical force. He asserts, "In the intervals between such acts of violence, the power of the state shall pass according to law."

This more sociological approach to the entanglement of military and economic force is complemented by a genealogical approach to the shifting contours of power. Foucault ([1997] 2003, 267) is particularly helpful here, questioning the ways in which warfighting and military institutions underpin civilian forms and asserting the profoundly martial contours of political imaginaries and logics. Many scholars have taken up the call to unearth the ways that war underpins peace in diverse domains: through material culture, industrial innovation, landscape, scopic regimes, and medical techniques and in social scientific discovery. Especially since the rise of industrial war and mass mobilization, in this is expansive terrain, as Mark Duffield (2011) notes, "everything from rope to jam had acquired a military significance." A part of this growing chorus, this book instead traces the ways in which calculation—specifically the martial expertise in calculation of the most banal but essential aspects of war in supplying the means of life (provisions) and death (munitions)—was imported from the world of state war into the world of corporate trade, redefining both in the process.

Imperialism admits this entanglement but also considers its shifting ground. "Imperialism," Raymond Williams (2013, 160) explains, "like any word which refers to fundamental social and political conflicts, cannot be reduced semantically, to a single proper meaning. Its important historical and contemporary variations of meaning point to real processes that have to be studied in their own terms." Nevertheless, Williams also helpfully distinguishes between two different meanings of imperialism that have some resonances and parallels in contemporary debates about "geopolitics" and "geo-economics." He notes that if imperialism is defined, as it was in nineteenth-century England, as "primarily a political system in which colonies are governed from an imperial centre . . . then the subsequent grant of independence or self-government to these colonies can be described, as indeed it widely has been, as 'the end of imperialism.'" However, a different conception yields a different diagnosis of the present. "On the other hand," he writes, "if imperialism is understood primarily as an economic system of external investment and the penetration of markets and sources of raw materials, political changes in the status of colonies will not greatly affect description of the continuing economic system as imperialist."

Logistics maps the form of contemporary imperialism. Over the course of the last century, logistics has come to drive strategy and tactics, rather than function as an afterthought. Meanwhile, over the last fifty years, corporate civilian practice has come to lead this former military art, redefining logistics as a business science. Yet despite all this change, logistics remains deeply tied to the organization of violence. If logistics was a residual military art of the geopolitical state, where geopolitics is concerned primarily with the exercise of power and questions of sovereignty and authority within a territorially demarcated system of national states, then logistics as a business science has come to drive geo-economic logics and authority, where geo-economics emphasizes the recalibration of international space by globalized market logics, transnational actors (corporate, nonprofit, and state), and a network geography of capital, goods, and human flows (Sparke 1998, 2000; Pollard and Sidaway 2002; Cowen and Smith 2009).

Transforming Territory

The paradigmatic space of logistics is the supply chain. This network space, constituted by infrastructures, information, goods, and people, is dedicated to flows. Casually referred to by those in the industry as a "pipeline," logistics space contrasts powerfully with the territoriality of

the national state. Today, the supply chain is understood to be both vital
and vulnerable and so in urgent need of protection. This networked space
surfaces over and over again as the object of supply chain security, rendering its trademark cartography. The corporate supply chain has a history in
the military and colonial supply line. It is no accident that the supply *chain*
of contemporary capitalism resonates so clearly with the supply *line* of
the colonial frontier. It is not only striking but diagnostic that old enemies
of empire—"indians" and "pirates"—are among the groups that pose
the biggest threats to the "security of supply" today. It is also incredibly
revealing that these groups frame their struggle in explicitly anti-imperial
terms. Indeed, the supply line or chain is the geography of transnational
flow but also of imperial force. The resurfacing of the supply line at the
center of contemporary geopolitical economy with the echoes of empire
connects present war with past forms and indicts the era of national territory as the historical anomaly.

FIGURE 1. (American) military supply line near Namiquipa, Mexico, 1916.
Source: National Geographic Creative.

FIGURE 2. Corporate supply chain near Vancouver, British Columbia, 2009.
Source: Photograph by Debra Pogorelsky.

How does this supply line—this network space of circulation—remake the world of nation-states and national territoriality? The growing importance of the supply chain in our political as well as economic geographies begs this question. Crucially, while logistics space collides with and corrodes *national territoriality,* it by no means marks the decline of *territory.* Saskia Sassen's recent work on the remaking of political and legal authority taking shape through processes of globalization is instructive (Sassen 2006, 2008, 2013; see also Elden 2009, 2013). Sassen traces transformations that she deems epochal in the recalibration of "the most complex institutional architecture we have ever produced: the national state" (Sassen 2006, 1). At stake is not the decline of territory but a more precise transition: the denouement of a particular historical-geographical instantiation of territory organized through nation-states—namely, territoriality. "Territory," Sassen (2013, 25) writes, "is not 'territoriality.'" If "territoriality" is a form associated with the modern state, Sassen (2013, 23) sees territory in itself as "a capability with embedded logics of power and of claimmaking." Key to these transformations is the rise of new "transversally bordered spaces that not only cut across national borders but also generate new types of formal and informal jurisdictions . . . deep inside the tissue of national sovereign territory" (ibid.). This book argues not simply that logistics spaces are one form of emergent jurisdiction among many that challenge the authority of national territoriality but rather that logistics is a driving force in the transformations in time, space, and territory that make globalization and recast jurisdiction. A ubiquitous management science of the government of circulation, logistics has been crucial in the process of time–space compression that has remade geographies of capitalist production and distribution at a global scale.

The politics of circulation are at the forefront of a number of threads of scholarship today—but which *forms* of circulation are we talking about? On the one hand, *circulation* refers to material and informational flows, and there is a growing body of scholarship considering the government of circulation in this vein. Much of this work emerges in conversation with Foucault's lectures collected in "Security, Territory, Population," in which he outlines the rise of a form of government concerned with the management of circulation (Foucault 2007, 65). Tracing the emergence of what he calls "security" in town planning, Foucault traces the encounter with "a completely different problem that is no longer that of fixing and demarcating the territory, but of allowing circulations to take place, of controlling them, sifting the good and the bad, ensuring that things are always in movement." More broadly, there is a dynamic and growing body of literature in the interdisciplinary study of "mobilities," which interrogates the radically undervalorized role of movement and circulation in everyday life (Sheller and Urry 2006; Sheller 2011). This sense of circulation (the movements of things, data, and people) is our common sense of the term, but it stands in some contrast to the notion at work in the study of the circulation of capital through its different forms. Indeed, this latter notion of circulation, perhaps most rigorously taken up in Marx's *Capital*, volume 2, is also at the center of contemporary debates—but about the political economy of crisis. While debates about circulation are experiencing resurgence, these different forms of circulation elaborated on in distinct literatures and networks rarely collide. Yet it is precisely the shifting relationship between the circulation of stuff and the circuits of capital that is at stake in the story of logistics. I suggest that on offer at this intersection is a vital political history of the economic space of our present.

Logistics entails not only "transversal networks" but a suite of other spaces that underpin circulation—nodes, chokepoints, "bunkers" (cf. Duffield 2011), borders, and overlapping jurisdictions such as cities and states. The making of logistics space challenges not only the inside/outside binary of national territoriality but also the "tidy" ways that modern warfare has been organized along national lines. In his classic account, Charles Tilly considers the long histories of European state formation that were defined by contestation between capital accumulating networks of mercantile cities and the territorially bounded coercion of military states. For Tilly (1990, 19), "Capital defines a realm of exploitation," whereas "coercion defines a realm of domination." Importantly, Tilly allows that "coercive means and capital merge where the same objects (e.g., workhouses) serve exploitation and domination." If, as I assert in this book, the revolution in logistics transformed the factory into a disaggregated network of production and circulation, then arguably the supply chain as reformed workhouse is a paradigmatic and expansive space for the entanglement of exploitation and domination. Indeed, while Tilly's intervention is typically remembered for its separation of these two organizations of power—capital/city and coercive state—he nevertheless marks the historical expansion of both forms. "Over time," he writes, "the place of capital in the form of states grew even larger, while the influence of coercion (in the guise of policing and state intervention) expanded as well." Indeed, as I argue in the pages that follow, the story of capital and coercion is not an either/or. As the title of this work hints, logistics space is produced through the intensification of both capital circulation and organized violence—although in ways that might be difficult to recognize.

Perhaps it is not surprising that some of the most promising insights on the spaces and scales of contemporary government come from critical scholars of *security*. Martin Coward's (2009) arguments about the urbanization of security are prescient in that they focus on the networked infrastructures that render contemporary life neither local nor global; it is at once urban and transnational. While infrastructure has long been vital to political economic life and the target of organized violence, Coward suggests that significant change has occurred in the relationship between infrastructure and the urban that makes them both *critical* in circuits of power and violence today. Historically, he writes, "infrastructures were targeted because they were an element in a war machine that happened to be concentrated in cities," whereas today, the city is targeted because it is constituted by critical infrastructure (Coward 2009, 403). Critical infrastructure is not simply proximate to urban centers but constitutive of the city (ibid., 404). What Coward describes is essentially the rise of logistics space wherein cities (logistics cities) have become key informational, infrastructural, economic, and political zones and thus the targets of attack. Mark Duffield (2011) offers some stunning insight into this very claim, suggesting that a reformulation of total war has given way to an "environmental terror" that targets the conditions of life through attack on vital infrastructures. Duffield (2011, 765) argues that environmental terror and its Nomos of Circulation (Evans and Hardt 2010) have a precise architecture in "nodal bunkers, linked by secure corridors and formed into defended archipelagos of privileged circulation." Duffield (2011) emphasizes the ways in which "secure corridors" delineate "global camps" and thus offers a map of the world that is also a map of logistics space. Logistics logics drive both war and trade and constitute a complex spatiality at once national, urban, imperial, and mobile—an "interlegality" (de Sousa Santos, quoted in Valverde 2009) of rough trade.

Questions of (logistics) space are also profoundly questions of citizenship. If national territoriality gave literal legal shape to modern formal citizenship, what are the implications of its recasting for political belonging and subjectivity? As the assemblage of a global architecture for the protection of trade flows brings new forms and spaces of security into being—the network spaces of logistics infrastructure and flow—it also provokes, at least potentially, new paradigms of citizenship (Partridge 2011). Supply chain security crosses over land and sea, encountering and recasting the government of national borders, but it also collides with the rights and livelihoods of groups, reconstituting those groups in the process. Protecting trade networks from disruption creates new spaces of security and in doing so problematizes the political and legal status of subjects. For instance, military, corporate, and civilian state managers deliberate whether pirates in the Gulf of Aden should be administered as "criminals" or "terrorists" when they disrupt shipping traffic. Their answers have produced a new category of problem—"the Somali pirate"—and a whole new arsenal of antipiracy initiatives that violently transform the lives of Somali fisherfolk, as they also remake international law. While supply chain security is highly contested and in flux, the problematization of disruption and possible responses are tied to the political and spatial logics of logistics. In other words, the network geography of supply chain security does not elude longstanding territorial problems of sovereignty, jurisdiction, and security, but it does work to dramatically recast these spatial ontologies.

After several decades of work in political geography and citizenship studies, it should not be strange to pose these questions in this way. John Pickles (2004, 5) suggests that "maps provide the very conditions of possibility for the worlds we inhabit and the subjects we become." Even more directly, Peter Nyers (2008, 168) eloquently argues that "acts of bordering are also acts of citizenship in that they are part of the process by which citizens are distinguished from others: strangers, outsiders, non-status people and the rest." Kezia Barker (2010, 352) likewise emphasizes viewing citizenship through a geographical lens, which she sees as "the unstable outcome of ongoing struggles over how constructed categories of people come to be politically defined in space." For Engin Isin (2009, 1), citizenship is not only about the strategies of rule through which rights are defined and distributed, but more important, it "is about political subjectivity. Not one or the other but both: political and subjectivity. Citizenship enables political subjectivity. Citizenship opens politics as a practice of contestation (agon) through which subjects become political." Questions of this sort are posed in these pages in only preliminary ways, but already here we begin to see some of the contours of the citizenship of stuff and its contestation.

Resilient Systems and Survival

The rise of a business science of logistics has been pivotal in the broader tilt toward a public–private partnership of geo-economic power. Yet the rise of geo-economic logics and forms does not mark the *replacement* of national states and their populations and territories, or even of geopolitics, but rather a profound reshaping. While global logistics corridors challenge territorial borders, and while a new paradigm of security is assembled to protect goods and infrastructure, the politics of populations and territories remain extraordinarily salient, as the brief preceding discussion about citizenship suggests. Struggles over territory, rights, and the laboring body are at the center of the citizenship of stuff, as the chapters that follow insist. Likewise, while this book traces the rise of a distinct paradigm of security that is concerned with circulation, the logistics system at its core is not only sociotechnical but persistently biopolitical.

An insistence on the biopolitics of logistics is *anything but* simple. With the securitization of supply chains, it is the circulatory system itself that becomes the object of vulnerability and protection, not human life in any immediate way. Efforts to secure supply chains might be understood in the context of the rise of a form of collective security that Stephen Collier and Andy Lakoff term "vital systems." This form of security seeks to protect systems that are critical to economic and political order ranging from transportation to communications, food and water supply, and finance. Vital systems security responds to threats that may be impossible to prevent "such as natural disasters, disease epidemics, environmental crises, or terrorist attacks" (Collier and Lakoff 2007). Vital systems security is thus distinguished by the wide range of disasters to which it aims to respond and by its emphasis on preparedness for emergency management rather than preventive or predictive responses that characterized risk-based models of insecurity. Lakoff (2007) explains that for vital systems security, the object of protection is not the national territory or the population but rather the critical systems that underpin social and economic life. Unlike population security and its welfarist rationality, vital systems interventions "are not focused on modulating the living conditions of human beings, but rather on assuring the continuous functioning of these systems." I intend to highlight this shift in government from concern for the security of national territories and populations to the security of the circulation of stuff but also to hail debates in the "new materialities" that insist on a more-than-human political theory (Mitchell 2002, 2011; Bennett 2010; Braun and Whatmore 2010; Coole and Frost 2010). This demands some engagement with the liveliness of the sociotechnical systems that constitute contemporary logistics space. Specifically, it begs the question of whether these systems have a meaningfully precarious *life* in ways that are more than metaphorical.

This question is taken up centrally, though in perhaps somewhat oblique ways, in the concluding chapter. Despite the fact that *inanimate objects* are largely what constitute its infrastructures, I argue that logistics space is nevertheless profoundly biopolitical. As Duffield (2011, 763) argues, "Biopolitics has changed"; it has "realigned around processes of remedial abandonment." I suggest that making sense of logistics as a "vital system" requires an elaboration of the "more-than-human" politics of nature. The politics of inanimate objects and information are a key domain of logistics, but I direct attention toward the lively instead. I make this move, in a sense, empirically—by addressing the convergence of logistical and biological politics through discourses of systems, survival, and resilience. Logistics systems figure as natural systems rather than "things," where *nature* is not just a metaphor but a metric. It is not just any nature at work here but a very distinct conception—a social Darwinism of circulation. A modern-day and hypermobile recasting of social Darwinism explicitly calibrates logistics systems to the nonhuman migrations that National Geographic (Kostyal 2010, 16) calls "the elemental story of instinct and survival." Looking to popular culture and advertising campaigns but also to the actual securitization of supply chains, the concluding chapter traces how survival through circulation is mapped on both the nonhuman and economic worlds at once.

Mark Duffield's recent work elaborates on the dangerous discourse of resilience, specifically the ways it links war and trade through nature. Duffield (2011, 763) argues, "Not only do we see a diagram of war in nature, nature itself has been rediscovered to function as a market." His insights are prescient. The conflation of a survivalist politics of circulation in nature and trade has troubling implications; it naturalizes trade flows, casting disruption as a threat to life itself, ideologically buttressing active efforts to cast acts of piracy, indigenous blockades, and labor actions as matters of security subject to exceptional force. And yet the ironies of this maneuver are also potent. If social Darwinist ideas of animal migrations serve to naturalize economic circulation, Darwin's ideas have also been interpreted as the transposition of capitalist social relations onto nature. More than 150 years ago, Karl Marx suggested that Darwin's work in the *Origin of the Species* described the relations of production that constituted the capitalist mode of production *as his "nature"* (Ball 1979, 473). Initially upon reading this work in 1860, Marx expressed his appreciation to Engels for Darwin's refusal of a teleological approach to nature. Just two years later, in 1862, he reports to Engels that on rereading Darwin, he found him "amusing." As Ball explains, "Darwin emerges, on Marx's rereading, as a nineteenth-century English Bourgeois-turned-naturalist." In a letter to Engels, Marx writes, "It is remarkable how Darwin recognizes among beasts and plants his English society with its division of labour, competition, opening up of new markets, inventions, and the Malthusian 'struggle for existence.' His [nature] is Hobbes' bellum omnium contra omnes, and one is reminded of Hegel's Phenomenology, where civil society is described as a 'spiritual animal kingdom,' while in Darwin the animal kingdom figures as civil society" (Marx, quoted in Ball 1979, 473). In perfectly circular fashion, "nature" is thus a metric for trade, which is *already* a metric for nature.

At stake in this survivalist circulation, and in these debates about the bios, are also the contours of contemporary organized violence. Biopower is centrally a matter of death as well as life, as Achille Mbembe's crucial insights on the management of killing and his elaborations on the politics and geographies of warfare teach us. If the limit of the inside/outside geography of modern war was the colony—for instance, that which Mbembe (2003, 23) describes in the context of jus publicum and the bounding of legitimate war (see also Badiou 2002; Mignolo and Tlostanova 2006; Asad 2007), where "the distinction between war and peace does not avail" (25)—then contemporary war, logistical war, imports this indistinction across its transnational networks of security. This is not to suggest that uneven and exceptional spaces have become smooth—global space is if anything as divided, segregated, and differentiated by rule and force as ever—but rather that the spatial logics of contemporary warfare and biopower are also shifting.

The concluding chapter explores the *circulation of the biopolitics of circulation* and its violent cartographies, yet this engagement with the "nature" of circulation is also an effort to open up alternatives to the technocratic antipolitics of logistics space. In this aim, the work of feminist and queer theorists is particularly helpful. I take up Elizabeth Grosz's recent (2005, 2011) work centrally, for while she does not directly engage the world of logistics, she is centrally concerned with the problem of social Darwinism that has become so vital to logistics logics. Grosz suggests that new materialist feminist futurities rely on disaggregating two key concepts in Darwin's work. In a move that shares rhythms with queer critique, Grosz insists on the autonomy of sexual from natural selection. Sexual selection locates creative transformation in desire without determination. If natural selection is the logic of mimetic reproduction, sexual selection charts unpredictable assemblages, both in the immediate realm of sex and sexuality and in the capacity for "artistic" practice to organize futurity. If sexual selection offers the profound political openings that Grosz suggests, it provides some potentially powerful ways for conceptualizing alternatives to the necropolitical, racialized, and heteronormative premises of natural selection that currently code the violent logics of logistics space. Thus the concluding chapter of the book asks what the unhinging of sexual from natural selection might mean for logistics space. Here I ask that if social Darwinist ideals of species survival are serving as discursive infrastructure for the assemblage of "resilient" global supply chains, how might we instead encourage them to "appear in all their queernesses" (Puar 2005, 126)?

This book only briefly engages the many movements that labor toward a different calibration of logistics and everyday life, yet in this engagement and in offering a map of logistics space, it intends to contribute to these counter cartographies. Logistics space is constituted through distinct political geographies—networks of circulation—and I explore how these same spatialities are also an opportunity for alternative alliances.

The Logistics of *The Deadly Life of Logistics*

This book mobilizes a variety of research methods and archives to trace a long history and global geography of logistics. To organize the study of such a vast terrain with both rigor and humility, the book targets key events in the emergence and transformation of the field. Each chapter focuses on a time and place where significant change takes place and where important experiments in the government of circulation are under way. My intention is to provide a sketch of an emerging network of power and violence with no pretense to comprehensiveness. There are dramatic and necessary limitations on this work, which I hope might be interpreted as invitations and open questions. First and foremost, and with some irony—the *geography* of my geography is profoundly partial. The project is bounded by the practical need to locate the analysis of a globalized system in place, although there is a deliberate choice here, too. The United States figures centrally in the stories that follow, as the book also traces the mobility of rough trade through Canada, Iraq, Dubai, and the Gulf of Aden. American actors and institutions have played a pivotal role in the emergence and transformation of the field, and despite the multinodal map of contemporary global power, U.S. imperialism remains profoundly salient (Smith 2004; Panitch and Gindin 2012). There are, however, countless places, events, and questions that should be addressed in the chapters that follow but that do not make appearance. The "known unknowns"—to paraphrase Donald Rumsfeld (and Matt Hanah 2006)—the things I am already aware deserve more attention than they get, are massive and multiple. Major events like containerization are only briefly addressed, despite clearly having a profound impact on the shape of this story. Likewise, the widespread sweep of port privatization during the last decades of the twentieth century is only addressed in passing. The power of finance capital in fueling logistics' life deserves its own book. No doubt there is also a list of "unknown unknowns"—things I do not even realize I have neglected but that should be included here.

If there are limits of time, space, and capacity in terms of *what* this book highlights, there are also profound limitations in terms of *how* this book is crafted. I take some comfort in Christopher Kelty's (2008, 20) comments on the study of "distributed phenomena" wherein he reminds us that *careful* and *comprehensive* are not the same thing. Kelty suggests that comprehensiveness is not only impossible but undesirable, and certainly unnecessary, when the object of study is distributed. "The study of distributed phenomena does not necessarily imply the detailed, local study of each instance of a phenomenon," Kelty writes. "Such a project is not only extremely difficult, but confuses map and territory." Indeed, the study of something as widely distributed as *distribution* itself raises complex methodological questions and demands reflexivity on the limits of knowing, yet, as Kelty argues, "it is possible to make any given node into a source of rich and detailed knowledge about the distributed phenomena itself, not only about the local site." The sites I study are nodes in networks of flow rather than discrete objects, and this implies that the site is never *simply* local or entirely contained. I also draw important lessons from Timothy Mitchell, who provides a model for careful conceptual work through events and places that refuses the abstraction of so much theory. In his beautiful book *The Rule of Experts*, Tim Mitchell (2002, 8) suggests, "The theory lies in the complexity of the cases," and I aim to follow his approach in opening theoretical questions through these empirical adventures. This book's rhythm, which may feel peculiarly empirical for theoreticians and strangely theoretical for empiricists, thinks through *things*—events, places, relations, and institutions.

Maps are critical infrastructure for the arguments presented in this book and essential architecture for its unfolding. While "a map is not the territory" (Korzybski 1973), maps are nevertheless crucially important in the production of space (Harley 1988, 1989; Kitchen and Dodge 2007; Lefebvre 1991; Wood 1992, 2010). Maps purport to represent the world, yet critical cartographers have reiterated that they are not in any simple sense representations; instead, "maps and mapping precede the territory they 'represent'" (Pickles 2004, quoted in Kitchen and Dodge 2007, 4). When maps work, they respond to something concrete in our lived experience but frame it or channel it in a particular way. They are "the products of power and they produce power" (Kitchen and Dodge 2007, 2). Maps are neither true nor false; they are "propositions" (Krygier and Wood 2011) that authorize "the state of affairs which through their mapping they help to bring into being" (Wood 2010, 1). Wood argues that the rise of the map as we know it today is "the rise of the modern state" (ibid.). Modern Western cartography emerges as part of state power, where maps serve to "replace, reduce the need for the application of armed force."

A central irony of supply chain maps is thus that they conceal histories of organized violence as they render them visually. It is the networked space of the supply chain that is mapped in the images that open each of the chapters of this book. Some of these render very particular spaces—for instance, the Gulf of Aden (chapter 4) or even the illustrations of Basra Logistics City (chapter 5). The rest are conceptual maps—diagrams of abstracted spaces that detail the designs of processes and relationships that are not obviously or immediately geographical in the same sense but that nevertheless have their spatialities. *How* each of these images work in the world to render actual spaces is elaborated in each respective chapter, but they collectively constitute key cartographies of rough trade. The images of specific places may seem more straightforward in this regard; the map of the Gulf of Aden renders the invention of a new space, a corridor of public and private security: the *International Recommended Transit Corridor* off the coast of the Horn of Africa. The plan for Basra Logistics City, on the other hand, lays out a vision for the transformation of the largest military detention center in Iraq into a glimmering hub of global oil trade. Yet the diagrams are no less significant in the making of space, even if in ways that are less immediately visible: the "system of supply" that animates the birth of business logistics in chapter 1, the network space that is the object of supply chain security in chapter 2, and the ordering of exceptional authority that defines the "process model" for secure ports in chapter 3. Together the images map a series of violent and contested geographies: spaces of movement and flow, and spaces of bordering and containment.

This book opens up a genealogical and geographical investigation of the modern art and science of logistics. Chapter 1 offers a sketch of the long life and mobile meaning of logistics. It traces a series of astounding transformations that characterize modern logistics in its infrastructures, technologies, landscapes, forms of labor, and expertise but also in the very meaning of the term. It outlines, first, the long military history of logistics as an art of war and the technopolitics of early twentieth-century petroleum warfare that placed it in the driving seat of strategy and tactics. This chapter then dwells heavily in debates in the fields of systems analysis, business, and physical distribution management (the latter briefly known as "rhocrematics") from the 1940s through the 1960s to trace the revolution in logistics and its remaking of spatial calculation and so too geopolitical economic life. Like chapter 1, chapter 2 also sets some technical ground for the more political chapters that follow. It traces the birth of "supply chain security," locating this increasingly important transnational paradigm of security at the core of the project of logistics space. The chapter thus examines the problem of disruption as part of the assemblage of the infrastructures, technologies, institutions, labor forces, and regulations that support the building of the "seamless" corridors and gateways of logistics space. As an ever-present threat to just-in-time circulation systems, disruption has come to figure as a threat to the "security" of supply chains. Disruption can stem from many forces, and one of the defining features of supply chain security is the interdisciplinary nature of the threats it aims to govern. Earthquakes, equipment failures, pirate attacks, rail blockades, and myriad other disparate forces of disruption are all governed under its rubric.

The distinct work of securing systems of supply in specific places is taken up in chapters 3, 4, and 5. These are key sites of experimentation—zones where circulation faces particularly potent disruption. Chapter 3 looks at the labor of logistics and situates recent initiatives to "secure" workers in a much longer tradition of managing the bodies and movements of productive labor. Logistics technologies have devastated the conditions of work across entire sectors, but I insist that we shift perspective somewhat to see this as centrally a reorganization of the geographies of (unfree) labor. If the boundaries of making and moving are both obscured in logistics networks that stretch around the world as the revolution in logistics suggests, we also see the rise of an extraordinary apparatus of management that is neither just public nor private and neither military nor civilian but something else. Yet the people that labor at logistics may be more "resilient" than these systems, as they continue to disrupt flows and construct alternative circulation. Workers have been intransigent in their claims for economic and social justice and can create bottlenecks that ripple powerfully through global logistics networks. Yet if the factory is a global system, then it is not just workers in the strict sense that may disrupt production. Indeed, piracy—taken up in chapter 4—has surfaced again as a global threat to the legally sanctioned rough trade of contemporary imperialism. Firmly within the global social factory, the crucial shipping corridor of the Gulf of Aden has become a hotspot for experiments in martial, legal, and "humanitarian" efforts. Europe and the United States have been particularly active in deploying physical and symbolic violence in ways that remake political space and echo the colonial violence of a century ago.

Chapter 5 explores the *urban* revolution in logistics. While it traces the urbanization of infrastructure and economy, it also insists that the study of the "global city" refuses a civilianization of vision. It suggests that there is significance to the rise of the "logistics city"—a hybrid form that combines the exceptional spaces of the military base and the corporate export processing zone. Both parasite and supplement, the logistics city provokes questions about the future of urban citizenship, circulation, and political struggle.

The conclusion—"Rough Trade?"—also investigates alternative futures, drawing on a very different archive. It looks to advertising (which emerged out of management sciences as did logistics) and specifically the corporate campaigns of a leading logistics company and the branding of logistics as alternately lovable and lethal in human and more-than-human worlds. Collecting themes raised throughout the book, the analysis explores visions of violence and desire in the social and spatial assembly of logistics space while highlighting paths toward alternative futures and perhaps even alternative economies of rough trade.

CHAPTER ONE

The Revolution in Logistics

"America's Last Dark Continent"

Techniques will not be discussed because the basic problems are not technical.

—Peter Drucker, "Physical Distribution"

The simple little diagram shown in Figure 3 changed the world. With its childlike simplicity of rectangles and relationships, this 1970 representation of an "Alternative Orientation to Integrated Distribution Management" announced the birth of a field that would transform the global space economy in the decades to come. The diagram remained buried for more than forty years in the archives of the *International Journal of Physical Distribution*—an obscure outlet with a small professional circulation that no longer publishes under the same name. This diagram has rarely even seen the light of day since it was originally published, and even then it has received the scrutiny of only a small cadre of specialists. This diagram never had a wide circulation and did not travel the globe; its power—its work in the world—was of a different order. In fact, it was not so much the diagram that changed things as the profound conceptual shifts it captures and concretizes. It is precisely these shifts that make the diagram worth digging out of the 1970s and dragging into our present, as it captures the core kernel of the logic driving the *revolution in logistics*.

Arguably the most underinvestigated revolution of the twentieth century, the *revolution in logistics* was not the upheaval of one country or political system but a revolution in the calculation and organization of economic space. With the revolution in logistics, a new means of calculating costs and benefits was widely adopted—initially by larger corporations

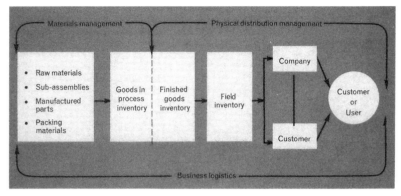

FIGURE 3. "Alternative Orientation to Integrated Distribution Management."
Source: LaLonde, Grabner, and Robeson 1970.

and eventually by virtually all the rest. This kind of calculation offered a
new logic for how, and so *where,* to do business. This diagram, and the
revolution that it announced, combined the stagnant fields of physical
distribution and materials management—the former holding jurisdiction
over the distribution of goods after production and the latter's authority
bounded by the production process—to create a new umbrella management science. No longer a problem locked in discrete segments of supply
chains, this new science would elevate its authority to the management of
circulation across the entire system of production and distribution. This
new science was called "business logistics."

From its long history as a military art of moving soldiers and supplies
to the front, logistics was transformed into a business science in the years
after World War II. With the introduction of the language of business logistics, the corporate focus on the cost of distribution in discrete segments
of supply chains was transformed into a concern with value added in circulatory systems that span the sites of production and consumption. The
shift from cost minimization *after production* to value added *across circulatory systems* entailed the ascent of logistics to a strategic role within the
firm. Logistics revolutionized was also logistics globalized, with profound
implications for how material life is made and sustained. More specifically, the revolution and globalization of logistics gave rise to transnational
networks of cargo flow that are increasingly governed through the frame
of security. At the same time, the revolution in logistics hardly marked its
"civilianization" but rather a different, even deepened entanglement of the
just-in-time geographies of production and destruction. These transformations in the field have propelled logistics from a discrete and specialized

military art to a ubiquitous science of circulation. With surgical precision, this diagram thus captures a leap in the calculation of economic space, a leap that has hardly been acknowledged to exist, even as it underpinned the globalization of production in the second half of the twentieth century.

Despite decades of debate about the production of space (Lefebvre 1984), conceptions of "spatiality" (Soja 1989), and the interdisciplinary "spatial turn" across the social sciences and humanities (Gupta and Ferguson 1992), space is still often naturalized in such a way as to preclude a set of pressing intellectual and political problems at the core of our present. It is this persistent, even stubborn assumption about the givenness of space that has allowed profound transformations in how we think, calculate, and organize economic space to remain hidden in plain view, untroubled. Yet to appreciate the significance of this diagram and the revolution in logistics that it graphically renders, we must take a different tack. This chapter tracks the profound transformation in calculative knowledge of space and economy in the three decades after World War II. It demonstrates the tremendous amount of intellectual labor—the years of research, debate, conferences, books and journal articles, and experiments—that enabled the rise of business logistics. It also tracks the labor of professionalization—the establishment of degree programs and research institutes, the initiation of trade journals and professional associations, and the creation of new corporate structures to reflect the rising power of logistics within the firm and within the economy. However, alongside this professional discourse and professionalized practice, this chapter also maps some of the broader political projects, logics, imaginaries, and interests that prompted and sustained the creation of this "clean" new science. Situating the rise of this management science in the context of persistent colonial and imperial politics and acute class and labor struggles within the United States, this chapter traces the transformation of the political, economic, and spatial logics of American-led imperial power and so sets out the social life of this powerful technoscience.

"Cold Calculation": Logistics at War

Historically, logistics meant something quite different than it does today. Its genesis was not as civilian science but rather as military art. There is only a paltry body of historical scholarship on the logistics of warfare. Military writers are typically oriented toward the monumental rather than the mundane, drawn to the most sensational aspects of organized violence. Logistics, in contrast, has figured precisely as the residual and uncomplicated, even bureaucratic tasks that need doing once the sexy work of strategy is done. Writing in 1917, Lt. Col. George C. Thorpe suggested that "strategy is to war what the plot is to the play," while "logistics furnishes the stage management, accessories, and maintenance." Thorpe saw the audience "thrilled by the action of the play and the art of the performers" while overlooking the critical but "cleverly hidden details of stage management." A masculine bravado typically characterizes the writing of military history. In Martin Van Creveld's (2004) words, the fact that "this kind of calculation does not appeal to the imagination" may be why "it is so often ignored by military historians" (1–2). Van Creveld (one of the very few historians of military logistics) notes that for every book on the topic there are hundreds on strategy and tactics (233). Yet as he argues and countless practitioners confirm, successful military campaigns require "not any great strategic genius but only plain hard work and cold calculation" (1). Logistics remains largely overlooked despite the fact that "logistics make up nine tenths of the business of war, and that the mathematical problems involved in calculating the movements and supply of armies are to quote Napoleon, not unworthy of a Leibnitz or a Newton" (233).

If we shift our attention from scholars of war to its practitioners, a different story emerges. Here we see the importance of logistics reiterated over and over again, yet often only in fragments of quotes and literary records. An entire history of the organization of ancient Chinese warfare remains to be written. Today we have only hints of the central role that provisioning played in ancient China well before the language of logistics was even invented. Sun Tzu's writings helped to shape a new form of warfare, defined by a deliberate art of war and a professional cadre of military officers, which together replaced the older emphasis on charismatic leadership (Wilson 2008, 362). Assessing the very practical costs and needs of waging successful military campaigns, Sun Tzu (1980, 72) writes, "Generally the way of employing the military is this: 1000 fast chariots, 1000 leather carriages, 100,000 sashes and suites of armor, transport and provisions for a 1000 li [about 500 kilometers], then total expenses, the employ of liaisons and ambassadors, glue and lacquer materials, contributions for chariots and armor, amount to 1000 gold pieces per day. Only after this can 100,000 troops be raised." The language of *logistics* came later. Its etymology is often traced to the Greek *logistikos*, meaning "skilled in calculating." Supply lines were a key consideration in military strategy for the Greeks and Romans, with fodder for animals a defining feature of the organization of war. Donald Engels (1980, 119) goes so far as to argue, "Supply was the basis for Alexander [the Great]'s strategy." This strategy revolved largely on his efforts to reduce the number of horses on campaigns and instead have troops carry as much of their equipment and provisions as possible. Nevertheless, Engels estimates that more than 1,000 horses were required simply to carry grain as fodder for the estimated 6,000 cavalry horses and 1,300 baggage animals that supported Alexander's campaigns. This created a situation where, according to McConnell, Hardemon, and Ransburgh (2010, 173), "strategy had to be adapted to account for horses' needs." Indeed, logistics was such a central force in the success or failure of campaigns that Alexander is reputed to have said that "my logisticians are a humorless lot . . . they know if my campaign fails, they are the first ones I will slay" (JAPCC 2011, 3).

The Roman Empire's military might was also largely underpinned by the cold calculation of logistics. Jonathan Roth (1999, 279) explains how "the Roman's success in conquering and maintaining their enormous empire lay partly in their military culture, their weapons and their training," and no doubt these are the elements that dominate popular conceptions of Rome's imperial power. However, "Rome's ability to provision large armies at long distances was, however, equally, of more importance to its success" (ibid.). The Romans used logistics "both as a strategic and a tactical weapon"—in fact, "the necessities of military supplies influenced and often determined the decisions of Roman commanders at war" (ibid.). If careful attention to the movement of men and materials and the provisioning of armies and animals was the basis for the strength of the Roman Empire, then logistical failure has also been blamed for the empire's decline. One recent major study argues that increased warfare and a growing number of invasions during the reign of Marcus Aurelius undermined the integrity of agricultural production and food supplies, gradually undermining the integrity of the empire itself (Thomas 2004).

The modern military face of logistics first took shape through Napoleonic warfare. Logistics was one of the three "arts of war" of the geopolitical state along with the better-known arts of "strategy" and "tactics," and it was essential for the building of national and colonial power. Napoleon is often quoted for saying, "An army marches on its stomach," signaling the key role of supply lines for war. In fact, providing sustenance for troops was such a problem that in 1800 Napoleon called for a whole new approach to food preservation. He offered a large monetary reward to the inventor who could design an effective system for conserving soldiers' rations. This was the context for Nicolas François Appert's invention of metal canning techniques.

Military strategists on both sides of the Napoleonic wars devoted increasing attention to logistics. Carl von Clausewitz ([1873] 2007, 78) is known to have said, "There is nothing more common than to find considerations of supply affecting the strategic lines of a campaign and a war."

In his lectures and writings, Clausewitz placed significant emphasis on the problem of "friction" for war fighting. Influenced by the physical sciences of his time, friction became a core concept for his theories. In fact, in his *On War,* friction is what makes seemingly simple tasks difficult. It is, Clausewitz writes, "the only concept that more or less corresponds to the factors that distinguish real war from war on paper" (119). Clausewitz proceeds to outline the wide range of minute problems, challenges, delays, and disruptions that characterize the everyday of warfare. These problems are inherently in the domain of logistics:

> Everything in war is very simple, but the simplest thing is difficult. The difficulties accumulate and produce a friction, which no man can imagine who has not seen war. Suppose now a traveler, who, towards evening, expects to accomplish the two stages at the end of his day's journey, four of five leagues, with post horses, on the high road—it is nothing. He arrives now at the last station but one, finds no horses or very bad ones; then a hilly country, bad roads; it is a dark night, and he is glad when, after a great deal of trouble, he reaches the next station, and finds some miserable accommodation. So in war, through the influence of an infinity of petty circumstances, which cannot properly be described on paper, things disappoint us, and we shall fall short of the mark. (50)

The extent to which problems of friction were directly matters of logistics is clear when Clausewitz writes, "The whole of military activity must . . . relate directly or indirectly to the engagement. The end for which a soldier is recruited, clothed, armed, and trained, the whole object of his sleeping, eating, drinking, and marching is simply that he should fight at the right place and the right time" ([1873] 2007, 38). This was a moment when notions of "species survival" framed the warring state. Clausewitz and Darwin both saw competitive struggle as the driving force of their social and natural worlds, with states and species, respectively, the agents of change (see Cowen and Smith 2009). German geopolitician Friedrich Ratzel deepened this discourse. Trained in zoology, Ratzel not only published a book on Darwin but came to invest his nation-state with a broadly Darwinian organicism and teleological drive for growth. Ratzel's concept of *Lebensraum* placed "Darwinian natural selection in a spatial or environmental context" (Smith 1980, 53).

Military strategists fighting with Napoleon, like the nineteenth-century writer Antoine-Henri Jomini, also devoted significant attention to logistics. Far from an afterthought, Jomini argued that logistics would occupy a leading position in the organization and execution of strategy and tactics. Jomini ([1836] 2009, 189) emphasized that logistics was dedicated to the important but unglamorous work of getting "men and materials" to the front. He furthermore makes a case for the ascending importance of logistics to warfare, arguing that "if we retain the term [logistics] we must understand it to be greatly extended and developed in signification, so as to embrace not only the duties of ordinary staff officers, but of generals-in-chief." Jomini asserted the growing importance of logistics in warfare as early as the 1870s, though it was really with the development of the petroleum-fueled battlefield that logistics became the driving force of military strategy. In addition to Jomini's formulation of "men and materials," we should emphasize that logistics has also always been centrally concerned with getting the *fuel* for men, animals, and machines to the front as well. In fact, the transformation in how war was *fueled* was definitive in the rise of logistics from a residual to a driving force in modern warfare.

Despite the long and important history of military innovations in the logistics of war, Van Creveld (2004, 233) argues forcefully that the most significant shift in the field took place not with Alexander or Napoleon but with the rise of industrial warfare fueled by petrol, oil, and lubricants (POL). It is with the rise of POL that "to a far greater extent than in the eighteenth century, strategy becomes an appendix to logistics." Manuel De Landa (1991, 105–6) concurs and suggests that logistics began to *lead rather than follow* strategy and tactics during World War I. For De Landa, this was one important implication of POL warfare and the ways it made the military critically dependent on supply lines. Nevertheless, while it was during World War I that POL began to reshape the nature of warfare, livestock continued to play a definitive role, and fodder remained an enormous logistical problem. The greatest volume of material shipped during World War I from the United Kingdom to France was not munitions (5,253,538 tons) but rather oats and hay for horses (5,438,602 tons; Goralski and Freeburg 1987, 282). If World War I marked the beginnings of the first massive experiment in POL warfare, then World War II saw the logistics of industrial warfare take center stage. Leaders from all sides extolled the definitive role of fuel in shaping the form and outcome of war. Commenting on the Allied operations, Churchill exclaimed, "Above all, petrol governed every movement" (cited in Goralski and Freeburg 1987, 284). Stalin offered similar reflections on the war: "The war was decided by engines and octane" (ibid., 68). Even as Germany entered the war still reliant on horse-drawn transport, Adolf Hitler quickly learned the definitive role of petrol: "To fight," he exclaimed, "we must have oil for our machine."

Critical in all this is the way in which the shifting technologies of violence reorganized the relationship between means and ends, and this was increasingly recognized within the heart of the U.S. Empire. As Fleet Admiral Ernest King would stress in his 1946 report to the Secretary of the Navy, World War II was "variously termed a war of production and a war of machines," but "whatever else it is . . . it is a war of logistics" (cited in "Logistics and Support" 2005). Just a year later, U.S. historian Duncan Ballantine (1947) reiterated the importance of logistics to the outcome of World War II, particularly for naval forces. The lesson from the "Second World War suggests that the naval commander must be indoctrinated in the problems of providing as well as making use of the means of warfare." Logistics, he explained, "is not something distinct from strategy and tactics, but rather an integral part of both." He cautioned against making a "specialist of the logistician," insisting instead that "logistics is part of the exercise of command." And indeed, on his way to the president's office, Dwight D. Eisenhower concurred, "You will not find it difficult to prove that battles, campaigns, and even wars have been won or lost primarily because of logistics" (Hawthorne 1948, xii).

While admitting that he might be making a "slightly exaggerated statement," Admiral Lynde McCormick of the U.S. Navy suggested "that logistics is all of war-making, except shooting the guns, releasing the bombs, and firing the torpedoes" (cited in Roloff 2003, 110). In the estimation of historians and theorists who have dwelled on the problem of logistics, McCormick's comments are prescient. In fact, De Landa (1991, 105) goes so far as to assert, "Modern tactics and strategy would seem to have become a special branch of logistics." While logistics had long been critical to warfare, with the rise of industrial war, military logistics has come to lead strategy and tactics: it has gone from being the *practical afterthought* to the *calculative practice that defines thought*. Changes in the material form and social organization of fuel saw logistics gradually become *the how that shapes the what*.

Cold *War* Calculation: McNamara and Management

During and after World War II, the field of logistics drew increased attention from forces beyond the bounds of the military. Business interest in logistics "commenced during World War II when immense quantities of men and material had to be strategically deployed throughout the world" (Miller Davis 1974, 1). Social and industrial technologies that were designed to support the American battlefield during and after World War II were critical. The U.S. military played a key role in the development of just-in-time techniques, first through the training of workers in occupied Japan to meet U.S. procurement needs and then by diffusing these techniques through contracting for Korean War supplies (Reifer 2004, 24; Spencer 1967, 33). The standard shipping container, another U.S. military innovation, has been repeatedly dubbed the single most important technological innovation underpinning the globalization of trade (Levinson 2006; "Moving Story" 2002; Rodrigue and Notteboom 2008). While it was not until the Vietnam War that the military use of the shipping container entrenched its standardized global form (Levinson 2006, 8, 178), experimentation with a container that could be transferred across different modes of transportation took place during World War II as a means to reduce the time and labor involved in transporting military supplies to the front. These specific technologies, alongside calculative technologies of managing complex forms of circulation and distribution, lured civilians in. Indeed, Grant Miller Davis (1974, 1) suggests that "entrepreneurial concern with the monetary and strategic value of logistics expanded rapidly during the late 1950s and early 1960s."

But when did logistics become a problem to be solved in the world of business management, and what problems did proponents seek to resolve by using military methods to rethink space and economy? What kinds of connections can be drawn between the history of logistics as an art of the geopolitical military and its more recent life in organizing global corporate supply chains?

Edward Smykay and Bernard LaLonde (1967, 108), two crucial players in the rise of business logistics, assert, "No one really knows when it was first recognized that the business firm had a logistics problem." They suggest that "since roughly 1960 the academic world has experienced a steady addition of writing in logistics-physical distribution," and that alongside this expansion of academic interest, "American business has experienced literally a 'revolution' in the organization and methods used to handle this important function." By applying the new methods of logistics, businesses were learning that "considerable costs can be saved, customers can be better served and the firm can more effectively play its role in society." As late as 1954, it was still possible to diagnose "a great deal more attention" being paid by business "to buying and selling than to physical handling," as Paul D. Converse did in his lecture to the Boston Conference on Distribution. Converse went so far as to suggest that "the physical handling of goods seems to be pretty much overlooked by sales executives, advertising men and market researchers . . . Problems of physical distribution are too often brushed aside as matters of little importance" (Converse 1954, 22, quoted in Bowersox 1968, 63). He described the same neglect of physical distribution in business magazines, which in his words devote "relatively little space to physical distribution." Yet, only a decade later, physical distribution could no longer be defined as an overlooked field; by the mid-1960s, the revolution was well under way.

In fact, it was on April 6, 1965, that management guru Peter Drucker would confidently assert, "Physical distribution is simply another way of saying 'the whole process of business.'" In a lecture to the newly formed National Council of Physical Distribution Management, Drucker argued that physical distribution was "today's frontier in business" (quoted in Mangan, Lalwani, and Butcher 2008, 338). The promise of physical distribution for Drucker (1969, 8) lay precisely in the fact that "the only model of a business we can so far truly design—the only operational system, in other words—is that of the business as physical distribution, as a flow of materials."

Not only was there a flurry of new writings on the topic, but there was also a surge of institution building in the field at this time. The growth in the power of logistics' technoscientific knowledge occurred alongside the rise of logistics as a social and institutional force, particularly visible over the last twenty years. Logistics firms are increasingly acting as full-service-systems managers of global supply chains. During this time, new associations sprouted up for logistics professionals, and enrollment leapt in a growing number of professional and academic programs. Trade magazines that formerly catered to shipping, distribution, or materials management now orient themselves to "logistics professionals," while firms that once specialized in shipping, distribution, or even manufacturing increasingly assume new corporate identities as logistics firms. Supply Chain Management is a mainstay in business and management schools, sometimes even replacing traditional economics departments (Busch 2007, 441).

The American Management Association was a "pioneer group" in the early development of business logistics. In 1959, they held a seminar on "Management of the Physical Distribution Function." Four years later, the National Council of Physical Distribution Management was founded, with more than "300 top executives and analysts . . . not only interested in the subject but actively engaged in physical distribution programs."[1] The universities also started to institutionalize logistics: the University of Michigan created the first distribution and logistics program in 1957, and increasing numbers of schools and students have followed suit since. A number of new trade magazines were also founded at this time, including *Distribution Age, Handling and Shipping, Traffic Management,* and *Transportation and Distribution Management.*

The founding of the Logistics Management Institute (LMI) in 1961 was a crucial event in the history of business logistics. After taking office earlier that same year, Secretary of Defense Robert S. McNamara began advising President Kennedy on the need for a federal institution devoted to the study of logistics. In a memo to the president, McNamara reported that the Department of Defense was encountering serious problems in procurement, logistics, and relations with the defense industry. McNamara argued that the LMI would produce the "same type of fresh thinking on logistics that is being provided by groups such as Rand on technical and operational matters" (LMI n.d.). He explained, "We can achieve major breakthroughs in logistics management where we spend half of the Defense budget by sponsoring the establishment of a special, full-time organization of highly talented business management specialists." The LMI was created a few short weeks later, with a powerful board that included an assortment of high-ranking military officers, Charles H. Kellstadt (former chairman of Sears, Roebuck, and Company) as chairman, Peter Drucker, Dean Stanley E. Teele of Harvard University, and Professor Sterling Livingston of the Harvard Business School. Today the LMI remains dreadfully understudied with a research staff of more than six hundred members and contracts with almost every part of government and, increasingly, the private and third sectors. The founding of the LMI was both an element in this retooling of logistics and a symbol of its growing influence.

A Science of Systems

What can now be identified as the era of the "revolution in logistics," the 1960s was a time of tremendous experimentation (Bonacich 2005; Poist 1986). The timing of this rising concern with logistics in business management can be explained in part by the wartime display of complex logistics planning and operations. But there were other practical factors that propelled logistics to the center of attention in business management in the postwar years. Quantitative techniques and the computers on which they relied were key (Stenger 1986). According to Donald Bowersox (1968, 64), neither computers nor quantitative methods "were to be denied the fertility of physical distribution applications." The "prolonged profit squeeze of the early 1950s," culminating in a recession in 1958, prompted big business in the United States to search for cost savings in their operations. At this time, logistics was identified as the solution to complex problems. Reflecting on this development of logistics as it transpired, Smykay and LaLonde (1967, 108) wrote, "The time is right, the harvest is full, and only awaits the picking."

It is not only the expansion of logistics research but the radical shifts in its theory and practice that were so important at this time. Transformation in the corporate spatial practice that marks the revolution in logistics occurred through thinking and calculating space anew. By the end of the

1950s, two highly influential articles helped to shift emphasis in the field from transportation, physical distribution, and what was known as "rhocrematics" (Brewer and Rosenzweig 1961; Bedeian 1974) to logistics (Lewis, Culliton, and Steel 1956; Meyer 1959). These articles emphasized that the stakes were much higher than just the isolated movement of goods out of the factory. Rather, they emphasized the opening up of a new space of action—the rationalization and deliberate management of spatial organization within the firm and beyond. But important as these early papers were, they still operated on the assumption of cost minimization. By the early 1960s, cost minimization had been replaced with a model that emphasized value added. The nature of this shift is subtle but substantial. As W. Bruce Allen (1997, 114) explains, "The typical analysis would be: x tons of widgets must be shipped from A to B; what is the cheapest full-distribution cost mode to ship by? A profit maximizing approach would ask questions of whether x was the best amount to ship and whether to ship from point A to point B was the proper origin and destination pair." The shift to a profit-maximizing approach was an important consequence of the introduction of systems thinking into the field of distribution geography in the early 1960s. It was the shift to a systems approach to logistics problems that revolutionized the field. With systems analysis, logistics and distribution were conceptualized wholly differently:

> In traditional orientations to business operations, the end of the
> production line, as they put it in the paper industry, is at the dry end
> of the machine. Physical distribution perspectives, however, throw
> entirely new light on the question, "Where does the production line
> end?" In the view of physical distribution managements, the end of the
> production line is at the point where the consumer actually puts the
> product to use. The petroleum industry is a good case in point. Gasoline sold at the pump is really the end of the whole process of products
> and distribution. Yet no one actually sees the product even when it is
> finally delivered to the tank of the car. (Smykay and LaLonde 1967)

Without a doubt, the single most important shift that took place in logistics thought and practice in the early postwar period was the introduction of a "systems perspective" (Smykay and LaLonde 1967; LaLonde, Gabner, and Robeson 1970). Leading practitioners commenting on the evolution of the field at the time and more recently identify the profound impact of a broad paradigm shift toward a systems approach (Bertalanffy 1951; Johnson, Kast, and Rosenzweig 1964; Poist 1986). Until that time, the field was known as "physical distribution management," defined by the American Marketing Association in 1948 as "the movement and handling of goods from the point of production to the point of consumption or use" (cited in Haskett, Ivie, and Glaskowsky 1964, 7). Until the introduction of a systems approach, physical distribution was concerned exclusively with the movement of finished products. Upon its formation, the National Council of Physical Distribution Management defined the field as the movement of "the broad range of finished products from the end of the distribution line to the consumer, and in some cases . . . the movement of raw materials from the source of supply to the beginning of the production line" (cited in Smykay 1961, 4). Key here is the sharp separation between concerns and processes of production and distribution.

Yet, as Smykay and LaLonde (1967, 17) explain, "under the systems concept, attention is focused upon the total action of a function rather than upon its individual components." A systems perspective gave rise to a new approach known as "integrated distribution management," a new name for the field of business logistics and, importantly, a rescaled space of action. Distribution was increasingly understood as an element of the production process rather than a discrete function that followed. Firms like Lockheed and Boeing began incorporating logistics calculation into production flow at this time, further breaking down any distinction between production and distribution (Miller Davis 1974, 1). As the simple orange diagram this chapter opened with suggests, business logistics brought the entire system of production and distribution into focus. As Ronald Ballou (2006, 377) explains, the introduction of the name *business logistics* was an attempt both to distinguish the field from military logistics and also, importantly, "to focus on logistics activities that took place within the business firm." The implications of these shifts are profound; by the end of the revolutionary 1960s, business logistics was defined as "a total approach to the management of all activities involved in physically acquiring, moving and storing raw materials, in-process inventory, and finished goods inventory from the point of origin to the point of use or consumption" (LaLonde, Grabner, and Robeson 1970, 43; see also LaLonde1994). As Miller Davis explained in 1974, intrafirm activities

> form a total system. That is to say, purchasing, inventory control, material handling, warehousing, site determination, order processing, marketing, and other functional activities within the modern firm have common relationships that must be perceived, identified and treated as an inclusive unit. (1)

The Logistics of the Revolution in Logistics: Total Cost

While systems analysis is recognized as pivotal to the transformation of the field, the sources of this thought are explicitly and conspicuously absent in industry accounts. When logisticians and supply chain managers tell their history, they inevitably highlight the impact of systems approaches and underspecify their genealogies. As Bowersox (1968, 64) explains, "It is difficult to trace the exact origins of the systems approach to problem solving." In fact, it is both systems thought and "total cost analysis" that are highlighted in these early discussions of "integrated physical distribution." Writers cite the importance of both in the emergence of integrated distribution management, yet the latter fades quickly into the background, and the connection between them remains unexplored. In practice, it would seem that total cost analysis was the applied means through which systems thinking entered the field.

The connections become clear if we trace the operation and effects of "total cost." Total cost analysis aims to account for the actual costs of distribution across all the activities of the firm in contrast to the delimited segment of activity traditionally associated with the field. In a highly influential 1965 paper, Richard LeKashman and John Stolle of the firm Booz Allen Hamilton explain, "The real cost of distribution includes much more than what most companies consider when they attempt to deal with distribution costs" (1965, 34). These authors argue that costs that "never appear as distribution costs on any financial or operating report, but show up unidentified and unexplained at different times and in assorted places— in purchasing, in production, in paper-work processing—anywhere and everywhere in the business," are in fact "all intimately interrelated, linked together by one common bond. They all result from the way the company distributes its products" (LeKashman and Stolle 1965, 33). Only four years later, Peter Drucker estimated that the total cost of physical distribution accounted for as much as 50 percent of the total costs of the entire production and distribution process. Key here is that a wide range of functions previously understood to be distinct from distribution were now part of its total cost, including inventory carrying and obsolescence, warehousing, transportation, production alternatives, communications and data processing, customer service, alternative facilities use, channels of distribution, and cost concessions. Total cost analysis accounts for distribution costs embedded into other functions and "disguised" (LeKashman and Stolle 1965, 37), thus one practical impact of total cost analysis was to break down any hard distinctions between production and distribution.

Figure 4, which appeared in the 1965 article by LeKashman and Stolle, communicates two key lessons about total cost. The first and perhaps most obvious is the incredible amount of data that would be required to perform total cost analysis. Such elaborate calculations would be impossibly labor intensive without the advent of computers, nonlinear programming,

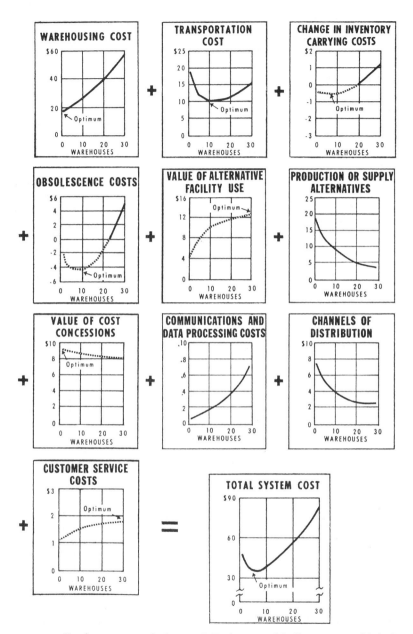

FIGURE 4. Total cost approach. Source: LeKashman and Stolle 1965, republished with permission of Elsevier; permission conveyed through Copyright Clearance Center Inc.

and simulation modeling. In fact, LeKashman and Stolle cite three reasons firms had not already adopted a total cost approach to distribution: first, because of the deeply embedded and intertwined nature of distribution costs in other activities; second, because of the traditional orientation of accounting departments toward production and finance; and third, the reason that they understand to be definitive. They explain, "The major reason why these distribution-related costs have continued to rise and to depress profit margins throughout our economy" is because "even a relatively simple problem in distribution system design can involve hundreds of bits of information that interact in thousands of ways. So there was no way of dealing with the distribution cost complex" until techniques and technologies were designed to help (1965, 37). The wider availability of these technologies helps explain the timing of the rise of total cost.

Writing in the late 1960s, Edward Smykay and Bernard LaLonde (1967) argued that computer technologies competed with physical distribution for the attention of business management at this time, yet it is clear that the latter was the domain for the application of the former and that the interest in physical distribution was inextricably tied to the transformative capacities of computer technologies.

At least as important as the rise of computer technologies that enabled new kinds of cost calculation, the collection of charts in Figure 5 reveals that a total cost analysis itself identifies for a firm the "opportunity to increase its profits that it could not have identified or taken advantage of in any other way" (LeKashman and Stolle 1965, 38). Total cost analysis produced new sources of profit with very different kinds of effects on corporate strategy, and this strategy was inherently spatial. Whether a firm invested in more warehouses, changed the location of production, or invested in more transportation infrastructure would all be decisions made relationally in the broader interest of total cost, or overall profitability. Total cost analysis would often yield counterintuitive decisions regarding location. In one example that LeKashman and Stolle provide, they insist that "only the total cost approach could have established, for example, that the earnings of this business could be increased by supplying its customers in the Dakotas from a plant in Ohio rather than from a much nearer facility in Illinois. Yet when total profits were calculated, this turned out to be an element in the most profitable use of the existing facilities of this company" (1965, 43; see Figure 5). Because of the "interdisciplinary" nature of the analysis, senior executive support was necessary to undertake total cost analysis, thus propelling logistical questions to a much higher level of management. In fact, with the adoption of total cost, corporate strategy became ever more defined by logistics.

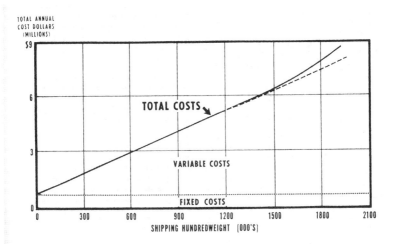

FIGURE 5

Total Plant and Warehousing Cost, Five Plants

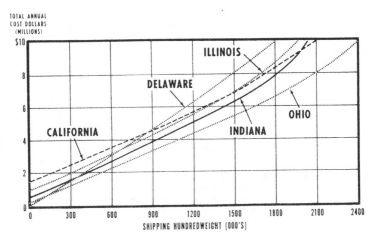

FIGURE 5. Total plant and warehousing cost, five plants. Source: LeKashman and Stolle 1965, republished with permission of Elsevier; permission conveyed through Copyright Clearance Center Inc.

Total cost analysis was thus crucial to the revisioning of the field during the 1960s and was a practical means through which systems approaches entered the field. This latter claim has significant implications, as it means that the source for systems thinking in early logistics thought also becomes clear. Total cost analysis was developed by researchers at the RAND Corporation as part of their post–World War II operations research. In fact, the total cost concept and total cost methods stem directly from RAND's work on Air Force weapons systems in the 1950s (see Fisher 1956). This suggests not any simple militarization of business but rather a more complex entanglement of market and military.

The rise of integrated distribution management meant that cost minimization was gradually replaced with a model that emphasized value added (Allen 1997). Logistics was transformed from a least-cost analysis of discrete segments of distribution into a science of value added through circulatory systems. The revolution in logistics saw transportation conceptualized as a vital element of production systems rather than a separate domain or the residual act of distributing commodities after production; it thereby put the entire spatial organization of the firm, including the location of factories and warehouses, directly into question. From this point onward, logistics became a "science of systems," and its more circumscribed concern with distribution transformed into an umbrella science of spatial management. In the words of two of the most important early figures in the field, "'Where does the production line end?' In the view of physical distribution management, the end of the production line is at the point where the consumer actually puts the product to use" (Smykay and LaLonde 1967, 98).

Social War and Technological Change

By reframing the way that economic space was conceived and calculated, the science of business logistics was critical in the remaking of geographies of capitalist production and distribution on a global scale. Business logistics helped build a global social factory. Rethinking "the system" in this way facilitated relocation and reorganization of the component parts of the supply chain, not just from Illinois to Ohio, but around the world. Of course, there was much precedent for the increasingly transnational organization of production and circulation, not only in the experiences of colonial trade regimes such as those in cotton, fur, and tea. A more recent and much more directly relevant event that fed immediately into the revolution in logistics was the American military's adoption of the shipping container for supplying the war effort. Initially developed to solve the logistical challenges of the U.S. military during and after World War II, the container would eventually help to transform the organization of civilian life. While there were earlier experiments with container technologies, it was the U.S. military's use that led to its development and standardization. More than fifty years after its introduction as an efficient means of moving military equipment to the front, the container has been celebrated as the single most important invention in the economic globalization of the decades that followed (Levinson 2006; "Moving Story" 2002; Rodrigue and Notteboom 2008). Containerization radically reduced the time required to load and unload ships, reducing port labor costs and enabling tremendous savings for manufacturers, who could reduce inventories to a bare minimum. Containerization was thus a necessary underpinning for the rise of just-in-time (JIT) production techniques. For JIT to become a globalized system, inputs and commodities had to be coordinated and transported quickly and reliably across space. U.S. military procurement laid many of the infrastructural foundations for this work during the Korean War (Reifer 2004, 24). With the military's use of containers to manage massive supply chains during the Vietnam War, container shipping became firmly entrenched (Levinson 2006, 8, 178).

If containerization was a technology that saw much of its early development in American wars abroad, the introduction of the standard shipping container was also part of a growing social war on transport workers at home. Much of the cost savings that came with containerization came directly from the reduction in workers' time needed to unload and reload ships. Struggles over containerization in ports in the United States and abroad were often explosive, animated not only by the specific question of the container but by the rights of workers to participate in decisions regarding the planning and management of technological innovation in their workplaces. From the perspective of owners and managers, time was of the essence. Slashing labor time by mechanizing port work was one direct outcome of containerization, but technological change also provided an opportunity to undermine the strength of organized labor, and so the conditions of work, and assert greater control over the flow of goods. There is a range of different experiences of containerization that vary with the strategies unions adopted—in some cases to fight against it, and elsewhere to fight for some control of this technological transformation (Bonacich 2005; Lim 2011; Reifer 2004). We return to these struggles over labor and logistics in chapter 5 and see how protecting the flow of cargo in the interests of efficient supply chains has in recent years come to be treated as a matter of national security (Amoore and De Goede 2008; Cooper 2006; Rice and Caniato 2003), with devastating consequences for transport workers. However, another aspect of this domestic social war on transport workers that was crucial for the revolution and constitutive of the globalization of trade requires brief scrutiny here: *deregulation.*

If containers were a physical technology that transformed both the social and spatial organization of trade and provided the opportunity for an attack on the strength of organized labor in the ports, then deregulation was a social technology with similar effects across many modes of transportation. The push for deregulation in the transport sector really emerged in force in the 1950s when "those with foresight planted a seed that the field of transport and logistics was important" (Allen 1997, 119). President Truman's 1955 Week's Report, and two reports commissioned under President Eisenhower, the 1960 Mueller and Doyle Reports, all advised that transport regulation was "holding back the economy" and recommended deregulation (Arthur 1962; Allen 1997). Presidents Kennedy and Johnson made similar assessments. Advocacy for deregulation was bipartisan. As Allen (1997, 108) explains, "The seed was planted— the rules didn't have to be the rules. Firms might compete on the basis of transportation." Fueled by the recession of the 1970s, the oil embargo, and rising inflation, which intensified concerns for cost control and competition, the lobby for deregulation gained strength. Following the lead of the Nixon and Ford administrations, Carter took on the cause and ran his 1980 reelection campaign on the grounds of fighting regulation to control inflation (Allen 1997, 108). While regulation in transport history may be more productively seen as a long history of reregulation, 1980 marked an important moment. Indeed, as James MacDonald and Linda Cavalluzzo (1996, 80) explain, "Between 1975 and 1983, Congress fundamentally altered the system of transportation regulation in the United States," with profound implications for owners and operators. With ideological fervor appropriate for reflection on a moment of ascendant neoliberalism, Clifford Lynch (1998, 3) exclaims, "The year 1980 brought with it the opportunity to do all these things. It was during this year that the transportation industry in the United States was deregulated. After over 100 years of outmoded and often inequitably applied laws, the nation's carriers were at last free to operate in a free-market environment. They were free to be creative and innovative. Most importantly, their customers were free to behave competitively." Just a few years later, the National Council of Physical Distribution Management changed its name to the Council of Logistics Management. In a 1985 editorial piece, they explain how "physical distribution's role in industry has changed dramatically, particularly since the advent of deregulation." The name was changed to recognize that *logistics* was the most encompassing term that described the management of firms' acquiring and distributing activities over space (specifically to include both inbound and outbound materials as well as management of the work itself). Indeed, they suggest that "the move to 'logistics' is a very positive step as it connotes a much broader range of activities than 'physical distribution' does. Communications, information flows, and data interchange are compelling managers to integrate the total materials/finished product cycle much more closely than ever before" (Cutshell 1985, 7). But the professional association also marks that the name change was "a move designed to expand its participation and concerns beyond national boundaries" ("NCPDM" 1985).

In contrast to the simple assessment of deregulation enhancing the "freedom of customers," a more careful examination reveals that deregulation was a complex process that took shape quite differently in different sectors of the transportation industry. As James Peoples (1998, 128) explains, "Deregulation has radically altered labor relations in the trucking, railroad, airline, and telecommunications industries, but what is interesting is the differing approaches to reducing labor costs that were used in each industry." Indeed, there were some common outcomes: deregulation of the U.S. transport sector had devastating consequences for workers, and on the whole it oriented the industry toward the transnational shipment of goods in place of a purely national focus. But the particular ways in which deregulation did its work and the specific outcomes vary. In the rail sector, MacDonald and Cavalluzzo (1996, 80) demonstrate that despite the fact that the 1980 Staggers Rail Act made virtually no direct mention of labor, it nevertheless led to a "dramatic decline in employment," the gradual erosion of wages, and the decline of the strength of unions' bargaining power. This was because the cost savings "resulted from a reduced demand for labor associated with changes in shipment methods" (ibid.). This is significant because rail is the one sector that had high rates of unionization and maintained them throughout the period of deregulation (Peoples 1998), and yet rail workers nevertheless experienced significant deterioration in their conditions of work. The trucking industry, on the other hand, saw a stark decline in the union membership rate from 46 percent to 23 percent over the deregulation period of 1978 through 1996 (Peoples 1998, 112). Weekly earnings in that sector during that time period fell from $499/week to $353/week in constant 1983–84 dollars (ibid.). This decline is directly attributed to the 1980 Motor Carrier Act, which encouraged a shifting of risk from owners to operators and prompted the widespread use of nonunion "owner operators" with closer resemblance to sharecroppers than the label of "self-employed" suggests. As Peoples (1998) reports, in the sectors where the workforce continued to expand after deregulation such as trucking and airlines, wages and union density were under direct attack, whereas in the rail sector, where wages and union density remained more constant, it was the number of workers that declined radically. Altogether this meant that across the entire transport industry cost savings that were reaped from deregulation were largely taken directly from workers. From the time before deregulation through to labor's total annual compensation in 1991, worker losses amount to up to $5.7 billion in trucking, $1.2 billion in railroads, $3.4 billion in airlines, and $5.1 billion in telecommunications (Peoples 1998, 128).

Another implication of the wave of deregulation that occurred from the late 1970s through the 1990s was the rise of intermodalism. Intermodalism refers to the organization of transportation across more than one mode, and it has been a vital element of the rise of global logistics. Before deregulation, intermodalism was discouraged by policies that created financial incentives against cooperation and joint planning. Deregulation fostered the rapid growth of intermediaries in the logistics industry, and yet even before the deregulation of transport was under way, industry analysts predicted the rise of intermediary operators as an almost necessary feature of intermodalism. Writing in 1970, LaLonde, Grabner, and Robeson suggest that "a new form of distribution middleman with intermodal capability and spanning a wide range of intermediate distribution functions will emerge to serve the needs of the multinational distribution manager during the 1970s" (48). The story of intermodalism brings us back to the emergence of the shipping container and wartime experiments. Jean-Paul Rodrigue and Theo Notteboom (2009) suggest that intermodalism was far from a new concept in the world of transportation and in fact that efforts to ease the transfer of goods from one mode of transit to another were active in the late nineteenth and early twentieth centuries. They suggest that the pallet was the first successful intermodal technology, which in the 1930s reduced the time required to unload a boxcar from three days to four hours. It was World War II that truly "demonstrated the time and labor saving benefits of using pallets" (2009, 2). Yet Rodrigue and Notteboom argue that while intermodalism had earlier precedents, it was "the advent of the container that had the largest impact on intermodal transportation" (2009, 2). True intermodalism took some time to develop because of the reticence of shipping companies to invest too heavily in container technologies prior to the standardization of both the box and its infrastructure. The maritime sector was gradually able to move ahead with a standard dimension container following the International Standards Organization's designation of two standard measures: the twenty-foot equivalent unit (TEU), which became the industry standard reference for cargo volume and vessel capacity, and the forty-foot equivalent unit (FEU), the most commonly used container today.

Yet U.S. rail was unable to adapt prior to deregulation. Rodrigue and Notteboom (2008, 4) explain that after the 1980 Staggers Act when the deregulation process was set in motion, "companies were no longer prohibited from owning across different modes and they developed a strong impetus towards intermodal cooperation." And indeed, as Figure 6 suggests, growth in intermodal rail loadings (with rail as the key link in the intermodal supply chain) has increased since 1965, but the rate of growth really takes off after 1980.

Deregulation of the rail sector in the United States was thus a lynch-pin in the construction of the global material infrastructure for business logistics. Celebrating the seamless system that intermodalism promises, Rodrigue and Notteboom (2008, 4) state, "The advantages of each mode could be exploited in a seamless system. Customers could purchase the service to ship their products from door to door, without having to concern themselves with modal barriers. With one bill of lading, clients can obtain one through rate, despite the transfer of goods from one mode to another." Deregulation of the domestic transport sectors has all these implications and others, but it also piggybacked on an attack on labor that was explicitly transnational in form and scope. It is perhaps not surprising that a profound reregulation of the shipping industry—a fractious and contested process that started in the interwar period and gave rise to the "flag of convenience"—served as the precedent on which the globalization of U.S. industry and deregulation of transport sectors unfolded. "Open registries" or "flags of convenience" were experimented with first by U.S. firms in Panama. Their use expanded significantly during and after World War II and then again following the oil crisis of 1973. In 1949, Panama had already become the fourth-largest shipping nation, following the United States, the United Kingdom, and Norway—yet the vast majority of registered ships were American owned (306 of 462; Cafruny 1987, 94). Jonathan Barton (1999, 149) asserts the significance of the flags of convenience debates, which "traditionally only concerned shipping but now has wider ramifications in terms of the globalizing of other sectors." The radical transformation in the geography of shipping regulation "has provided a model of interstate failure to regulate flexible, globalizing, geoeconomic

Year	1965	1970	1975	1980	1985	1990	1995	1997
Loads (millions)	1.7	2.4	2.2	3.1	4.6	6.2	8.1	8.7

FIGURE 6. Rail intermodal loadings. Source: Association of American Railroads, reprinted in Plant 2002.

forces." And yet, this can only be understood as a convenient or successful failure, as the implications for the economy more broadly are significant and proceed apace. Indeed, by allowing firms to geographically circumvent "nation-state legislative and economic controls, the Open Registries issue provides an intriguing yet disturbing example of the problems of international agreement and international management of the transboundary geoeconomic ecumeme" (Barton 1999, 149).

Guy Heinemann and Donald Moss (1969–70, 416) explain that flags of convenience offer ship owners advantages including "immunity from direct taxation, lower repair costs, circumvention of strict Coast Guard safety requirements, and avoidance of high wages paid to American seamen." "Beyond the purely economic benefits," Barton (1999, 148) asserts that flags of convenience "provide an advantageous blanket of anonymity for ship owners since the associated difficulties of the investigation of shipping casualties and the tracing of owners, holding companies and operating companies makes for a complex web that international maritime agencies are left to unravel." More than half of the world's ships are flagged in this way, even as a majority of the world merchant fleet is owned by ship owners in Greece, Japan, the United States, Norway, and Hong Kong, statistics that "demonstrate the separation of the traditional concept of national shipping and the modern form of globalized shipping" (Barton 1999, 145).

Alan Cafruny (1987, 96) outlines the immediate stakes of the flag of convenience for labor: "The creation of an international market enabled owners to subvert the national gains won by militant seamen's unions internationally and, especially in the Unites States." In other words, "flags of convenience thus placed America's maritime unions on the defensive." Maritime workers have fought these developments since the 1950s; the Seafarers International Union and National Maritime Union launched a global boycott of vessels in 1958, which had most impact within the United States, "where 129 vessels were picketed, rendering the docks around these vessels unworkable when other dock workers refused to cross the picket lines" (Heinemann and Moss 1969–70, 417). After another round of actions in 1961, the president issued a Taft-Hartley injunction in order to break eighteen days of disruption to the industry. The expansion of flags of convenience was not only protected by the U.S. government but actively engineered by the same. Cafruny (1987, 94) outlines how an active coalition between "extractive multinationals, large independent shipowners, and the executive branch"—"implicitly endorsed" by the inactivity of Congress—established this powerful precedent in the postwar period.

That maritime labor felt the impact of the rise of flags of convenience is hardly a surprise—labor was the key target rather than collateral damage. Figure 7 not only suggests how critical the cost of labor was to postwar considerations of the shipping industry—especially in the United States— but the British figures also expose how much race and nationality was an organizing principal for maritime work. Cafruny (1987, 94) explains that the 1954 report from the Department of Transportation and Maritime Administration that carried this table found that a central reason for the dramatic disparities in wages derived from the capacity of shippers outside the United States to employ "non-nationals."

A New Imperial Imaginary: Cartography and Spatial Metaphor

Even as there has been a profusion of interest in the role of models, maps, and other "conceived" spaces in the production of human geographies (Elden 2007; Lefebvre 1991; Huxley 2006), transformations in the ways that the economic space of globalized capitalism has been conceived and calculated are almost entirely neglected outside the applied field of business management. The work that perhaps comes closest is writings on the concept of "time-space compression" (Bell 1974). David Harvey has used the concept to explore how globalization processes and the rise of advanced capitalism organized through the speed of supply chains and JIT production techniques have dramatically transformed experiences

	Number of Crew	Total Monthly Wages (USD)
United Kingdom, mixed crew	80	5,541
United Kingdom, white crew	54	6,444
Japan	56	6,273
Norway	43	7,145
Netherlands	55	7,567
Italy	41	7,713
Denmark	43	7,990
France	47	10,274
United States	48	29,426

FIGURE 7. Comparison of wage costs aboard United States and foreign flag vessels, 1953. Source: U.S. Department of Commerce, reprinted in Cafruny 1987.

and representations of space. His notion of space-time compression identifies "processes that so revolutionize the objective qualities of space and time that we are forced to alter, sometimes in quite radical ways, how we represent the world to ourselves" (1989, 240). Yet the history of business logistics reveals that changing representations of space were not only an outcome of space-time compression but also a foundation for changing lived relations of space-time.

Henri Lefebvre (1991) offered one of the most compelling analyses of the role of technical and professional conceptions of space in the production of space more broadly. His influential "triadic" conception of space puts emphasis on the role of scientists', technicians', bureaucrats', and managers' representations of space in shaping perceptions of space and spatial practice. Scholars from geography and other social science disciplines increasingly mobilize discursive methodologies to understand how economic space is produced and regulated and to explore how economic actors define and legitimize their methods and theories through their representations of economic problems and solutions (Amin and Thrift 2004; Barnes 2004; Buck-Morss 1995; Callon 1998; Gibson-Graham 1996; Mitchell 2005). But despite longstanding interest in the production of space (Gregory 1994; Harvey 1973; Lefebvre 1991; Massey 1977; McDowell 1999; Smith 1984; Soja 1989; Thrift 1996;), recent work on the rise of "geo-economic" calculation (Neil Smith 2005; Sparke 2006), and growing interest in social and political theory on the "performance of the economy" (Barnes 2002; Callon 1998; Mitchell 2005; Strathern 2002; Thrift 2000), there is a dearth of scholarship on the representations of logistics space.

We have already seen how powerful systems thinking was for the formation of business logistics. Rethinking distribution as an element of an integrated system of production and circulation, rather than a discrete and bounded activity, opened up the possibility of organizing the system differently. But what kinds of understandings and associations does the notion of a system bring with it? Did particular meanings already associated with the notion of a system impact how the physical distribution system was conceived and practiced? Systems theory emerged out of natural sciences, and it wasn't until the 1960s that it moved into social scientific work. Ludwig Von Bertalanfy's systems theory is a different variant of systems thinking than the systems analysis of RAND and operations research; nevertheless, they share common conceptual underpinnings and overlap in popular and research worlds (Hammond 2002). In his classic text, *General Systems Theory,* Von Bertalanfy (1973, 46) defines a system as "an arrangement of entities related in such a way as to form a unity or organic whole." The biological framing persisted in the organic models of organizations as organisms, and this was a goal, not an accident. "Whether a living organism or a society," Von Bertalanfy explains, "characteristics of organizations, are notions like wholeness, growth, differentiation, hierarchical order, dominance, control, competition." He proceeds to cite "Iron laws" that "hold good for any organization," and the first he cites is the Malthusian law of population.

Biological models for human society are hardly new—for instance, the "body politic" has long been a powerful political metaphor with tangible effects (Rasmussen and Brown 2002). Systems theory places an emphasis on the "subjective bounding of the system, and a fundamental emphasis on flow" (Naim, Holweg, and Towill 2003). In a recent paper on systems thinking in supply chain management, Naim, Holweg, and Towill (2003) write, "Systems are intra and interconnected by flows, or exchanges of information and matter. It is these flows that determine the extent of integration in the operating environment." Systems theory thus posits a biological imperative to flow, wherein disruption becomes a threat to the very *resilience* of the system. This notion of an organic imperative to the integrity of the system becomes important in more recent attempts to protect supply chains from disruption (Collier and Lakoff 2007; Pettit, Fiskel, and Croxton 2010), and this has implications for the way securitization has unfolded, as we explore in chapter 2 and then in more detail in the concluding chapter.

But if the biological contours to the metaphor of the system would in many ways infuse the assembly of business logistics, the frequent deployment of another set of metaphors played a definitive role in ensuring that

Physical Distribution – Forgotten Frontier

Guidelines to profit improvement are revealed through varying company approaches to control information, personnel competence, distribution economics, and the overall distribution problem.

FIGURE 8. "Physical Distribution—Forgotten Frontier." Source: Neuschel 1967.

business logistics would remain tethered to its military past. In the writings that came to define the field in the 1960s through the early 1970s, colonial and military metaphors were rife. The landmark work on logistics and physical distribution carried titles about "new frontiers" and "dark continents," a reminder of the history of this new business science as an old military art. Writing in *Fortune* magazine in 1962, management guru Peter Drucker (1962, 72) identified logistics and physical distribution as America's "Last Dark Continent": "We know little more about distribution today than Napoleon's contemporaries knew about the interior of Africa. We know it is there, and we know it is big; and that's about all."

These colonial metaphors are perhaps more telling than their authors would suspect. From its history as a military art in service of the national, territorial, geopolitical state, logistics became a technology of supranational firms operating in relational geo-economic space. In contrast to the

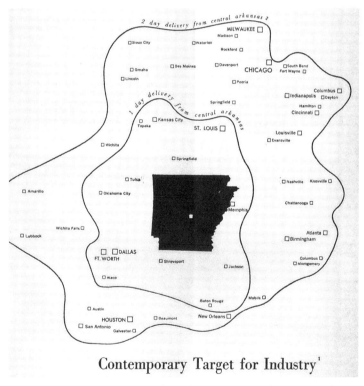

Contemporary Target for Industry[1]

FIGURE 9. Contemporary target for industry. Source: Advertisement from *Fortune* magazine, June 1968.

absolute territory of geopolitical calculation associated with colonial rule, geo-economics relies on the unimpeded flows of goods, capital, and information across territorial boundaries. As Neil Smith argues in his analysis of American imperialism, geo-economics denotes a shift from direct territorial control to rule through markets (Smith 2004; 2005, 71). Territorial rule becomes a tactical option rather than a strategic necessity. Geo-economics thus does not operate "beyond space" or "after geography"; rather, geo-economic political geographies transform rather than dispense with spatial calculation, and the work of logistics is concerned precisely with the production of space beyond territory. Indeed, the revolution of logistics is precisely a revolution within capitalism, a revolution in the spatial logics of global economic and political power. These metaphors provide a glimpse into the changing and persistent politics of imperialism, a theme we will revisit in chapters to come.

After the Revolution

In 1991, following Operation Desert Storm (widely heralded as a logistical war par excellence), the corporate world once again looked to the U.S. military for lessons in logistics. Yet this time, they only found their own models, language, and lessons thrown back at them. In an interview with a leading business magazine, lead logistician General William Pagonis touted the lessons of corporate logistics management, mobilizing concepts such as "profit ratio" and "customer satisfaction," casually explaining their translation into the art of war. Indeed, the interviewer notes, "Pagonis demonstrates what senior managers of world-class companies have always known: good logistics can be a source of competitive advantage, and excellent logistics management has many similarities to and ideas for other management disciplines, including general management" (Sharman 1991, 3). In his report on contingency operations logistics, Major Brian Layer (1994) makes a similar claim, asserting that over the past few decades U.S. military logistics lagged behind the "logistic innovations" that have "revolutionized civilian distribution practices." However, "despite the deficit," Layer argues, "US operational artists can benefit from these innovative logistics ideas . . . many successful companies provide impressive logistic design models." Like leading civilian companies that "look to logistic design as a tool for gaining competitive advantage over their rivals," Layer argues that "military planners should look to their own logistics systems as a means to gain operational advantage over the enemy."

Yet tempting as it may be to tell a tale of the "civilianization" or "corporatization" of logistics over the past six decades, this narrative would be a partial truth. The revolution in logistics hardly marked its "civilian-ization" but rather a different and even deepened entanglement between military and market methods.

As we will see in the chapters that follow, if we went into the logistics revolution of the 1960s with a corporate world eager to learn from military knowledge, we have emerged from the other side with an art and science that is deeply hybrid in its influence, with logisticians that receive their training in both military academies and business schools, and with a logistics industry that provides the backbone for both corporate and military strategy, such that it would be futile to try to disentangle who said what. As we will see in the concluding chapter, logistics is furthermore the sector of current U.S. military work that is most likely to be contracted out to private military companies, the proliferation of which also challenges this military–civilian divide. And finally, as chapter 2 explores in some depth, the entanglement of military and civilian logistics is particularly stark in the recent rise of "supply chain security," a form of security that aims to protect the material infrastructure and commodities flows of global trade.

CHAPTER TWO

From National Borders to Global Seams

The Rise of Supply Chain Security

The diagram in Figure 10 appeared as part of a 2006 *New York Times* article on the growing challenge of securing global supply chains (Fattah and Lipton 2006). Assembled using data from the RAND Corporation, U.S. Customs and Border Protection (CBP), the Government Accountability Office, and AMR Research, "Securing the Flow of Goods" illustrates the transnational journey of an imaginary shipping container from source to destination. The diagram highlights the myriad sites along the route where "security concerns" arise: opportunities for tampering with the contents of containers, sites where inspection technologies are outdated or inadequate, and places where physical security (gates, fences, locks, cameras) around ports and other transshipment facilities is lacking. The diagram also showcases a variety of security initiatives that have been designed in response to these perceived risks, but in stark contrast to typical national security initiatives, the border does not serve as the "geographical pivot" here. The national border has not vanished, but it requires some effort to determine its exact whereabouts. The border can be found, presumably, between the zones labeled "at sea" and "United States"—the site where CBP does one of its many marked screenings and inspections. A literal move away from borders, and away from territorial models of security on which they rely, is characteristic of broader attempts to secure the transnational material and informational networks of global trade. This diagram helps mark the rise of a new paradigm of security—supply chain security—that is increasingly challenging geopolitical forms organized by nation-state territoriality.

At least two other things are notable about this graphic representation of security in the global supply chain. First, it is striking how closely this

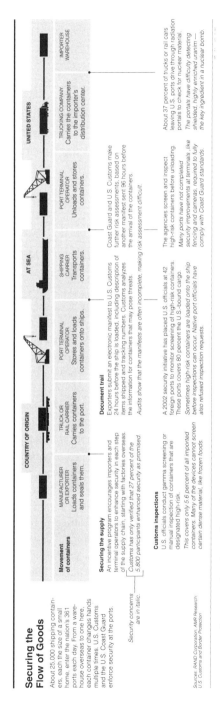

FIGURE 10. "Securing the Flow of Goods." Source: Fattah and Lipton 2006. Copyright 2006 *New York Times*. All rights reserved.

diagram resembles the one that opened the previous chapter. "Alternative Orientation to Integrated Distribution Management" rendered the conceptual shift of the revolution in logistics immediately visible; the formerly separate fields associated with managing materials through the production process and distributing them afterward were folded into the new umbrella field of business logistics and a new vision of the supply chain as a system. "Securing the Flow of Goods" assumes that same systems context. It maps the same activities in the same formation, starting with the manufacturing process and working through distribution to the buyer. "Securing the Flow of Goods" takes the same series of movements as the diagram from chapter 1 but stretches them around the world and across national borders.

This takes us to one final feature of the diagram that demands scrutiny. While these diagrams are similar, a clear difference is the focus on security here. If the diagram from chapter 1 rendered the revolution in logistics visible, then this one clearly marks the securitization of globalized and revolutionized logistics. The demand for security has become ubiquitous in the early years of the twenty-first century. From states' claims to national security in the face of terror, to the demands of nongovernmental organizations for human security to protect civilians against casualty, to claims to income security by activists in search of a living wage, to the growing demand for local food security from social movements, *security* is high on the political agenda. Yet despite this contemporary common sense, the supply chain is much more than just another site of securitization. In a neoliberal context wherein economy has become policy, the protection of the material flows of trade is paramount. The stretching of logistics systems across borders into "pipelines of trade" means that supply chain security recasts not only the object of security but its logics and spatial forms as well. This diagram prompts us to explore these shifts and ask, when did national governments, supranational governing bodies, transnational shipping and logistics corporations, and retailers begin to devote extensive efforts to "secure the supply chain"? What are the implications of the rise of supply chain security for politics, space, and citizenship?

"Securing the Flow of Goods" thus provokes questions about a series of profound shifts in the relationships between security, space, and economy that animate the following investigation. This chapter traces efforts on the part of national states, supranational governing bodies, and transnational corporations to actualize the promise of the revolution in logistics—to make logistics systems "seamless." It is one thing to *conceive* of logistics as a system, however, and another to enact the regulatory reform, extend the physical infrastructure, and enhance the speed of circulation in that system. This latter labor was initiated with the rise of intermodalism and the deregulation of the transport sector, addressed in chapter 1 (Allen 1997; Levinson 2006; Rodrigue and Notteboom 2008), yet by the 1990s these efforts took shape on a whole new scale. Transnational trade agreements were both a sign of the growth of cargo flows and an important element in amplifying them. The capacity for countries to participate in the physical circulation of global trade became itself a measure of development, and by the turn of the century the World Bank was producing global indexes of national competitiveness based entirely on the speed and reliability of logistics systems. This growing emphasis on global logistics has not simply expanded the scale of economy—for instance, from a national to continental or even global space. Rather, it provoked a newfound emphasis on the infrastructural networks of trade and renewed interest in "corridors and gateways," both anchored in enormous logistics infrastructure projects led by states acting with or like corporations (cf. Cowen and Smith 2009). But if states and corporations have invested heavily in infrastructure and regulation to enhance seamless cargo circulation, they have also invested in the creation of supply chain security to protect that circulation. Indeed, a system built on the speedy circulation of cargo through smooth space entails new forms of vulnerability. As the Organisation for Economic Co-operation and Development asserts, world trade is fundamentally dependent on a system of maritime transport that has been made "as frictionless as possible," which renders that system fundamentally vulnerable, as "any important breakdown in the maritime transport system would fundamentally cripple the world economy" (2003, 2). Disruption is the Achilles heel of global logistics systems.

If the revolution in logistics allowed for the disaggregation and redistribution of what had previously been defined, separately, as production and distribution, then the globalization of logistics followed directly from that shift and redistributed component parts of the supply chain across the globe. Because of its reliance on the speed of supply chains, business logistics has provoked tremendous experimentation with the protection of these globalized networks. This experimentation has given rise to "network" or "systems" models of security, wherein borders are reconstituted and governed differently. Indeed, while these models of security prioritize flow, they are organized through new forms of containment—new kinds of borders and security zones. The rise of business logistics directly challenges geopolitical calculation and the national and territorial forms of security that historically gave it form.

Globalizing Logistics

In the wake of the revolution in logistics, global trade went through a period of phenomenal growth. In 1970, the total volume of international seaborne goods slightly exceeded 2,500 tons; by 2008, that figure reached 8.2 billion tons (IMO 2012, 6). The United Nations Environment Programme (UNEP) reports that in 2006 world shipping constituted 90 percent of global trade volume and documents the same phenomenal expansion of international trade using dollar figures; imports jumped from under a billion dollars in 1973 to an excess of twelve billion in 2006 (Vidal 2008). The World Shipping Council, an industry lobby group, reports the remarkable speed of expansion in global container traffic that took place in the years following the first Atlantic crossing by a container ship in 1966. In 1973, U.S., European, and Asian containership operators transported 4 million twenty-foot equivalent units (TEUs), but only a decade later in 1983, the figure jumped to 12 million TEUs, and container technology had circulated to the Middle East, the Indian subcontinent, and East and West Africa. The *Journal of Commerce* reports that by 2010 global container traffic hit the remarkable figure of 560 million TEUs (Barnard 2011).

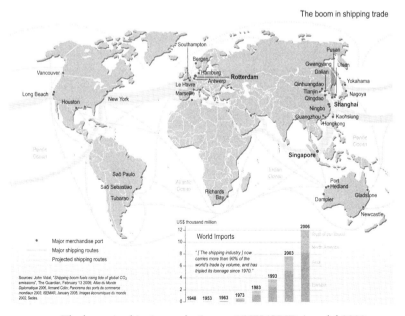

FIGURE 11. The boom in shipping trade. Source: UNEP/GRID-Arendal 2009.

That there are connections between logistics and the globalization of trade is increasingly clear to a broad public beyond the walls of management schools (Dicken 2003; Makillie 2006). Yet the transformations marked by the revolution in logistics and the ways in which these underpin rather than simply correspond with the globalization of production and trade remain hidden in plain view. It is significant that the world's largest company, Wal-Mart, is frequently described as a logistics company disguised as a retailer (Lecavalier 2010). Wal-Mart imports more tonnage into the United States than any other company, has the largest private satellite system in the world devoted to managing inventory movement, and creates global standards in the field—for instance, with the implementation of the bar code two decades ago (Bonacich and Wilson 2008, 9). Edna Bonacich and Jake Wilson (2008, 3) are right to point out that a "flurry of textbooks" have been published on the topic over the last decade, in addition to a proliferation of professional programs and trade journals devoted to logistics. However, they miss the mark when they suggest that this bout of activity indicates that the revolution in logistics itself is a recent event. As chapter 1 demonstrates, the most significant conceptual and calculative shifts underpinning the logistics revolution took place in the 1960s, while the elevation of logistics to an executive level within large corporations and the work of building professional organizations, lobbying for deregulation, and investing in intermodal infrastructure was already well under way in the 1970s. It is indeed recently that we have seen the popularization and generalization of logistics across the corporate sector. Today it is not only the large industry leaders that take the field seriously but companies of all kinds and sizes that are looking to logistics and competing on the basis of entire supply chains. Think tanks are also jumping into action, declaring that logistics is vital to national competitiveness. The Brookings Institute (Robins and Strauss-Wieder 2006, 8) queries, "Because the ability to compete and thrive in the emerging global economy now depends on the strengths of a nation's freight system, this dynamic situation generates one crucial question: Can U.S. infrastructure handle the volumes and adequately extract economic value from goods movement?" A series of popular advertising campaigns have made logistics accessible if not intriguing to a broader public. With ads on television and You-Tube, DHL explains that they are "passionate" about logistics, while the United Parcel Service (UPS) declares, "We love logistics"—affective corporate performances that I return to in the concluding chapter. Indeed, there is a growing common sense that the competitiveness of firms, nations, and supranational regions is contingent on their capacity to mobilize "seamless" supply chains, to circulate *stuff* in a timely and reliable way.

Notable in this flurry of attention to logistics is the growing interest of government, particularly entrepreneurial nation-states and supranational bodies like the World Bank and United Nations. The World Bank has become one of the most serious advocates of the science, calling logistics the "backbone of international trade." Their aggressive call for export-led growth strategies imposed through structural adjustment programs since the 1970s makes it almost surprising that their take-up of logistics didn't occur sooner. The consensus on the pivotal role of logistics to global trade is now established and frequently reiterated. In a review of Indian logistics infrastructure, global consulting firm Deloitte (2011, 3) suggests that while there are many factors that facilitate export-oriented growth, "the most important enabler is the improvement in transportation infrastructure (mainly ports, roads, airports and railways), telecommunications and power."

It wasn't until 2007 that the World Bank issued their first Logistics Performance Index (LPI), titled "Connecting to Compete: Trade Logistics in the Global Economy" (Arvis et al. 2007). The authors explain the vital role of logistics for development in the opening pages of the report, emphasizing that the capacity to "connect to what has been referred to as the 'physical internet' is fast becoming a key determinant of a country's competitiveness." The "physical internet," a term used by the *Economist* to describe the networked nature of global logistics systems, is said to bring "access to vast new markets; but for those whose links to the global logistics web are weak, the costs of exclusion are large and growing" (Arvis et al. 2007, 3). This global ranking of the competitiveness of national logistics systems has had a significant impact in drawing more attention to logistics infrastructure from governments, particularly in the global south. Praising their own efforts in the field, the World Bank authors report that their first LPI prompted several countries to launch programs to improve their logistics performance, cultivated greater cooperation between public and private sectors in the logistics field, and prompted demand for a second LPI, released in 2010 and to be updated every two years. The map in Figure 12 is a graphic representation of the LPI rankings drawn from the 2010 report. With the darker colors representing higher performance scores, the stark unevenness of global logistics systems shadows the stark unevenness of global political economy. The LPI is centrally concerned with the "logistics gap" between high- and low-income countries, particularly given that the World Bank locates its concern for logistics performance in a broader project of "poverty alleviation." The report highlights "the importance of trade logistics for developing country competitiveness and the ways in which the sector can help countries reap the benefits of globalization and fight poverty" (Arvis et al. 2010, 12).

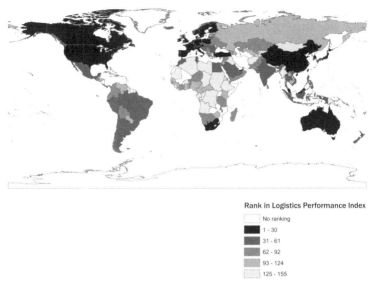

Rank in Logistics Performance Index

☐ No ranking
■ 1 - 30
■ 31 - 61
■ 62 - 92
■ 93 - 124
☐ 125 - 155

FIGURE 12. Map of global logistics performance index. Source: Arvis et al. 2010.

The critiques of the World Bank's export-led development models are extensive and come from all corners of the world (Sparr 1994; Plehwe, Walpen, and Neunhöffer 2006; Potter 2007). These will not be rehearsed here, but it is worth highlighting the extension of these models and in fact the deepening of the logic through the focus on the logistics of trade. The World Bank is increasingly taking aim at logistics systems and their infrastructural components and financing public–private infrastructure partnerships. By way of example, the World Bank is currently financing a massive logistics plan in Vietnam. The plan took shape at the behest of Nike, which employed two hundred thousand workers and produced ninety-four million pairs of shoes in the country in 2010. The company began lobbying the government to invest in infrastructure in order to strengthen their supply chain. USAID's Vietnam Competitive Initiative (VNCI) is facilitating private investment and privatization of the infrastructure—in their own words, "assisting the Ministry of Planning and Investment (MPI) to improve public procurement to attract private investment." The VNCI, in coordination with Nike and shipping giants Maersk and APL, coordinated and sponsored a "study mission" for Vietnamese officials to learn "about new models for PPP in ports and logistics infrastructure." One of the goals of these infrastructure investments is to increase the capacity of the ports around Ho Chi Minh City in order to increase the speed of goods circulation from the 2007 level of three million TEUs to thirteen million TEUs in 2013. The study mission also visited Singapore and met with the Singapore Economic Development Board, Ministry of Industry and Trade, Ministry of Finance, and Marine Port Authorities, as well as stakeholders responsible for infrastructure and export development, financing, project development, and project management such as PricewaterhouseCoopers, Lovells Lee and Lee, Fitch Ratings, and other key exporters and logistics providers. VNCI also worked with the Asian Development Bank to train sixty government officials in "PPP methods" and will support "a new PPP administrative unit that will be created in MPI for more efficient competitive procurement of PPP infrastructure projects" (ADB 2012).

In sum, American and global organizations are financing large-scale infrastructure investments in Vietnam to satisfy transnational production companies like Nike in their needs for enhanced logistics capabilities but so too to support the expansion of logistics companies like Maersk and APL. This project reveals a range of dynamics at play in contemporary logistics projects: the leadership of foreign investors in defining priorities for public investment, private ownership and financing of infrastructure, and public–private partnerships created to plan and govern projects. These are all familiar if not defining features of neoliberal government. The unwavering commitment to the promise of global capitalism to distribute social goods, a general faith in the efficiency of markets, and more broadly the elevation of market rationalities as unquestioned organizing principles of government are all hallmarks. Yet while neoliberalism has entailed a dramatic privatization of government, this has clearly not meant the emaciation of the state, another theme reflected here. Indeed, as Thomas Lemke (2001, 201) reminds us, "neo-liberal forms of government do not simply lead to . . . a reduction in state or its limitation to some basic functions"; rather, the state in the neoliberal model not only retains its traditional functions but also takes on new tasks and functions. While the role of the state within classic liberalism is tethered to the security of national and individual property (Cowen 2006), the neoliberal state takes on crucial new roles in making markets; in Lemke's words (2001, 197), "Government itself becomes a sort of enterprise whose task it is to universalize competition and invent market-shaped systems of action for individuals, groups and institutions," as we see with the Vietnamese project. The United Nations (UN Industrial Development Organization 2009, xv) captures elements of this role for the state in the context of public–private logistics partnerships when they assert, "Logistics can be disrupted by government-created delays or speeded by government-supplied infrastructure." Jeremy Plant (2002, 29) lobbies for more of this public supply for private gain, suggesting that "intermodalism needs policy advocates who argue an essentially Hamiltonian message, the need to increase the infrastructure by public means for the use of private operators in the achievement of community goals."

Alongside the shifting role of the state, investment in global logistics projects is also clearly contributing to the rescaling of government from national space to supranational regions. This enlarging of "free trade" zones to capture new markets and exploit new resources or labor forces has been cast as a constitutive feature of neoliberalism (Brenner and Theodore 2002; Peck and Tickell 2002; Sparke, Roberts, and Secor 2003). The free trade agreement between the United States and Vietnam ("Agreement" 2000) notes that Vietnam is "taking steps to integrate into the regional and world economy by, inter alia, joining the Association of Southeast Asian Nations (ASEAN), the ASEAN Free Trade Area (AFTA), and the Asia Pacific Economic Cooperation forum (APEC), and working toward membership in the World Trade Organization (WTO)," subsequently achieved in 2007. Accordingly, the United States and Vietnam extended "national treatment" to each other's products and producers.

These general observations about the neoliberal nature of globalized logistics are not without merit, but they also avoid the more nuanced shifts that are under way and attention to their effects. A more careful investigation of the globalization of logistics reveals something much more precise emerging—a new cartography of the political. This is not just about enlarging the zone of free trade in order to capture new markets, resources, or labor forces but about the creation of corridors, networks, or "pipelines" for the circulation of stuff. The significance of this network geography becomes clear when we investigate the very practical efforts that have emerged to protect these circulation systems and the radical implications they have for citizenship and security.

Gateway and Corridor Cartographies

Perhaps ironically, it took a business school professor to describe this emerging map of the North American space economy. Rather than territorial blocks of land regrouped into megaregions, Stephen Blank (2006) suggests that a transnational network of corridors and gateways offers a more apt visual rendering. The irony stems from the fact that it was geographers who were debating (and mapping) corridors and gateways four decades ago in a disciplinary conversation that has largely disappeared since. In the late 1960s and early 1970s, the role of gateways and corridors in the geography of economic activity formed an important pillar of the "urban systems" debates (Burghardt 1971; Whebell 1969). The decline of these debates in academic geography precisely at a time when supply chains were experiencing radical transformation and scrutiny in the corporate world is no coincidence but one of the uninterrogated effects of the revolution in logistics. As "distribution geography" was folded into logistics management, a split occurred between applied research that aimed to improve the efficiency of corporate circulation (Allen 1997; Ballou 2006; LaLonde, Grabner, and Robeson 1970; Pettit, Fiksel, and Croxton 2010) and a more critical trajectory of radical analyses emerging in geography committed to transforming rather than enhancing global capitalism (Dalby 1999; Elden 2007; Gibson-Graham 1996; Harvey 1989; Mitchell 2005). The study of transportation still occurs within geography departments, though it stands far from the cutting edge of the field. Professional logistics programs are typically located in business schools, and as Lawrence Busch (2007, 441) suggests, supply chain management programs are at times replacing traditional economics departments.

In a review of current "gateway and corridor" logistics initiatives, Trevor Heaver (2007, 1) explains, "The term 'gateway' was once used mainly by geographers to capture the image of a port serving a hinterland. Now, it has become popular in business and politics to capture the critical role that numerous activities on and beyond port terminals play in the flow of goods to and from hinterlands through the port communities." Heaver is right to suggest that the gateway concept has expanded in important ways in recent years. As David Gillen et al. (2007, 11) note, today gateways and corridors are "not just about transshipment of goods across the region" but about "creating value added services and the development of a significant logistics industry that among other things reduces the cost of the border to shippers." However, the key role of transportation infrastructure has remained constant. Writing in 1971, Andrew Burghardt describes a gateway as "an entrance into (and necessarily an exit out of) some area . . . located on a site of considerable transportational significance, i.e. either at a bulk-breaking point or at a node of transport" (269). Burghardt contrasts this model to that of the "central place" because of the prominence of central place theory at that time. He notes, "The central place . . . was not thought of in terms of a site of particular transportational significance" (270).

This is not to suggest that scholars have avoided interrogation of the shifting geographies of globalization. On the contrary, there are vast debates in this area. However, the gateway and corridor cartography that is at the core of globalized logistics has hardly featured in critical scholarly work. This cartography furthermore represents much more than simply a geography of trade routes. While the business school professor is right to suggest that a corridor cartography offers the best map of economic integration, it also offers a powerful mapping of forms of mobility and security that are actively reworking the geopolitical state. This network geography bounds the emerging *political space* of logistics.

Dynamic debates on the rescaling of the state and the "new regionalism" have explored these themes, but they have largely focused on the enlarging of political territories—the rescaling of the region, for instance—rather than the reconfiguration of the relationship between space, politics, and economy. Recent work on "geo-economics" has come closest to this question of gateway and corridor cartographies in that scholars are exploring a different logic of spatiality than that which underpins geopolitical thought and practice. If geopolitics is concerned primarily with the exercise of power and questions of sovereignty and authority within a territorially demarcated system of national states, then "geo-economics" emphasizes the recalibration of international space by globalized market logics and transnational actors (Cowen and Smith 2009). As Matthew Sparke (2000, 6) suggests, geo-economics entails "new forms of describing and inscribing territory that are increasingly common in the context of globalization—forms of description and inscription that treat spatial relations with the same top-down, view-from-nowhere, visual preoccupations of classical geopolitics but that are also characterized by a wholly different, non-state-centric identification with the border-crossing cartographies and deregulatory dynamics of today's transnationalized economies." Sparke has emphasized cross-border regional integration as a "distinct geographical component" of geo-economics in his work on the "remapping" of regions—particularly "Cascadia" straddling the Western U.S.–Canadian border underpinned by the North American Free Trade Agreement's (NAFTA's) continental integration—and his work examines a series of supranational trade maps that he argues "rescale" the region.

International trade agreements like NAFTA were crafted in response to already expanding integration but have also been pivotal in enhancing the volume of cross-border trade. The growth in cross-border flows was not in itself a surprise for the North American Free Trade Agreement's architects, but the dramatic rise of cross-border goods movement *within companies* that occurred in the wake of its implementation was. This "deep" or "structural integration" has come to define North America's "complex cross-border supply chains" (Blank, Golob, and Stanley 2006, 5). NAFTA is a late chapter in the long history of state-led transportation policy in North America. Canadian and U.S. transport policies were both initially oriented toward building a national system of east–west movement for colonial settlement, but today they are increasingly oriented toward a continental system of north–south flows. While NAFTA did not provide any direct financial commitments to transportation infrastructure (Brooks 2001), it did establish thirty working groups and committees that have addressed a wide range of regulatory standards in the areas of labor, hazardous materials, and technology. Large-scale lobby groups have emerged to demand more federal action, such as the Coalition for America's Gateways and Trade Corridors. There are substantial efforts to map and build North American logistics corridors led largely by private-sector coalitions working in conjunction with state and local governments, though often with federal funds. The most significant is North America's SuperCorridor Coalition (NASCO), also known as the Mid-Continent Corridor, but colloquially referred to by critics as the "NAFTA superhighway." CANAMEX is another significant North American corridor initiative that crosses the Cascadia region (see Figure 13). The emerging maps craft a different spatial imaginary than blocks of transnational territory, as Blank argues, and they represent much more than the simple mapping of supply lines. In addition to physical infrastructure enhancement, these corridor projects take a sustained focus on "soft infrastructure" such as the integration, standardization, and synchronization of customs and trade regulations, not to mention the entire realm of efforts to secure the actual space of these logistics corridors, which will be addressed shortly.

Logistics corridor projects and their visual rendering in technical and popular cartography are popping up all over the world. Projects are under way across Africa, where USAID has commissioned logistics diagnostics studies as part of their work in "trade facilitation." The Maputo Corridor Logistics Initiative (MCLI) is one of several major logistics corridor projects currently under way on the continent in which USAID has played a key role (others include the East Africa Corridor, West Africa Transport Logistics corridor, and the Trans-Kalahari Corridor). MCLI is a coalition of private and public shareholders from the rail, port, and roads sectors that connects Johannesburg to the port city of Maputo, Mozambique. The MCLI's lobbying efforts have been successful in transforming infrastructure as well as the management of the Mozambique–South Africa

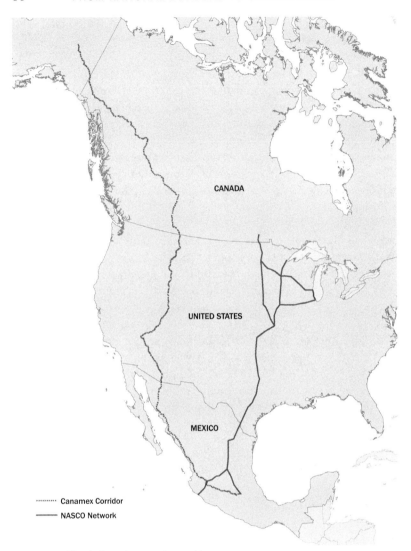

FIGURE 13. North American trade corridors.

border. Most significant in this regard was the creation of a "one stop border post" in 2010 for logistics (implemented later in the same year for passenger travel), which allows a common processing site for the two countries. Underpinning their "Seamless and Integrated Asia" initiative, the Asian Development Bank has been active in facilitating logistics corridor projects (ADB 2009, 2010). The bank conjures the legacy of the Silk

Road to mark the defining role that transnational trade routes have played historically in the region in their report on "Asian connectivity." One of the many major projects they are helping to finance is the Mekong corridor, sometimes referred to as the ASEAN logistics corridor, which crosses Myanmar, China, Laos, and Vietnam (see Figure 14). Agreements between these countries allow for the creation of a single stop for joint inspections of customs, quality inspection departments, and border control.

It is hardly surprising to learn that China has been a leader in corridor and gateway projects. Often imagined as a factory for the world, China is producing an extraordinary share of the world's exports—as much as one quarter of the global total (UNCTAD 2010). However, the lessons of the logistics revolution were not lost on China; rather than world factory, China might be better conceptualized as a logistics empire. China boasts the world's largest container and crane manufacturers, is now the third-largest ship-owning country after Germany and the second-largest shipbuilding country after Japan, and has surpassed India as the largest ship-recycling country (UNCTAD 2010, xvi). China has been actively assembling its own gateways to extend logistics corridors into other

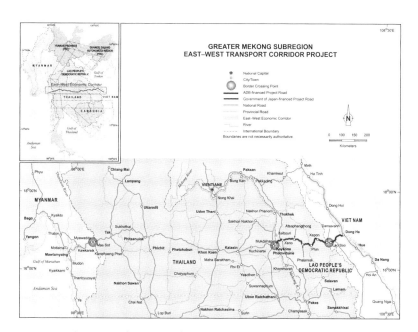

FIGURE 14. Greater Mekong Corridor Project, stretching from Mawlamyaing, Myanmar, to the Vietnamese coast, with border crossings. Source: ADB 2008.

regions of the world. In the highly publicized bid for control of Greece's largest port just outside of Athens, the port of Piraeus, China acquired not only "a gateway into Europe" but also a gateway into "the highly promising market of Southeast Europe and the Black Sea" (Faiola 2010). This bold entry of China into Greece saw the Chinese shipping giant China Ocean Shipping Company (COSCO) assume full control of container operations for thirty-five years at a cost of $5 billion.

This logistics gateway not only brings Chinese goods into Europe and the Black Sea region but also extends Chinese labor practices and management methods into Greece. Standing at the Piraeus container terminal, dockworker John Makrydimitris pointed toward his feet and said, "There is Greece," and then pointed to a metal fence just yards away and added with a laugh, "and there is China." Indeed, the Union of Dockworkers of Piraeus sees the deal as "importing the Chinese labor model to Greece." At the COSCO terminals there is no union recognition; industry standards in everything from wages, to training, to working hours have been completely undermined (Morris 2011). But the Chinese gateway is reshaping labor relations beyond the borders of the COSCO terminals as well, says Nick Georgiou, president of the Dockworkers' Union: "The result is that companies not run by the Chinese are being influenced by what the Chinese are doing in lowering the labor costs and reducing workers' rights" (quoted in Lim 2011). COSCO chairman Wei Jiafu agrees; in 2010, he told a gathering of the World Economic Forum, "By going global, we are also transferring our culture to the rest of the world" (quoted in Lim 2011). Greek Minister of State Haris Pamboukis asserts that Piraeus provides a model for future agreements. China's influence over Greek politics grows alongside Chinese investment, a direct result of Greek leaders' hope that China could save Greece from total financial collapse. Yet Pamboukis defensively insists, "Piraeus is not a colony" (quoted in Lim 2011).

The Asia Pacific Gateway and Corridor Initiative

Among all the transnational corridor and gateway projects that are being assembled in the world today, the Asia Pacific Gateway and Corridor Initiative (APGCI) offers perhaps the best glimpse at the stakes involved in the building of logistics space. The APGCI is officially a project of the Canadian federal government (Woo 2011), but this radically underdescribes the authority at play. Like the logistics project in Vietnam, the APGCI was first initiated by a small group of transnational corporations who are also directly involved in governing the large-scale public investment and who are furthermore the beneficiaries of the megaproject. Like the Chinese "gateway into Europe," the APGCI facilitates the circulation of wholly different labor regimes across the territories it spans. As we will see in chapter 3, the APGCI has been the vehicle for a coalition of maritime employers (composed of many of the same corporations that initiated the APGCI) to attempt to import the "Dubai model" of unfree labor into the Canadian logistics sector. The APGCI also provides a window into the shifting logics and techniques of imperial rule. Efforts to "secure" gateways and corridors from disruption throw the politics of protecting the circulation of globalized goods into direct conflict with ongoing anticolonial struggles over lands and livelihoods. The APGCI's experiments with the old and new politics of securing trade networks collide directly with indigenous sovereignty struggles. Perhaps most striking, the APGCI tells the story of the reorganization of state sovereignty and national security to fit the form and function of transnational logistics space. Rather than territorial borders at the edge of national space guaranteeing the sovereignty of nation-state, a new cartography of security aims to protect global networks of circulation. As the conceptual map in Figure 15 shows, borders do not disappear in the APGCI but are superseded by transnational networks, flows, and urban nodes.

The APGCI is a major public/private initiative that aims to increase the capacity, productivity, speed, and reliability of cargo flow between Asia and North America, and according to a provincial policy director I interviewed,[1] $15 billion in infrastructure investment has already been committed to the project from federal and provincial governments and the private sector (see also Moore 2008). The APGCI provoked a complete reorganization of Canada's federal transportation ministry away from a provincial territorial model over the last decade. Transport Canada (TC) has undergone a process of internal transformation in order to accommodate this network model into their organizational structure and operations.[2] TC is now organized around three major gateways (Asia Pacific, Atlantic, Continental), of which the West Coast APGCI is the most significant. The initiative emerged out of conversations and then a more formal alliance of shippers, terminal operators, and other logistics companies in Vancouver. With most of the world's thirty-largest companies working in British Columbia's ports, this was clearly a local meeting of global capital. In 1994, Maersk, COSCO, DP World, Hanjin, TSI, Maher Terminals, Hapag-Lloyd, K-Line, and fifty-three others represented by the British Columbia Maritime Employers Association (BCMEA) met with the Port of Vancouver, Fraser Port, CN and CP Rail, International

Canada's Asia-Pacific Gateway and Corridor

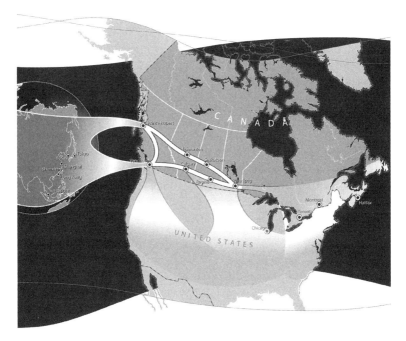

FIGURE 15. Asia-Pacific Gateway and Corridor Initiative conceptual map. Source: Asia Pacific Gateway and Corridor Initiative 2009.

Longshore and Warehouse Union, Western Economic Diversification, and the Asia Pacific Foundation and established the Greater Vancouver Gateway Council (GVGC). The GVGC's mission was to provide "seamless logistical services" within the local vicinity of Vancouver (Gow 2009).

A few years later, after undertaking "probably a million dollars" worth of research to look at the opportunities and to identify what was needed, the GVGC "then turned around and came to the provincial and federal government and said, 'you really need to get onside this; you really need to take this on as your own initiative. You need to start investing in what's needed—both from a policy and legislative perspective, but also from an infrastructure perspective'" (Gow 2009). The GVGC research culminated in a 2001 plan for $7 billion in capital investment over twenty years. Just five years later, the government of British Columbia announced a $3 billion investment and released a Pacific Gateway Strategy Action Plan, while the federal government formally announced the APGCI and over the next two years committed an unprecedented level of funds for national infrastructure projects: $33 billion in 2006 and 2007 alone. These public funds are crucial to enabling private gain in the corridor, yet government has played an even more critical role in ensuring planning and strategy on the scale of the system. Lisa Gow, executive director of the BC Pacific Gateway Branch, states that a key role of the government is to plan for "operational system efficiency, as opposed to operator efficiency." She insists that "the operators have done a really, really good job about improving their own efficiency, but there's no incentive for them to look at the broader system efficiency." One of the tangible outcomes of the early alliance was the scrutiny applied to the system and its growing visibility. The APGCI "mapped the entire container trucking system in the Lower Mainland" to find problem areas for improvement, "some of them in the trucking system, some of them in the ports, and a whole bunch of opportunities for eliminating a lot of the duplication of activity that's happening" (Gow 2009).

Corporate partners remain central in governing the APGCI through the Gateway Executive Council. The council is made up "only of executives" and meets quarterly to plan collaboratively. "It's very—it's formal. It's a formal structure," Gow reports. "All of the decision-making is collaborative; it's consensus based. So it is as open as you can be with direct competitors sitting in the room with each other. They have been surprisingly forthright with the amount of information that they're prepared to share with each other. It doesn't always come easily, but it does work." The Executive Council is also the international face of the Gateway, and members travel together on "missions." "We've actually been doing what we call missions, which is we actually go out into Asia. We go into the U.S. Midwest . . . missions are a big one for us," Gow explains. Missions provide the opportunity for corporations and government to work with common "comprehensive marketing and communications." They are "both strategy and tactical, a plan that's been developed for all the partners. We have developed an agreed-on common logo, common branding. We have common positioning statements that all of the partners use in their outreach. So we all are 'Canada's Pacific Gateway.' We use that; the feds use that; the private sector uses that." One 2008 Asian mission took the APGCI Executive Council to Dubai, which Gow described as "like Disneyland. It was very interesting—*very* interesting." With Dubai Ports as a member of the APGCI Executive Council and thus treated as "part of the overall family," the travel abroad was also a trip "home." The mission provided the opportunity for the APGCI to market itself, while it also allowed government representatives to see dramatically different labor and legal regimes for port and transport regulation.

Dubai has some really interesting approaches. Obviously it's a wholly different governing structure from what we're dealing with here, but they are thinking huge. I mean, talk about comprehensive planning. It's an entity that, when they do things, they think of everything. They hire the best in the world; they get advice, people to come in. And they don't just develop a port. They develop a system—it's infrastructure, and ports, and it's free trade zones, and it's accommodation, and it's transportation of people, and it's energy—and the whole bit gets thought about as they do it. So it's really quite comprehensive.

Dubai may well be a "Disneyland" for capital, with its radical social order where workers and citizens are separate classes of people. An extreme attempt to remove workers from the realm of citizenship and so too the economy from the political, with a labor force that is 90 percent noncitizen, Dubai ensures a "love it or leave it" approach for elite professionals and pitiful conditions of work and wages for the rest. If the factory has been stretched across supply chains and distributed around the world, then the radically different labor regimes are already "inside" the factory, and as we will see in chapter 3, corporate members of the APGCI see themselves as simply standardizing the supply chain in their efforts to bring the Dubai model to North America.

The vision for the APGCI, articulated first by logistics corporations, then by the GVGC, and finally by government, is to enhance and expand trade between Asia and North America. The Canadian government asserts that the country is "geographically positioned to prosper as the crossroads between North America and growing Asian economies." The language here is significant—Canada is not positioned *at* the crossroads but *as* the crossroads. This is important precisely because it is the activity of goods movement that is coveted, regardless of the final destination of the goods. With the revolution in logistics, the disaggregation of the categories of production and distribution and their reassembly into component parts of supply chains that can then be redistributed across space, the circulation of goods is no longer simply a matter of transportation. Logistics—the management of supply chains—is a booming industry in itself with value added and spin-off economic activity. An early consultants' report on the APGCI illustrates the importance of both the geographic position of the initiative between two empires and the value of the "traffic" between them. "Situated between Asia and the U.S.," they explain, "our ports and airports on the west coast are also ideally situated to capture a portion of the growing traffic between these major trading partners" (InterVISTAS 2007, 2). The goal of the APGCI is not simply to increase and enhance trade but also to siphon off some of the immense volume of goods bound for the United States and circulate it through Canadian logistics systems. Indeed, the Canadian government frames their discussion of the rationale for public investment under the banner "The Shanghai to Chicago Opportunity."

By any measure, the volume and value of trade between China and its largest trading partner, the United States, is vast and growing. During the first decade of the twenty-first century, the total value of trade between the countries expanded fourfold from $121 billion in 2001 to $456 billion in 2010 (U.S.-China Business Council n.d.). If Canada has a history as handmaiden to the British Empire and then to the American one, the APGCI suggests another major shift in this story. Yet despite the widely noted warming of the Canadian government in its relations to China, this shift is not simply away from American Empire toward the Chinese. Rather, the Canadian state is actively orientating itself toward the geo-economic logics of logistics.

Nowhere is this attempt to orient national investment and infrastructure toward the Chinese–American circuit more stark than with the "Chicago Express." This northern corridor of the APGCI runs from Prince Rupert, British Columbia, to the American rail hub of Chicago, and its nickname reveals the intentions that fueled its construction. According to Gow (2009), "The intent was it was going to be about 94 percent, 95 percent U.S.-driven":

> Essentially the idea is to come in, offload goods, move them direct to rail (the majority of their product comes in and out on rail), put it onto rail, haul it down to Chicago as quickly as you possibly can, make a couple of stops along the way—so they'll make a stop in Winnipeg; they'll make a stop in Chicago, Memphis—and then on the way back, fill the containers with exports from those various jurisdictions—so they'll pick up paper and other products out of Memphis and Chicago; they'll stop in Edmonton for agricultural and other products like that; and then they'll make a stop in Prince George, pick up lumber products for export—and then put it back on the ship. So very much an express service. I think they commit to five- or six-day delivery in Memphis.

As Figure 16 shows, the "Chicago Express" extends well beyond the Canadian border on both ends. It promises to reduce transport time by as much as two to three days for containers journeying from Asia to the United States, in part achieved from the geographic proximity of northern British Columbia to East Asia, but also because of the lower levels

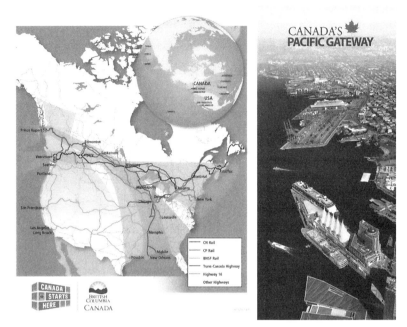

FIGURE 16. APGCI Northern Corridor, known as the "Chicago Express."
Source: Asia Pacific Gateway and Corridor Initiative 2009.

of congestion in Prince Rupert compared to others ports on the coast. However, the "Chicago Express" can only promise this time savings if the border cooperates, and so the border has been a major focus of APGCI planning from the get go. Like in the APGCI concept map, the national border is represented here, but only with the faintest line, as if receding into the background. This is in contrast to the bold golden ray that broadly follows transportation infrastructure and crosses from the Pacific Ocean through the Port of Prince Rupert and across the Canadian West before dropping down to Chicago, Memphis, and finally New Orleans. This visual representation captures something more than just the corporate fantasy of transnational goods flow. Efforts to actualize this image—to make the border fade into the background as a means of strengthening logistics space—are having serious impact. CBP agents are now stationed at the Port of Prince Rupert and carry out their inspections alongside their Canadian counterparts when containers reach the North American shore. As Pacific Regional Director General for Transport Canada Mike Henderson explained to me,[3]

A good example are the trains, the container trains now that come out of Rupert down into Chicago . . . and they cross the border at Fort Frances–Ranier in northwestern Ontario. I've been down there a few times to watch them, and those trains, when they leave Rupert, they almost don't stop. They only thing they really see are moose. They get to Winnipeg, they stop briefly, then they continue on. When they cross the border, the train doesn't stop. It slows down, rolls through, and then continues right down to Chicago. The biggest selling point of that service is that they can get containers from Prince Rupert to Chicago in less than 100 hours—much faster, for example, than we've moved containers from Seattle to Chicago or L.A./Long Beach to Chicago. So they've gone through all the gymnastics with U.S. Border Patrol, border security. Before those containers arrive at the border, the U.S. knows everything that's in them, where they've come from, who packed them.

Concerns about security have animated APGCI planning from the get go, in part because of the timing of its development in the wake of 9/11. Responding to popular concerns about the security of cross-border movements has been one key consideration. Yet it is concerns about the security of the logistics system itself and not the impact of cross-border cargo movement on the people or places they travel to that has taken precedence. Concern for the security of cargo movement is clearly articulated in the 2007 consultants' assessment of the gateway, which insists that government must consider the following:

- Aggressively pursuing opportunities to implement new approaches to minimize or eliminate dual clearance processes
- Taking a lead role in encouraging harmonization and mutual recognition of transport and border security policies in the Asia Pacific region
- Aggressively pursuing perimeter clearance with the U.S. (InterVISTAS 2007, 3)

In response, the APGCI formed a "Security Sub-sector Roundtable," which hired consultants to study supply chain security in the gateway in 2009. This report suggested that much like the broader role of government in the gateway—to coordinate individual firm approaches into an overall systems approach—the government's role in security was also to create a common vision and plan for the myriad stakeholders who would actually carry it out. The report suggests, "Security within the Gateway is currently planned and delivered largely by individual facility or supply chain components," whereas "the concept of a network or holistic approach to supply chain security is fundamental" to a gateway strategy

(APGST 2009, 6). They warn that the "the lack of a comprehensive, net-work approach to security increases the risk within the Gateway, leaving the supply chain only as secure as the weakest link."

What is clear in the work of the APGCI and in broader discussions about the security of global trade is that the very nature of the system, and the benefits it conveys to corporations, is rooted in the speed of circulation, which produces a new kind of vulnerability. Global logistics has an Achilles heel—a vulnerability that derives precisely from its reliance on fast flows. Indeed, in the words of one of the key actors in the APGCI, "it's that whole concept of the seamless movement of goods . . . Every time you get a connection, there's a possibility of something to happen" (Gow 2009).

Securing "Seamless" Systems: Supply Chain Security

Back in fall 2002, it was still meaningful for the *Economist* to assert, "There is a tension between the needs of inter-national security and those of global trade" ("Moving Story"). This tension, acute at the national border, lay specifically in the conflicting imperatives of the control of territory and the speed of supply chains. In other words, this tension is fundamentally between geopolitical and logistical models of spatial calculation. The timing of this assertion was meaningful; it was precisely at a moment of heightened conflict between open and closed borders, just as the claim was on the cusp of redundancy. Those at the heart of the global logistics industry repeatedly flagged this apparent conflict between global trade and national security, concerned for the impacts of the latter on the former. Some speculated about the end of just-in-time production systems in the context of post-9/11 securitization. In 2003, Brian Parkinson (UNECE 2003, xlii) of the International Chamber of Shipping exclaimed, "The measures developed to combat terrorism, in addition to terrorism itself, may threaten trade, which is an engine of growth and offers the best chance of steady progress for both developed and developing economies."

This tension was certainly not new, as Mark Salter (2004, 72) suggests: "The problem of borders" has long been "a result of two powerful governmental desires: security and mobility." Scholars had furthermore already begun to point out that in an era of mobility, "security" could no longer operate through a paradigm of "blockading borders" but instead would serve to "channel and monitor flows" (Bigo 2001). And yet, it was not until later in the first decade of the twenty-first century that a fundamentally different kind of security—a security devoted to the protection of trade flows—would emerge in earnest and put the *Economist* equation into question. The design of a model of security devoted to the protection of supply chains undermines any simple juxtaposition of international security and global trade. Rather than a competing force, the material flows of the economy and the transportation and communication infrastructures that underpin them are increasingly the object of security. Indeed, after just a decade of experiments with "supply chain security," the game had changed. In the introduction to the U.S. National Strategy for Global Supply Chain Security (DHS 2012), President Obama explains, "We reject the false choice between security and efficiency and firmly believe that we can promote economic growth while protecting our core values as a nation and as a people."

The seeds of supply chain security were planted with the revolution in logistics; more stuff moving longer distances, mixed with the accelerated speeds of just-in-time production techniques, prompted growing pressure at the border. A systems approach to supply chains furthermore put the whole network of production and distribution (now stretched across the planet) into the spotlight, as we saw with the *New York Times* diagram that opened this chapter. However, a more precise genealogy would locate the emergence of supply chain security in the first decade of the twenty-first century. It was at this time that supply chain security was named as such and that the first textbooks, articles, and experts in the field emerged (Thomas 2010). The mounting pressure at the border, the *Economist*'s "tension" between trade and security, became an outright impasse in North America in September 2001.

Yet it was not the events of September 11—the loss of life, the destruction of urban infrastructure, or even the trespass of state sovereignty—that were definitive in the birth of this paradigm of security. Rather, it was the events of September 12, 13, 14, and after—the closure of the American border, the collapse of cargo flow, and the deep impact on trade, particularly in the cross-border auto industry (cf. CRS 2005; Flynn 2003, 115)—that marked the crisis and prompted response. The deep integration of the North American economy facilitated by NAFTA that stretched just-in-time supply chains across the continent was suddenly at risk. The immediate costs of the delays were calculated at the scale of the individual truck, by port, by gateway, by sector, and for the economy as a whole (CRS 2002; Globerman and Storer 2009; RAND 2004). But in addition to the direct costs of disruption from border closure, there was mounting concern for the longer-term costs associated with post-9/11 border tightening. For a system based not simply on connectivity but the speed of connectivity, border security can itself be a source of insecurity for the supply chain. In the world of logistics and supply chain management, trade disruption (not the twin towers) was the key casualty of 2001. In response, national governments, international governing bodies, logistics companies, transnational retailers, private security companies, and polyglot think tanks embarked on an almost feverish experimentation with policies, standards, practices, and technologies to preempt disruption and recover circulation in its wake.

What is supply chain security (SCS)? The World Bank defines it as "the concept which encompasses the programs, systems, procedures, technologies and solutions applied to address threats to the supply chain and the consequent threats to the economic, social and physical well-being of citizens and organized society" (IBRD 2009, 8). While opaque, this definition is nevertheless useful in that it exposes a key assumption and maneuver at the core of this emergent paradigm: that the security of global trade is directly connected to the security of citizens and society. In fact, SCS goes beyond positing a connection between the protection of trade flows and national security. SCS specialists now conceptualize the security of supply chains as fundamental to national security, deeply entwined if not actually interchangeable (Haveman and Shatz 2006), while governments articulate visions of security that emphasize the protection of trade flows. One of the four key objectives of Canada's 2001 Anti-Terrorism Plan, Bill C-36, is "to keep the Canada–U.S. border secure and open to legitimate trade." Meanwhile, the aptly named Security and Prosperity Partnership (SPP) of North America was "premised on our security and our economic prosperity being mutually reinforcing" (CRS 2009). The SPP was replaced in 2011 by the U.S.–Canadian Beyond the Border Action Plan—a "shared vision for perimeter security and economic competitiveness." This entwining of the economic and the political raises questions about supply chain security as a paradigmatically neoliberal form.

Supply chain security takes the protection of commodity flows, and the transportation and communication networks of infrastructure that support them, as its central concern. Initiatives target shipping containers, seaports, and the integrity of intermodal transportation systems. SCS takes shape through national and supranational programs that aim to govern events and forces that have the potential to disrupt trade flows. Because it is oriented toward threats that may be impossible to predict like volcanic eruptions or terrorist attacks, SCS mobilizes preemption techniques to mitigate vulnerability (see Cooper 2006; Amoore and De Goede 2008) and preparedness measures to build resilience and recover circulation in the wake of disruption (see Collier and Lakoff 2007; Pettit, Fiskel, and Croxton 2010). Supply chain security relies on risk management to identify dangerous goods and disruptive people and keep them away from circulatory systems, alternately targeting high-risk containers, shippers, and workers. But as we will see in chapter 4, military deployment is also part of the paradigm; naval forces policing trade routes in the Gulf of Aden are a key link in the chain of trade security. The mix of military and civilian security is a feature of the transnational geography of supply chains. Indeed, as the diagram that opened this chapter suggests, what unites supply chain security initiatives is the space of the circulatory system that extends "from the factory gate in a foreign country to the final destination of the product" (Haveman and Shatz 2006, 1).

From the Borderline to "Seam" Space

Implementation of the first-ever global architecture for supply chain security began in 2002 with a quick succession of national and international policies and standards that targeted shipping containers, seaports, and the integrity of intermodal transportation systems. Since 2002, the United States has enacted eleven plans to specifically address supply chain security in addition to a series of programs that target particular sites within transport and trade networks. These national initiatives were followed by mandatory global standards for supply chain security issued by the International Maritime Organization in 2004, the International Standards Organization in 2005, and the World Customs Organization in 2005, all at the direct behest of the U.S. government (IMO 2004). This global vision for supply chain security is represented in Figure 17, a map of risk zones, chokepoints, and gateways of trade. Notable in both the visual rendering and the accompanying text is the wide range of supply chain disruptions that are collapsed under the lens of "security." This is a key feature of the broader logic of SCS; myriad events, actors, and forces that have the capacity to disrupt the flow of goods are all interchangeably addressed under the rubric of security, be they labor actions, volcanic eruptions, terrorist attacks, piracy, indigenous land claim standoffs, and even national border delays. Explaining the scale of the global risks represented in their map, PricewaterhouseCoopers (PwC) reports in "Securing the Supply Chain" (2011, 16),

> Attacks on supply chains are often looking for a big return on a small investment. Because they're so vital to trade flow, logistics hubs like airports or ports offer the ideal target. The possible consequences of disrupting a logistics hub, for example, can be seen by taking a look

at the port strike in 2002, where 29 ports on the US West Coast were locked out due to a labor strike of 10,500 dockworkers. The strike had a massive impact on the US economy. Approximately US$ 1 billion was lost per day and it took more than 6 months to recover.

The use of labor disruptions as a means to quantify "attacks" on the supply chain follows directly from the prior move of positing global trade as vital to national security. It allows for the exchangeability of radically different acts and actors, which have in common only the threat they pose to smooth circulation. A legal act asserting workplace democracy, when viewed through the lens of SCS, is not just like an attack—it *is* an attack on the integrity of flows. Indeed, this same group of port workers has been the focus of a sustained social war, and they have at times been explicitly deemed "terrorists" for disruptions to key nodes in the global supply chain. We return to the particular stakes for this group of workers and for workers and labor more broadly in the context of supply chain security in chapter 3. For now it is worth investigating what is perhaps the most startling "threat" to SCS: the national border. The enormous financial, political, technological, and affective investments in

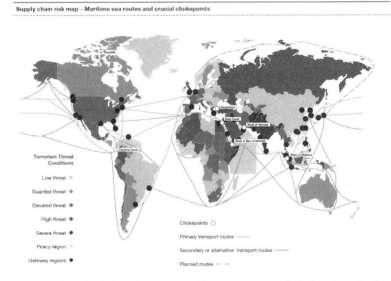

FIGURE 17. Supply chain risk map—maritime sea routes and chokepoints. Darker shades on the map signify more significant risk. Solid points mark "gateways," and hollow points mark chokepoints in global supply chains. Source: PwC 2011.

security under the rubric of the "War on Terror" have generated enormous interest in the topic of border "thickening" and "tightening" with a particular eye to delays for trade. Indeed, the border is flagged as one of the most significant obstacles to trade movement, such that in the context of expanding inspections and regulations, border security poses a threat to supply chain security.

And yet, after a decade of active experimentation, supply chain security is actively reconfiguring the geographic space of border security, as well as the legal and social technologies for governing border space. New security programs seek to govern integrated global economic space while at the same time retaining politically differentiated sovereign territories. Efforts to recalibrate security around the network space of supranational supply chains challenge longstanding territorial notions of state sovereignty by extending the zone of border management outward into the ports of foreign states, inward along domestic transport networks, into the space of "logistics cities" (Cowen 2009), and through the creation of exceptional zones—"secure areas"—around ports where normal laws and rights are either mediated or suspended (Cowen 2007).

For years now, military and civilian agencies have been actively rethinking security in order to respond to changing notions of threat. Specifically, the territorial paradigm of security that literally gave shape to modern nation-states is undergoing radical transformation. Within the territorial model of security, the border defined the legal, spatial, and ontological limits of national sovereignty. The very distinction between police and military, war and peace, crime and terror took shape in the division of inside/outside state space (Giddens 1985, 192; Foucault [1997] 2003, 49). With sovereignty and formal citizenship both ordered by the borderline, the "inside/outside" distinction was a core ideology of the geopolitical state (Cowen and Smith 2009). The border as territorial limit was the official basis for the division between police and military force and between crime and terror, while it also forged "domestic" legal space. Yet despite the formative nature of this territorial division, the same states were forged through its trespass, most starkly through colonial expansion when "outside" became "inside" and when the military was often interchangeable with police forces (cf. Badiou 2002; Mignolo and Tlostanova 2006; Asad 2007). The geopolitical state relied simultaneously on the sovereign territoriality of the borderline and on the trespass of the distinctions it created. But even as the division of authority and violence organized by the distinction of inside/outside was a sovereign fantasy as much as the everyday reality of the geopolitical state, it nevertheless had actual effects. The border was never managed in the definitive manner that the distinction of inside/outside would suggest and was never merely a line in absolute space (Agnew 1999; Newman 2006), but we can nevertheless trace important shifts in both models and practices of sovereign space. SCS raises profound questions about the changing meaning of security as well as the transformation of its social and spatial practice.

For the security of systems, the territorial border can be a problem rather than a solution. Military and civilian security experts insist that old categories are creating problems for law enforcement and international security work, and it is precisely the blurring of tactics and technologies of police and military that is needed in response to insecurity today. As U.S. Army Lieutenant Colonel Ralph Peters (1995, 12) argues, "We are constrained by a past century's model of what armies do, what police do, and what governments legally can do. Our opponents have none of this baggage, whether they are druglords or warlords." A decade later, in 2006, U.S. Army Lieutenant Colonel Thomas Goss called this new border space "the seam": a liminal zone between inside and outside space, where old divisions no longer hold. In "the seam," the border between police and military authority is blurred, and so too is the line between crime and terror. Thomas Goss offers as a test case Figure 18, which notably uses the maritime border.

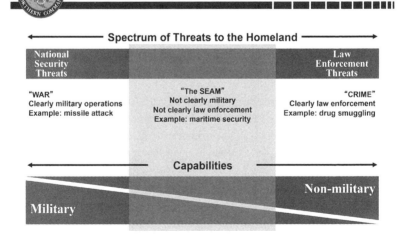

UNCLASSIFIED//FOUO
Figure 1: Current National Challenge

◄——— **Spectrum of Threats to the Homeland** ———►

National Security Threats   **Law Enforcement Threats**

"WAR"   "The SEAM"   "CRIME"
Clearly military operations   Not clearly military   Clearly law enforcement
Example: missile attack   Not clearly law enforcement   Example: drug smuggling
                               Example: maritime security

◄——— **Capabilities** ———►

Non-military

Military

UNCLASSIFIED//FOUO

FIGURE 18. Homeland security threats spectrum. Source: Goss 2006.

The maritime border is the paradigmatic space for experimentation and reform precisely because of the magnitude of the challenge of "opening and closing" access to trade flows. With 90 percent of all global trade and 95 percent of U.S.-bound cargo moving by ship, the challenge of securing maritime supply chains is profound. Indeed, *all* the eleven plans cited in a recent Department of Homeland Security (DHS) report that were developed after September 2001 to support supply chain security target maritime and port security (DHS 2007). No doubt, there has been tremendous experimentation in securing the movement of people since 2001 (Balibar 2002; Salter 2004; Sparke 2004; Walters 2004). These efforts have unleashed a variety of highly racialized programs that introduce new forms of biometric surveillance. Yet concern for the security of stuff (for commodities and supply chains) has been the subject of more and more national and supranational policy action.

Institutions like the Organisation for Economic Co-operation and Development (OECD) and RAND circulate a strikingly similar diagram to Goss's (see Figure 19). Here again, what was historically a borderline bifurcating two distinct spaces and their attendant norms and laws is transformed into a space unto itself that fits neither side of the old divide. In this model, the maritime border is not simply an example of the problematized space; rather, in this second diagram the port exists as the space in between national territories. In both cases, the maritime border becomes a space of transition: a zone subject to specialized government.

This experimentation with border space does not aim to dismantle border security per se, but it acknowledges the limits of a territorial model while attempting to rework its meaning and practice to support systems that span national space. DHS (2007, 2012) has adopted a three-pronged strategy of risk management, cost-benefit analysis, and layered security

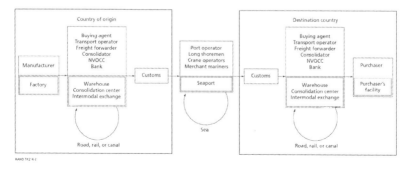

FIGURE 19. "Evaluating the Security of the Global Containerized Supply Chain." Source: RAND 2004.

with the aim of keeping dangerous cargo out, addressing infiltration from within, and securing infrastructure.

In the immediate aftermath of September 2001, U.S. officials began quickly and quietly designing new security plans for ports that would reshape not only domestic space but global security practices. The Container Security Initiative (CSI), a program defined and administered by American authorities, posts CBP agents in dozens of foreign ports to inspect U.S.-bound cargo. The CSI aims to "extend [the U.S.] zone of security outward so that American borders are the last line of defense, not the first" (DHS 2009). According to Deputy Commissioner of the U.S. Customs Service Douglas Browning (2003), with the CSI, customs officers "identify and pre-screen high-risk cargo containers that pose a risk of containing terrorists or terrorist weapons *before* they are shipped to the U.S. This simple concept represents a major revolution in standard practice. Currently, most customs services around the world—including the U.S. Customs Service—target and inspect high-risk containers as they sit in the port of *entry*." While their name never appears on the promotional literature, the Logistics Management Institute (LMI) took a lead role in the design of the CSI. In fact, the Container Security Initiative, a cornerstone of American SCS, is a perfect example of the new collaborative approach to security across the state and the corporate sector. As the LMI's vice president of operational logistics, Ray Schaible,[4] explained to me, "We were working with APL, American Presidential Lines, on that, because they had the large container company and everything, and we worked through MARAD, the Maritime Administration, and then with Transport Security Administration. So it was kind of a consortium, but we were the lead on it, to develop that whole concept of pushing the borders out." Schaible pointed to the importance of targeting high-risk containers before they even begin their journeys to U.S. soil: "A container—once it gets on a ship, and it's a suspect container, it's very difficult to deal with." The desire to intercept "suspect containers" prompted the design of the CSI and "caused the Coast Guard and other inspectors to be placed at overseas ports." Schaible highlighted the key challenge of increasing control over the flow of cargo without reducing its speed: "When we went into the CSI, the commercial companies were very concerned with slowing down the movement of items through their supply chain, because it costs them money when they slow down the inventory. And so you can't inspect 100 percent of the containers, for example, coming through. So you have to have a way of selecting which containers you want to look at." The means of selecting containers, of deciphering high and low risk, centered entirely on financial documentation. Companies with a steady level of trade, that act in predictable ways, receive a low risk score, while those that have less predictable behavior are targeted for scrutiny. Schaible explained, "It caused us to look at the documentation, and try to identify bad-acting actors through documentation that was flowing through the system. And the financial world, in particular, financial documentation. So if you saw an outlier there, or something didn't look right—you know, if you had a lone container coming from a place you've never heard about before—you might want to take a look at that. And that was . . . a risk analysis type thing." The CSI is now active in fifty-eight ports, which account for 85 percent of all containers arriving in the United States.[5]

Another extraterritorial security program that extends the border outward, the Customs-Trade Partnership against Terrorism (C-TPAT), was initiated in April 2002 and offers expedited processing of cargo for firms that comply with requirements for securing their entire supply chain. "Under C-TPAT, companies follow CBP guidelines for securing their supply chains going back to the origin of the cargo. Customs validates the security of the operations. C-TPAT now has 7,200 member companies. Being a member of the program is one of the criteria Customs uses to designate a company as a 'trusted partner,' a status that normally results in fewer cargo inspections and expedited treatment of shipments" (Mongelluzzo 2012). C-TPAT participants include importers, carriers, customs brokers, and freight forwarders and cover "every part of the logistics

FIGURE 20. Ports participating in U.S. Container Security Initiative. Source: DHS 2007. Adapted and used with permission.

chain from manufacture to final distribution" (Browning 2003, 172). They are subject to fewer cargo inspections because they receive a lower risk score in the CBP Automated Targeting System. Security is privatized as agents are made responsible for the security of the nation; participants in the C-TPAT sign an agreement that commits them to conduct a self-assessment of security in the logistics chain (CRS 2005, 10–11). Browning (2003, 171–72) explains, "The fact remains that most of the supply chain we hope to secure is managed by private-sector concerns so, while CSI allows us to work with other governments to look for potential security risks, C-TPAT opens the dialogue with the trade community so that it can mobilize its resources to enhance security in parts of the logistics chain where the ability of customs administrations to intervene is limited."

C-TPAT is part of a broader shift toward the privatization of security. Privatization is hardly a novel feature of neoliberal government (Burchell 1996, 29), but the privatization of national security enacted through SCS is unprecedented. Private companies not only are involved in managing programs, designing or manufacturing technologies, and supplying tools but are partners in the very design of policy and the identification of the problems to solve. This is particularly noteworthy in the field of national security. For classic liberalism, national security was an exceptional realm of state action in a political landscape of individualism. According to classic liberal political theorists, national security was one of the exceptional domains where the state should command a monopoly. In fact, security was the core rationale for the liberal state and treated as a prerequisite for individual freedom. Even the eminent neoliberal Milton Friedman supported the collective organization of security, arguing that "I cannot get the amount of national defense I want and you, a different amount" (Friedman 2002, 23). However, while states still play a central role in planning and coordinating security, in the context of SCS they take their cues directly from private sector actors, who are invited to advise on the design of programs and participate in the governance of public–private security partnerships.

The privatization of security is also part of its international harmonization. In 2008, the C-TPAT was harmonized with the Canadian Partnership in Protection (PIP) program following a mutual recognition agreement between Canada and the United States. PIP was first developed in 1995 to promote international trade compliance with customs regulation but was renovated more recently to focus explicitly on security. "After the events of 9/11, the PIP program's focus shifted to place a greater emphasis on trade chain security," the Canada Border Services Agency website explains. In 2002, PIP membership became a prerequisite for participation in the Free and Secure Trade (FAST) program, which facilitates expedited border clearances into Canada for preapproved (low-risk) importers, carriers, and drivers, thus linking the program to a broader infrastructure of security and significantly elevating its importance. Since the 2009 harmonization, a single application can be used to apply to both C-TPAT and PIP, which entails, in effect, the standardization of two formerly national programs to govern international space. The harmonized C-TPAT and PIP also entails the deep integration of information-sharing security across the two states. Mutual recognition arrangements have since extended the reach of the programs to include Japan and the European Union (both formalized in 2012), Korea, and Singapore. In fact, the *Journal of Commerce* (Mongelluzzo 2012) describes the C-TPAT as "probably the most-duplicated security program of the past decade . . . Canada, Jordan, Mexico, New Zealand, Singapore, Japan, Korea and, most recently, the European Union, have developed similar programs."

This privatization certainly crosses borders. Like the PIP, which allows firms to apply for "trusted trader" status that expedites their border crossings, the Canadian government has implemented the Security Emergency Management System (SEMS) to regulate the security of facilities and operators within national space. Similar to the PIP, the SEMS promotes the reduction of inspections for stakeholders deemed low risk. Under the program, companies develop their own security plans and occasionally report on their compliance to government. "It's a lot easier for business," one senior manager from Transport Canada's Security and Emergency Preparedness division explained to me.[6] "We have some facilities that are fantastic: they take that security environment, the security attitude, very serious . . . So what we're doing is we're saying if this stakeholder has no infractions or incidents or deficiencies in the last three or four years, maybe what we do is we risk manage that facility and we say, 'You know what? We're not going to inspect you this year.'" These programs are key elements in the retooling of the state in the field of security. In place of the old "enforcement attitude," TC is oriented toward "voluntary compliance," where the private sector becomes "the owner of their program, rather than us walking in with a checklist and saying, 'Okay, is your fence up? Is your marine facility access controlled?' . . . That is our ultimate goal."

Whereas the national border (the privileged spatial boundary within a territorial model of security) was governed directly by the geopolitical state, the security of the corridor cartography of the supply chain is delegated to the components of the system. This is in part a feature of the geography of the system itself—the potentially endless number of sites and spaces that require attention if the goal is to secure trade networks. Yet it is also a feature of the introduction of risk analysis into the domain of security. Working with the assumption that there will inevitably be security incidents, risk analysis asks, what is the most effective way to target limited resources to have the greatest impact? In the senior manager's words,

> Are we going to put a Transport Canada inspector at every bridgehead, at every canal, at every facility, 24 hours a day? Is that going to stop actions? Is that going to stop terrorism? At what point does it become cost-effective? At what point do you say it's not costeffective? So a lot of the things that we're doing are what's called risk-based management.

A Global Architecture of Supply Chain Security?

In addition to these efforts at extending U.S. border practices outward— scanning cargo at the point where a container enters the international supply chain and delegating responsibility to the private sector—American officials pressured supranational governing bodies to develop new policies where the noncompliance of member nations results in their isolation from global trade. Indeed, the key pillars in the emerging global architecture of SCS all emerge directly or indirectly from the United States, provoking many accusations that this global system is plainly oriented to U.S. national interests (Boske 2006, 16). The UN International Maritime Organization administers the International Ship and Port Facility Security (ISPS) code. The ISPS code offers an alternative to direct U.S. presence and control abroad, even as it was crafted at the direct behest of the United States. The ISPS code defines basic standards of security to which international ports and ships must comply. In 2004, the code came into effect globally. It was adopted by 152 nations and requires the compliance of 55,000 ships and 20,000 ports. Among other things, the code calls for strict standards for accessing and handling cargo, although it leaves the details of policy design to signing member states. Nevertheless, authorities in a number of countries have designed remarkably similar programs, following direct conversations that bring the models of border space explored in the last section into practice. These programs aim to engineer secure "seam space" by targeting "high risk" workers in these critical nodes in global logistics networks. Security programs for port workers in the United States, Australia, and Canada were passed into law in January 2007, September 2006, and November 2006, respectively. In each case, this followed several years of struggle between federal authorities, maritime employers, and labor over the fate of the programs in question, as well as information sharing between these three states around policy design. All three programs create special security zones around ports—in effect, exceptional spaces of government—where normal civil and labor law can be suspended (Cowen 2007, 2009). The details of these programs will be explored further in chapter 4, but for now it is worth emphasizing that these zones function like the in-between spaces in Goss's and the OECD's models—not quite inside or outside law. They also inch toward the kind of control of disruption that SCS promises when it equates the risk of labor actions and terrorism.

A focus on security crises as moments of profound political experimentation responds not only to the current profusion of policy action but also to the growing scholarly interest in the role of crises like war in the development of political forms. At times of perceived crisis, state claims for the protection of the nation and its people can expedite dramatic reform of rights and entitlements (Titmuss 1958; Rose 1989; Tilly 1990; De Landa 1991; Foucault [1997] 2003; Cowen 2005, 2008; Cowen and Gilbert 2008). The revolution in logistics follows suit. Gradual reforms during the past four decades, fueled by the revolution in logistics, were piecemeal and now culminate in sweeping and centralized change enacted in response to the security crisis of 2001. While reform of government and citizenship at times of crises is hardly novel, the nature of reform under way with supply chain security is nevertheless groundbreaking. Rather than working directly to secure states or populations, this model of security works to protect international trade, which its proponents presume to be vital to the security of states and populations. Supply chain security is seeing older territorial forms of security challenged and reworked from within the state's military and civilian agencies.

What began as the piecemeal efforts of different strategies at various sites by a wide range of actors is becoming an integrated national and international architecture of risk-based, layered, and networked security, focusing particularly on container movement. If we return to the diagram that opened this chapter, we can see that the growing emphasis on global logistics systems through the construction of gateways and corridors has created a new challenge for security. This logic was in fact introduced with the birth of business logistics and the emphasis on the efficiency of the system rather than the performance of its component parts. What we have seen in this chapter is the extension of the logic of the revolution of logistics over the course of the 1990s and into the twenty-first century, first through the expansion and enhancement of the system itself through global logistics corridor and gateway initiatives. Efforts to build a "seamless" system of circulation are just that—efforts. The complex transnational networks of people, places, and infrastructures that constitute that system cannot ever be fully controlled; the seamless global circulation of stuff is a project, not a reality, but it is nevertheless a project with definite effects. We have already seen a massive reorganization of where the border works, how, and for whom. In the realm of supply chain security, the border has been reshaped, molded to fit transnational networks of circulation, perhaps best conceptualized as a "pipeline." The management of the security of this pipeline has been internationalized, digitized, and largely privatized. As we will explore further in chapter 3, the territorial border is increasingly managed as an exceptional zone that is neither inside nor outside national space, subject to the authority of both police and military with acts potentially classified as crime or terror. In the chapters that follow we will delve deeper into particular spaces of the supply chain where particular actors are challenging the global logistics paradigm and where SCS experts are experimenting with new social and legal technologies.

CHAPTER THREE

The Labor of Logistics
Just-in-Time Jobs

Work stoppages have a significant negative impact on the Gateway not only in the short run as traffic is diverted to competing ports, but in the long term as well, since reliability is critical for gateways to attract and retain customers. This measure is not limited to the ports themselves; labor disruptions at railways or trucking firms, by border/security officers or by any other component of the supply chain would have an impact. The ideal target for this would be zero work stoppages.

—InterVISTAS

The constant managerial obsession with discovering ever more "perfect" systems of visibility, inspection and control speak not of the weight of domination bearing down upon weak, disciplined subjects but of the resilience and potency of worker resistance.

—Alan McKinlay, *Managing Foucault*

The people who move the world can also stop it.

—Jo Ann Wypijewski

Figure 21 offers a conceptual map of the application process for a Transportation Worker Identification Credential (TWIC). The TWIC is a pivotal element of the United States' layered and risked-based approach to supply chain security in the broader "War on Terror," which the U.S.

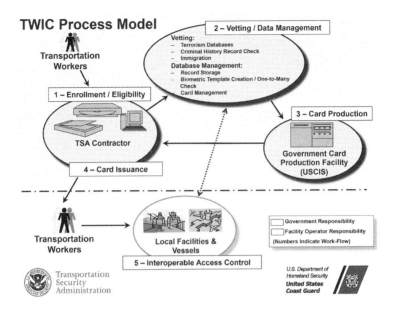

FIGURE 21. Transportation Worker Identification Credential process map.
Source: Courtesy of the U.S. Coast Guard.

administration is actively rebranding as "overseas contingency operations" (Anderson 2011, 206). It brings the United States into compliance
with the International Maritime Organization's 2004 International Ship
and Port Facility Security (ISPS) code, itself implemented at the direct
behest of the United States (Boske 2006). The diagram reveals many key
elements of the program—the multiple "vettings" of workers involved in
the TWIC, the multiple databases to be managed, and the many actors
involved in administering the initiative: the Department of Homeland
Security, the Coast Guard, intelligence agencies, and so on. The diagram
reveals that a key set of activities within the turquoise zone of "government responsibility" are in fact to be managed by a contractor working
for the Transport Security Administration, though it does not mention
the contractor selected: the notorious Lockheed Martin. Like the TWIC
program itself, this diagram opens up the minutia of workers' movements
for greater scrutiny and state control. The TWIC rewrites the limits of
state surveillance and supplants labor protections, but it does so without
presenting itself as labor law. Most important, the TWIC blurs the border between crime and terror and between police and military authority.
These borders between different authorities and legal codes for governing

insecurity are fundamentally geographic; they are the once-sacred borders of national sovereignty. With almost identical versions of the TWIC implemented in many ports around the world, the credential aims to secure the critical "seam" of the maritime border, preempting disruption by keeping "dangerous people" away from logistics systems (Cowen 2007, 2009). These programs are framed as exceptional measures targeted to a highly specialized group of workers, yet they establish precedents in critical nodes in the global social factory and are a wedge in an ongoing restructuring of work and labor. As one installment in the broader architecture of supply chain security initiatives, the TWIC aims to protect the speed and integrity of the circulatory systems of supply chain capitalism (Tsing 2009).

There is nothing new in the observation that capitalist logics aim to speed up circulation. As Marx a century and a half ago in 1867, capitalism perpetually refigures the relationship between space and time in the interests of speed. And yet, these general tendencies within capitalism that were heightened with the globalization of logistics and the rise of just-in-time production systems over the past four decades have been taken up with new force within a context of the securitization of trade. The logics of supply chain security redefine disruption of the logistics system as a matter of national security, sanctioning a social war on workers.

This chapter investigates the ways in which the recent securitization of supply chains intersects with the growing pressure on labor productivity that accompanied the revolution in logistics, containerization, and just-in-time production techniques over the last four decades. The central focus here is the body of the worker; from the caged bodies of workers in warehouses to the crushed bodies of longshore workers on the docks, this chapter explores the messy and violent everyday labor of the "seamless" logistics system. It offers a sketch of the ways in which the broader goals of accelerating the circulation of capital through the seamless movement of stuff are recast and intensified through the securitization of supply.

Death and Disruption

At 10:43 p.m. on June 9, 2007, Earle Hopson, a business agent of the International Longshore and Warehouse Union (ILWU), sped through the streets of East Vancouver en route to a night shift on the busy downtown docks. The ILWU—formed in 1937 around principles of antiracism, rank-and-file democracy, and economic justice—represents all West Coast dock workers from the southernmost ports in California to the most northerly facilities on the continent in places like Kodiak, Seward, Dutch Harbor, and Anchorage. At the gates of the globe's greatest consuming nation and its "foyer" to the north,[1] the ILWU handles (quite literally) a vast share of the world's trade. ILWU members load and unload ships; transfer containers to trains and trucks; plan port space; serve as electricians, foremen, and safety inspectors; operate tug boats; and undertake myriad other forms of labor that keeps *stuff* circulating. Their labor is a linchpin in systems of global commodity flows. When ILWU members act politically, they can create impassible chokepoints that have ripple effects through entire systems of production and distribution. The vital location of their labor alongside their intransigent international political orientation make the ILWU a powerful force, and a thorn in the side of corporate managers, in the vast and complex arena of global trade.

Earle spent eleven years as a casual worker "climbing the boards" to become a member of the union. A decade or more of precarity (of irregular, uncertain, and inadequate hours) is par for the course in the industry. Only the most persistent return to the hiring halls, week after week and year after year, slowly logging shift hours and ascending to become candidates for stable employment and full political standing. "Climbing the boards" refers literally to the process whereby a worker's timecard is inserted into the slots of an alphabetized system of boards that organize the status of casual employees—with "AA" at the top and working all the way down the alphabet. There can be hundreds, even thousands of casuals on the boards at any given time, depending on the size of the local and the state of business in the port. This long initiation process combines with the union's uncompromising stance in matters of economic, racial, and social justice to make thick affective ties between those who achieve membership. It is rare to meet an ILWU member who doesn't present a union logo on their body. T-shirt, jacket, cap, or pin, the docker's hook graces all these forms and is a waterfront worker's fashion standard. The union's tight embrace of the Wobblies motto, "An injury to one is an injury to all," highlights this collective spirit. The language of family and home exceeds metaphor; blood ties across generations of waterfront workers often connect union members. When kinship is not biological, it is still defined in familial terms—as adoptive or chosen family, often marked by shared spaces. "Up and down the coast, we all think of our dispatch hall as our home," Earle explains. I have visited enough locals and heard it repeated often enough to know it is true. "If it's not for my union," Earle continues, "I might as well not have kids, I might as well not have family, I wouldn't have my house, I wouldn't have my daughters." But the evening in question was not one of peaceful familial ties. This was instead a moment when bonds between dock workers were violently torn apart. This was an increasingly common event of graphic death on the docks.

"The one that messed me up real good was Lucio," Earle explains. "I went up the boards with Lucio . . . Lucio—he fell from a crane doing a specialty job."

Just before pulling up to the union office that evening, Earle received a call from Serge, the daytime business agent: "Meet me at the Pacific Elevator, there's been a horrible accident. It's Lucio." Earle continues,

> I sped over there . . . but I got stopped by the train. So it was me, Serge, and Johnny—Lucio's brother, and the ambulance. Stuck behind this train. We're on the phone with our employers. Johnny kept saying "cut the train, cut the train." The guy is like near death, could be dead. I get out of my car and I'm running down the length of the train looking for a switchman. Couldn't find him. They were completely down at the other end. Me running at that time—not a good sight. [Earle laughs.] I had just quit smoking and was like 300 pounds. So I finally gave up looking for a switchman, and I came back, and we eventually cut the train after like 5 or 10 minutes.
>
> We get through, we park and then Johnny starts running, and I start running. We get up on board the vessel . . . and we know where it is because that's where everybody is standing . . . and I get there, and I see my friend, my guy, lying in a pool of his own blood . . .
>
> And you know I had never dealt with this before . . . but just talking to the past business agents who had . . . the guys I grew up with. And they said, "First thing you do is get everybody away, if you can." So I tried getting everybody away and then I went to Johnny, Johnny was all over his brother . . . and I was trying to get him away. So I just pulled him away and held onto him. And the first aid attendants and the paramedics worked on him. And . . . it . . . It seemed like forever.
>
> And then finally . . . and I'm watchin' Lucio, and I've got Johnny in a bear hug. And I hear him start screaming out my name now, and I look over and as he's screaming he's got this horrific look on his face, his face is just contorted—he's in so much pain and anguish.
>
> That's what fucked me up for the longest time . . . So I continued to work my shift . . . and I started smoking again that night.

As a business agent (the formal intermediary between workers and employers), it was Earle's job to negotiate situations just like these: to manage relations between outraged workers and the employer, Dubai Ports World. But this was not an event that could in any meaningful way be "mediated," and this is not simply because of Earle's own trauma and rage. In this collision of metal and body is also a collision of interests and efficiencies. Disruption has already featured prominently in this tale of globalized logistics. Efforts to preempt disruption and recover systems of commodity circulation in its wake underpin the entire enterprise of supply chain security investigated in chapter 2. Disruption marks the interruption of normal life. The problem of disruption in a world built on fast flows takes on epic proportions; the reliance on speed combines with the interconnectivity of supply chains to propel disruption in one seemingly discrete locale to system-wide crisis. Typically, in the world of globalized logistics, disruption means that flows of stuff stop. Yet the disruptions at play in Earle's story hold grotesque irony; the stationary train became an impassable wall for the obstructed ambulance. The very infrastructure built to make stuff move long distances becomes an impassible barrier to local connectivity. Lucio's dying body could not be reached because the infrastructure of just-in-time global logistics systems blocked the way. And yet, the train blocking the local road is not the only form of disruption; Lucio's broken body, a final disruption of life itself, also interrupts the workings of the port. "Productivity" disrupts itself. While Earle returned immediately to work after Lucio's lifeless body was taken away, the ship couldn't move for days.

The Body as Battleground

Lucio's broken body marks a particular and bloody conflict between growing demands for greater productivity in the ports and the deaths these demands produce. The loss of Lucio is a tragic tale but one that regularly repeats. Port workers' bodies frequently fall from heights, get crushed between machinery, are trapped under collapsed stacks, are impaled on metal rods, and are severed when cargo shifts on ships. Those who don't succumb to immediate injury often expire after years of exposure to toxins that that come naturally with industrial employment. HIV also has a powerful life in transport industries, including longshoring—a feature of the combined mobility and unfreedom of so many workers in this sector (ITF n.d.). The effects of trauma—like the loss of Lucio—are also embodied; workers manage grief and anxiety with substances like nicotine. Port, transport, and logistics are consistently ranked among the most dangerous industries by governments that monitor workplace health and safety (HSE 2012; WorkSafeBC 2011). In the United States, port work is second only to mining in the number of annual industry workplace deaths and injuries (Bonacich and Wilson 2008, 182). In California, warehousing and trucking were listed on the "highest hazard occupation" list of the Occupational Health and Safety Association for 2009–10 (Lydersen 2011; UEPI 2011). The association cites extreme heat stress and lung cancer from diesel exhaust among health risks for people working in warehouses and driving trucks and locomotives.

The high stakes of logistics work is in part a feature of the inherent dangers of laboring in an environment of big machines and metal boxes. Heavy equipment and human flesh have never made for easy bedfellows. Yet the danger is also due to the speeding up of supply chains in recent years. While the speed of circulation of capital has been a concern for as long as capital has accumulated, the revolution in logistics has changed the game. According to Edna Bonacich and Jake Wilson (2008, 159–60), the logistics revolution "without a doubt, has made business enterprises more efficient." They highlight the reduction of inventories, transport costs, and prices of consumer goods that the revolution provoked. Relying on principles of just-in-time production pioneered in U.S.-occupied Japan, the revolution in logistics has made goods flow faster.

Technological advances, alongside changes to labor regulation, have led to increased intermodality—or a more "seamless" system of infrastructure

FIGURE 22. Gantry cranes in the Port of Elizabeth, New Jersey, 2006. Source: Photograph by the author.

and physical circulation. Ships are unloaded in a fraction of the time that they were a few decades ago—from weeks to just a few days for a standard container ship. Cargo moves from ship to rail or truck in minutes, and distribution centers are often fully automated. In some, goods are continuously circulating on conveyor belts. Yet how this speed is achieved and at what cost are precisely what makes logistics a terrain of struggle. After asserting that the revolution in logistics has been good for business, Bonacich and Wilson (2008, 159–60) also ask whether the effects have been positive for labor, and their answer is clearly negative. They highlight three trends that have intensified globally in logistics labor in the wake of the revolution: (1) increased contingency, deriving from the rise of temporary, contract, and generally precarious forms of labor; (2) weakened unions, as a specific result of the former but also an active contributor to making logistics labor more precarious; and (3) racialization, as a result of the deliberate targeting of more economically precarious communities by companies but also because racialized workers are already concentrated in precarious forms of work. Without a doubt, conditions of work in this sector vary dramatically at a global scale—and these trends therefore articulate differently in different places. We return to questions of the unevenness of labor regimes in an increasingly integrated global system shortly, but for now it is enough to say that aggressive privatization and deregulation are compromising conditions of work in this sector.

The deregulation of the transport sector in the United States was central in engineering these effects. Chapter 1 established that deregulation of the U.S. transport sector was not only a feature of the revolution in logistics but a process underpinning it. While it took shape differently in marine, trucking, rail, air, and telecommunications, across all these sectors it served to undermine the strength and scale of organized labor, led to a decline in conditions of work, deepened racialized wage gaps, opened the field to intermediary operators, and oriented the industry toward the transnational rather than national shipment of goods (LaLonde, Grabner, and Robeson 1970; Peoples and Saunders 1993; Peoples 1998; Bonacich and Wilson 2008; Rodrigue and Notteboom 2008).

The revolution in logistics also marks the rise of corporate retail and logistics giants with aggressive and punitive approaches to labor management. The world's largest corporation in terms of both revenue and employment, Wal-Mart is notorious for its low wages, poor benefits, and highly gendered and racialized labor force (Ortega 1998; Fishman 2006). Wal-Mart may be widely known as a mammoth retailer, but in the world of business management it is known as a logistics company (Bonacich

2005; Davidson and Rummel 2000; Dawson 2000, 2006). Wal-Mart has the largest civilian satellite network, second only to the U.S. Department of Defense. And it is through complex systems of pull production that rely deeply on real-time IT connection between seller and producer that the corporation distinguishes itself. Wal-Mart rose to its current size of close to nine thousand outlets and more than two million employees over the course of only five decades—its exponential growth from a single store in the early 1970s is a testament to the power of the logistics revolution. Wal-Mart has been setting a path for the industry (Fishman 2006; Hernandez 2003; Spector 2005) in both its own employment and contracting practices and those of the logistics sector more broadly through its key role in lobbying government through industry employer groups like California's West Coast Waterfront Coalition (Bonacich and Wilson 2008)—notorious for their aggressive labor relations with the ILWU.

All these shifts and others have contributed directly to the deaths on the docks. As Paddy Crumlin, president of the International Transport Federation, asserts on the ITF website, "The health and safety of men and women port workers can be threatened when casual or untrained labor don't follow health and safety best practice, also when they work for long hours or

FIGURE 23. A container ship in the Port of Vancouver, British Columbia, 2007. Source: Photograph by the author.

without adequate breaks, dealing with increased workloads as employers seek to do more work with less people." Indeed, increased demands for productivity are typically accompanied by cost-cutting initiatives, which can directly impact the level of training of port workers as well as the level of maintenance and inspection of equipment and infrastructure.

The Labor (of) Movement

This all begs the question of why logistics labor is subject to such intense scrutiny. What can be said about the role of logistics labor in global trade? Much has already been written, at least in general terms, about transport labor and the critical role of speedy circulation in the accumulation of capital. While popular imaginaries of work and labor typically conjure scenes of the *manufacture of commodities,* transportation has long been understood as a source of value and a form of production in itself. In chapter 6 of *Capital,* volume 2 ([1887] 1993), Marx outlines how use value, realized in the consumption of commodities, may require a "change in location" and thus an "additional process of production, in the transport industry." Transport produces surplus value, in part through the dead labor of technologies and infrastructures. Marx famously described how it was in "modern industry" that "man succeeded for the first time in making the product of his past labor work on a large scale gratuitously, like a force of nature" (Marx [1887] 1993, 366; see also chapter 1). But more crucial here is the value added "through the labor performed in transport," or in other words, through the "replacement of wages and of surplus-value." Thus in Marx's formulation and in contrast to reductive assumptions, "change of location" is a particular kind of commodity and the transport industry both serves production and is a form of production unto itself.

We might also interpret Marx as arguing that the labor power exploited to produce this commodity has a special importance in the context of the circulation of capital. Capital is *value in motion,* as David Harvey emphasizes (2010), and without a doubt Marx's work on the circulation of capital, specifically in volume 2 of *Capital,* insists on this mobility. Indeed, "the entire character of capitalist production is determined by the self-expansion of the advanced capital-value," Marx ([1887] 1993, 144) explains. And in order for accumulation or "production on an expanded scale" to take place, capital must circulate through the different forms signaled in the equation M-C-M (money capital—commodity capital—expanded money capital). While volume 1 of *Capital* focused specifically on the production process—the "productive consumption of the purchased commodities by the capitalist"—the circulation of capital through its different forms is the "direct object of our study" in the less trafficked volume 2. Not only does capital at its most basic need to circulate in order to accumulate, but the process of circulation can dramatically impact the extent and degree of accumulation possible. "The process of circulation," Marx writes, "sets in motion new forces independent of the capital's magnitude of value and determining its degree of efficiency, its expansion and contraction." In other words, the speed of circulation, "the particular speed with which that capital throws off its commodity-form and assumes that of money," plays a vital role in the process of accumulation.

Marx's discussion of the circuits of capital is largely abstracted from its particular material forms. "Circulation" as described here cannot be understood as simply or immediately *physical* mobility, in the way that the term is often used today. It is rather the transformation of value into different forms that constitutes the circulation of capital. Circulation certainly takes on material forms, but not in any obvious or predetermined way. Commodity capital likely has the most marked materialities and spatialities. We can trace the physical movement of commodities, for instance, more easily than the physical circulation of finance capital. And yet, the seeming simplicity of "following commodities" may also be misleading, as they may be bought and sold many times over the course of a simple journey from producer to consumer, meaning that various forms of capital are at play. Marx ([1887] 1993, 226) addresses this point directly when he suggests that the circulation of commodities can "take place without their physical movement . . . a house that is sold from A to B circulates as a commodity, but it does not get up and walk." More to the point, he suggests that "moveable commodity values like cotton or pig-iron, can remain in the same warehouse while they undergo dozens of circulation processes, and are bought and resold by speculators." In other words, "what actually moves here is the property title to the thing and not the thing itself." Finance capital has profound materialities; it makes its mark on the landscape, though in contradictory ways. Global events like the subprime crisis insist that capital of all forms works geographically, and yet it is the productive capital of the transport and communications industries—which Marx reflects on together—that bring us closest to thinking through the materiality of circulation. Transport (and communications) serves as part of the production process, but with the special capacity to speed up the physical circulation of commodities; reaching markets faster may also impact the speed of capital circulation from commodity to money form. The transport industry is exceptional in that it forms "on the one hand an independent branch of production, and hence a particular sphere for the investment of productive capital. On the other hand it is distinguished by its appearance as the continuation of a production process *within* the circulation process and *for* the circulation process" (emphasis in original).

While the material forms of capital circulation remain largely implicit in his writing, without a doubt, these circuits are for Marx not simply a matter of an abstract speed but of a material space-time. Marx noted 150 years ago that capitalism perpetually refigures the relationship between space and time in the interests of speed. In his *Outline of the Critique of Political Economy* ([1939] 2005, 539), he insists on this kind of relational (and imperial) understanding of the time and space of capitalism. Capital, he writes, "must on one side strive to tear down every spatial barrier to intercourse, i.e. to exchange, and conquer the whole earth for its market." But capital not only expands the space of accumulation; it also transforms space-time to reduce the *time that space takes* in the interests of accelerating circulation. In this passage, frequently cited by geographers, Marx continues by outlining that capital "strives on the other to annihilate this space with time, i.e. to reduce to a minimum the time spent in motion from one place to another" (539).

Stretching the Factory

These general tendencies toward the speed of capital circulation are heightened with the globalization of trade over the past four decades, giving us theories of "time-space compression" from diverse writers including Daniel Bell (1974) and David Harvey (1989). They provide important context for understanding the push to productivity in places like ports. While these debates about the speed of capital flows and the reconfiguration of relational space in the context of increasingly global trade continue (especially in critical geography), arguably a much larger literature has focused specifically on the reorganization of global labor in manufacturing. This is marked especially in research, writing, and advocacy regarding the "new international division of labor," off-shoring, the rise of *maquiladoras*, and the phenomenon of "runaway factories" (Amin and Thrift 2004; Antràs, Garicano, and Rossi-Hansberg 2005; Dicken 2003; Harrod and O'Brien 2002; Harvey 1989; Sassen 1991; Wilson 1992; Wright 2002). These all mark the incredible profiteering that has come by way of moving manufacturing to low-wage regions of the world to exploit radically uneven geographies of wages, social protections, and labor regulation. Without a doubt, these debates have been generative, allowing for far more nuanced conceptions of the geographies and relations of production in an era of global trade. But to begin to appreciate the implications of the logistics revolution and the rise of global supply chains for the reorganization of logistics labor requires that we probe a different kind of shift: the dramatic recasting of the relationship between *making and moving*, or production and distribution. At stake here is the rescaling and networking of production itself—the disarticulation of production into component parts that can be stretched out and rearranged in more complex configurations. In other words, the spatial arrangement of the reconfigured relationship between production and distribution is at the center of this question.

The globalization of logistics marks not simply the global distribution of production but the invention of the supply chain and the reorganization of national economies into transnational systems that stretch the factory across national borders and even around the world (Cooper et al. 1997). The image of the factory as located in a single place is less relevant than ever before. Instead, the functions of the factory have been disaggregated and dispersed across space according to the logics of total cost. Commodities are increasingly manufactured across multiple states precisely to incorporate radically uneven modalities of labor into the production process (Harvey 1989; Smith 1984). That production is now organized multinationally is hardly a new point, but the full implications of this shift, for our concepts and methods of inquiry, particularly when understood in the context of the rise of logistics, have not been fully appreciated.

Conceptual and calculative labor of the kind explored in chapter 2 was central in all this; it created the capacity to count the "total cost" of the "business logistics system" that propelled corporate management to rethink their calibrations of production and distribution (Drucker 1969; LeKashman and Stolle 1965; Smykay and LaLonde 1967). Systems approaches and total cost calculations transformed the field precisely by bringing the border between production and distribution under conceptual attack. If we return to the arguments mounted by leading management theorists of the time that were operationalized in logistics cost calculations, we see that the movement of materials at any and every stage of production (before, during, and after manufacturing) were all to be counted together. With total cost, all physical movement of materials (and eventually, information) is accounted for, rather than the much more limited cost of the transportation of finished products to consumers that characterized the old field of physical distribution. As corporate management of the 1960s and 1970s learned through total cost analysis, there could be profit in moving facilities further away from consumers (LeKashman and Stolle 1965).

The revolution in logistics didn't simply make transportation more important; it directly and deliberately blurred the boundaries between transport and other forms of productive labor. Undermining the distinction between materials management in production (understood as the movement of materials and information within the production process) and physical distribution (understood as the movement of materials and information into and out of production processes and facilities) was key (Harland 2005; Houlihan 1987). All movement of stuff across the business system became the territory of business logistics, and thus it would be calculated centrally. This meant, de facto, that the *production process* was no longer located strictly within or bounded by the fixed space of the manufacturing facility. This "stretching" of the factory prompted a subtle but powerful transformation; it relied on and bolstered the rise of geo-economic calculative imaginaries. Indeed, this conceptual shift had practical impact in how it reshaped the measurement of cost and value.

Thomas Reifer (2011, 7) boldly suggests that "if Marx were writing today," he might launch his entire investigation of capital from a different starting place. For Reifer, the transformations in the organization of global political economy through the logistics revolution have been so extensive and profound that he considers how the *container* might replace the commodity. He suggests that today Marx "might have begun *Capital* by noting that the wealth of nations in the 21st century increasingly appears as an immense collection of containers. Thus, Marx might have begun his analysis of capital by analyzing the container, its contents and the network of global social relations of which it is an integral part." This suggestion is provocative, and there is much to be gleaned from the study of the container in political economy and beyond. Nevertheless, the revolution in logistics ushers in a different kind of rescaling of the analysis of capital and value. It marks the birth of the supply chain— the disaggregated, dispersed, partially fictional logistics network as the basis for corporate competition. The supply chain does not hold the unity or seamlessness invested in it, but it is nevertheless very real.

It could be said that the key kernel of the revolution in logistics in fact echoed insights that Marx articulated 150 years ago: that transportation creates value, the value of a "useful effect" (Marx [1887] 1993, 226), which makes it a form of production rather than an activity that follows. In a sense, the revolution in logistics that began in the 1960s saw business management learning the lessons of Marx's *Capital*, albeit in a very particular historically and geographically situated way, emerging out of the specific genealogies of mid-twentieth-century American military arts and business sciences. When W. Bruce Allen (1997, 110), in one of the very few scholarly articles that examines the revolution in logistics outside of the applied field of business management, writes that "finished goods or raw materials held in inventory . . . are just dollar bills in disguise being warehoused," he restates a basic principle of the circulation of capital. It is notable that Allen's article, which documents such a critical and underinvestigated transformation in global capitalism, had been cited only twelve times (twice by this author in earlier work) at the time that this book was written. This begs the question of how the separation between production and distribution occurred to begin with, or in other words, how materials management (the labor of moving things within the production process) became a distinct field from physical distribution (the labor of moving things from production to consumption; see chapter 1). A genealogy of this separation in the work of neoclassical economists, or in the early field of management, is beyond the scope of this chapter. Certainly there is a question of the scale of movement and of distance at work here, as well as a distinction between internal and external movement (vis-à-vis the factory). It also begs some scrutiny of how embodied labor in the logistics sector is being recalibrated to the stretched, networked, global factory (Bonacich 2005; Bonacich and Wilson 2008; Reifer 2004).

Mapping for Management

As the factory itself is rescaled into a network of continuous production, a business system, and a supply chain, the labor that moves materials across that system is also scrutinized anew. If frequent bodily injury on the docks is a feature of greater demands for supply chain productivity, so too is a growing arsenal of managerial techniques and technologies of automation that target the body of the worker. Indeed, we are seeing renewed interest in the minutia of workers' movements and attempts to calibrate them to global logistics systems. In a recent contribution, Neilson and Rossiter (2010, 4) argue, "At the level of labor management, logistics registers the calculation of time against the performance of tasks and movement of things." It should not come as a surprise that workers' bodies elicit so much attention; they were a central concern in the earliest articulations of scientific management. "The first man in recorded history who deemed work deserving of systematic study and observation," according to management guru Peter Drucker (1973, 181), was concerned precisely with the efficiency of workers' bodily movements. Frederick W. Taylor's 1911 *Principles of Scientific Management* focuses on the relationship between the movement of workers' bodies and the movement of things. In fact, Taylor frames his intervention as precisely a concern for efficiency of the former in an era when the latter was commanding widespread attention. He speaks to these concerns in the opening pages of his *Principles*: "We can see and feel the waste of material things. Awkward, inefficient, or ill-directed movements of men, however, leave nothing visible or tangible behind them. Their appreciation calls for an act of memory, an effort of the imagination. And for this reason, even though our daily loss from this source is greater than from our waste of material things, the one has stirred us deeply, while the other has moved us but little" (6). Manuel De Landa (2005, 120) suggests that this common tendency to date the emergence of the management of the worker's body with Taylor betrays a troubling civilianization of the story. Instead he notes that Dutch commander Maurice of Nassau "had already applied these methods to the training of his soldiers beginning in the 1560s. Maurice analyzed the motion needed to load, aim, and fire a weapon into its micromovements, redesigned them for maximum efficiency, and then imposed them on his soldiers via continuous drill." Perhaps not surprisingly, De Landa traces the link from the discipline of the battlefield to the discipline of the factory through the field of military logistics and procurement. He suggests that the demands for standardized parts for military equipment promoted the standardization of production in this specialized arena of production, which also had the benefit of undermining craft worker control of the labor process. Indeed, De Landa argues that the "the actual history" of the "American system of manufactures" is different from the mythology surrounding it, "involving as actors not civilians working individually but a network of military officers and weapon factory superintendents working in the context of institutional organizations, such as the Ordnance Department and the Springfield and Harpers Ferry armories" (122).

Yet while there were significant precursors to Taylor outside the civilian realm, and some important martial genealogies to Taylor's innovations that support a broader rethinking of the relationship between militaries and markets, scientific management remains critical in understanding the rise of management. Interest in Taylor's scientific management was widespread and helped to usher in the era of the standardized work of the assembly line. Taylorism, as it was known, was concerned with the efficiency of work in production and promoted a set of specific principles (Braverman 1974, 112). Taylor sought to "separate the conception of work from its execution" (Bahnisch 2000, 54) so that control could be centralized in management. Taylor (1985, 158) argued that management should appropriate "all of the great mass of traditional knowledge, which in the past has been in the heads of the workmen, and in the physical skills and knack of the workmen." Betraying an "acute fear of the undisciplined working body" (Bahnisch 2000, 62), Taylor ([1907] 1995, 10) asserted, "The management must know better than every workman in our place." His methods served not only to expand the authority of management by extending its control into the intimate actions of workers, thus "reducing work to gestures and movements of the disciplined objectified body" (Bahnisch 2000, 54). Taylor also dissected work, dividing tasks into their component movements, rearranging and regularizing those movements to streamline gestures, and subjecting them to rapid increases in pace. In this way, workers' actions were removed from their own design and control and were instead "choreographed by the assembly line, the stopwatch and the clock, and the colonizing subjectivity of management" (ibid.).

In this way, scientific management enacts a politics of work built on the disciplined and objectified body, but as Mark Bahnisch (2000, 63) has argued, Taylorism also "proceeds by acting on class and sexed subjectivity." Taylor's bargain pivoted on the promise of valorized masculinity. The worker was assured that his masculinity, achieved through his hard physical labor, was valued and then rewarded through pay incentives, even as he was constituted as "pure body" without any capacities for conceiving of his own labor. In a famous discussion about pig iron work, this paternalism for the physical laborer is explicit: Taylor (1911, 59) explains that the man fit for this occupation should be "so stupid and phlegmatic that he more easily resembles in his mental makeup an ox."

The discipline of workers through scientific management relied on particular spatialities. This is already implied through the focus on the body and movements of the worker, but it is worth considering more carefully. The most immediate spatial problem for Taylor was the space of the factory, which he subjected to complete reordering. To separate conceptual labor from physical execution, and to divide work into constitutive and repetitive tasks, the space of work was subject to intense scrutiny and ordered anew. If Taylor was to "contain these anarchic bodies," he would have to construct "a space to confine them through the organization of the physical factory . . . from the lowest form of labor up to the highest, dividing all their tasks and movements, specifying as many as 600 bodily movements in the working day" (Bahnisch 2000, 62). But there are also other spatialities implicitly at work in Taylor's scientific management. Often unremarked is the fact that Taylor very deliberately casts the question of scientific management as a matter of *national* efficiency. "We can see our forests vanishing, our water-powers going to waste, our soil being carried by floods into the sea, and the end of our coal and iron is in sight," Taylor (1911, 2–3) remarks. "But our larger wastes of human effort, which go on every day through such of our acts as are blundering, ill-directed, or inefficient, and which Roosevelt refers to as a lack of 'national efficiency,' are less visible, less tangible, and are but vaguely appreciated," he continues. He proceeds to explain that *Principles of Scientific Management* "has been written, first, to point out through a series of simple illustrations, the great loss which the whole country is suffering through inefficiency in almost all of our daily acts."

The nationalism of scientific management was not simply a matter of words but also infused Taylor's basic logics. The assumption of a national economy—a project in the making at the time he was writing (Mitchell 2005)—infuses assumptions about the problem of efficiency. These surface in the most basic promise of scientific management: that improving efficiency benefits employer and employee. Indeed, Taylor's key promise was the possibility of an "essential 'harmony of interest' between capital and labor based upon increased productivity" (Noble 1977, 271). Taylor argued that "soldiering"—the deliberate wasting of workers' own efforts to slow down production in order to avoid making themselves redundant—would be undermined by a virtuous cycle of productivity. The logics of competition at work here are unspoken but nevertheless profoundly geographical: "To illustrate: if you and your workman have become so skillful that you and he together are making two pairs of shoes in a day, while your competitor and his workman are making only one pair, it is clear that after selling your two pairs of shoes you can pay your workman much higher wages than your competitor who produces only one pair of shoes is able to pay his man, and that there will still be enough money left over for you to have a larger profit than your competitor" (Taylor 1911, 6). This simple logic assumes many things—central among these is that conditions of work remain broadly even across different workshops. Without saying so, Taylor's argument requires a common labor market and thus some form of common government. With the rise of national economies, national borders came to mark often radical unevenness in labor regimes. This uneven development across nation-states—and constituted by them—is precisely the source of the gap that corporations have more recently taken advantage of in outsourcing production internationally. It is precisely the act of moving production outside one national space and into another that allows them to escape common labor standards and regulations. Outsourcing allows the capitalist to dramatically *increase* worker productivity and radically *reduce* their share of profits at the same time. This explains the formation of *maquiladoras* immediately beyond the southern borders of the United States. No doubt, labor markets are highly uneven regionally *within* nation-states, and capitalists can often exploit feminized and racialized workers at much higher rates even within the same local place, but the most dramatic gaps in conditions of work have been organized internationally in the geopolitical era.

In addition to subtle spatialities, this passage also assumes the benevolence of the capitalist in sharing the increased profits of newfound productivity with workers. Needless to say, these were hotly contested assumptions of scientific management—not only in words but in practice. Bahnisch (2000, 64) emphasizes the effects of Taylor's scientific management in terms of governing work and workers in new ways. He argues that the "achievement of Taylorism was to contain and discipline the working subject, separating the consciousness of the labor process and its embodiment in labor." But despite the success of these techniques and technologies in compelling workers to recalibrate their own labor and bodies, they were also resisted. As David Noble (1977, 272–73) explains, workers responded to Taylor's scientific management in various ways: "The unorganized depended upon insubordination and sabotage; the organized used the strike." Noble proceeds to document the many labor actions that met the implementation of scientific management in factories across the United States, including Bethlehem Steel—the same company where Taylor got his start.

Like the Taylorist motion studies of early twentieth-century scientific management, today's "process mapping" opens up the production process to managerial scrutiny (Graham 2008). Process mapping might be understood as a *rescaled motion study* in the interests of *transnational* efficiency. It works at multiple scales: from the scale of the worker's body to the intermodal system, aiming to calibrate the former to the latter. "With globalisation," a report by P&O Nedlloyd Logistics (2004, 3) asserts, "today's supply chains have rapidly extended their coverage beyond the traditional geographical areas." It is in this context that they praise the merits of the process map, "essentially a visual aid for picturing work processes . . . developed from the need to generate visibility of where time is used within the supply chain. Time compression, i.e. the removal of wasted time from the business processes, could then be applied" (2). The report continues by extolling the merits of the process map for management: "The mapping enables managers to see the total picture." Mapping the "total picture" is crucial in measuring supply chain performance; visual representation is a means toward control, achieved by "transferring the complex reality of performance into a sequence of limited symbols" (Lebas 1995, quoted in Chan 2003, 180). In other words, process mapping aims to make the system visible so its component parts can be measured and managed. Indeed, Felix Chan (2003) suggests that mapping supply chain processes is inherent to managing them and so locates process mapping as an essential component of the rise of (global) supply chain management since the 1990s.

Process mapping relies on the intermodal automation of logistics systems, while it also serves to further integrate those sociotechnical systems. Process mapping also helps to build logistics systems by integrating formerly distinct processes and thus managing "wasted" time and resources. Unlike Taylor's scientific management of a century ago, workers' bodily movements are not explicitly the focus of attention; process mapping doesn't dwell in the details of the motions of the arms or movement of the torso in its quest for efficiency. Nevertheless, the body is centrally implicated in the process map—though transformed into numbers representing costs. Managing the performance of supply chains entails "quantifying effectiveness and efficiency of action" (Neely et al. 1995, quoted in Chan 2003, 180). The movements and labors of workers' bodies are aggregated and quantified, and in this way central to the work of management.

If the process map allows for managerial scrutiny of supply chains through the visual representation of the "total system" (Miller Davis 1974), a range of computer systems are now used to manage enormous data flows that constitute that system. Enterprise resource planning (ERP) systems aim to integrate all departments and functions of a firm into a single computer system, allowing real-time communication across the company (accounting, finance, sales, distribution, etc.) as well as the tracking and tracing of performance (Bradford and Florin 2003; Grabski and Leech 2007; IGI 2010; Wang et al. 2007). New generation ERP systems are also geared toward allowing firms to communicate and integrate with other firms. ERP systems have been described as the "digital nerve system that connects the processes across the organization and transmits the impact of an event happening in one part of the enterprise to the rest accurately" (Mabert, Soni, and Venkataramanan 2001, 76). They are said to bring firms advantages such as reduced cycle time; faster information transactions; and standardization of manufacturing, warehousing, and labor management, while they also support electronic commerce. ERP systems change the way a firm operates though the automation of these functions in an era of extraordinarily complex supply chain organization, rather than through technological change in the simple sense. Despite their virtual rather than physical form, ERP systems are nevertheless a serious investment. In the late 1990s Allied Waste invested $130 million in their ERP system, while Nike spent $400 million on theirs in 2001. ERP systems build industry best practices right into the software (Brown and Vessey 2003), a marker of the profoundly neoliberal nature of this technology (Higgins and Larner 2010; Larner and Craig 2005; Rose 1996). Thinking through the implications of these systems for labor, Brett Neilson and Ned Rossiter (2010, 5) suggest, "Immaterialities of labor and life are coded into the quantitative parameters . . . through the brute force of instrumentality or calculation: no matter how a worker might feel, quotas have to be met and global supply chains must not be adversely affected. Feeling at once exceeds measure and is constantly drawn back into its purview. This is again the tension of living and abstract labor." At every site and scale of the supply chain, new technologies have been implemented that simultaneously automate work and integrate different forms of labor into the chain. The warehouse is a case in point. It is now generally referred to as a "distribution center" in keeping with the shift in its purpose in the context of just-in-time production from storing inventory to sorting and redistributing commodities. The distribution center keeps stuff in motion, often quite literally. Distribution centers rely on a whole range of communications technologies to manage inventory and its circulation. Mobile robotics systems developed by U.S. military research for defense purposes now organize and assemble shipments in automated corporate facilities (Everett and Gage 1999). Human labor and the human body are themselves automated; labor-intensive work like picking and packing is now guided by computer managed voice software that directs the minute movements of warehouse workers via headsets connected to small portable computers. As one manager of a large grocery chain who recently implemented "voice picking" explains, the technology has not only "increased the accuracy, it's also increased the productivity, because the selector has no time to actually talk or communicate with everybody else" (Trebilcock 2012). The advantage of the technology for this manager was precisely that the worker communicates "with the system itself, so it keeps him more focused on his job at hand."

Supply chain managers offer a number of reasons for their interest in automation in addition to the quest for accuracy and discipline. Labor supply is critical. "Human resources" is a top priority for management, but humans are an unreliable resource. Automation allows managers to "stabilize the workforce," particularly important in regions where there are competing pulls on employment (McCune, Beatty, and Montagno 2006; U.S. Congress 1957; USOPM 2009). Geography is critical in another regard. As one manager explains, "It's about space" (Trebilcock 2012). With rapid global urbanization, "just finding space close to a major urban area is pretty hard these days if you need to put down a 1-million-square-foot warehouse," he says. "A compressed footprint is a greener facility." Finally, technology has become more widely available as it becomes more affordable. Not long ago, supply chain automation was limited to the largest operations, but as it becomes more affordable for smaller firms, it also becomes implemented as an industry standard (Duclos, Vokurka, and Lummus 2003; Viswanadham 2002). Seaports and inland ports alike are relying ever more on automated container transport systems (Hino et al. 2009; Zhang, Ioannou, and Chassiakos 2006). Leaders in the field like Wal-Mart introduced electronic data interchange, whereby orders are automatically sent to producers when inventory levels drop below a set level, crucial to the rise of the pull system of production and distribution (Amin 1994; Aoyama and Ratick 2007). Radio frequency identification (RFID) tags emit low-range radio frequency with information about container contents and have been in use for some time.

The quest for efficiency and productivity implicates logistics labor through the introduction of new managerial techniques, but as the preceding discussion suggests, labor is also transformed with the introduction of new technologies—new machines. Many of these have been rolled out over the course of the last decade, though the advent of technology reshaping labor is hardly new (Castells and Hall 1994; Downey 2002). There is no better example of a technology that has served to automate logistics labor as it also constructed a transnational system of trade than the standard shipping container, introduced half a century ago, as explored briefly in chapter 1. The container, a U.S. military innovation, has been repeatedly dubbed the single most important technological innovation underpinning the globalization of trade (Levinson 2006; "Moving Story" 2002; Rodrigue and Notteboom 2008). While shipping containers have a long history of experimentation, the standardization of an intermodal container that could be transferred across different modes of transport was first experimented with during World War II as a means to reduce the time and labor involved in transporting military supplies to the front. It was not until the Vietnam War that the military use of the shipping container entrenched its standardized global form (Levinson 2006, 8, 178). Containerization reshaped work dramatically across the logistics sector;

the slow, dirty, and physically intensive labor of moving bulk cargo was quickly transformed into the fast and dangerous work with metal and machines. The container's impact on the speed of goods circulation was phenomenal, making the time it takes to move goods from one mode of transport to another a fraction of the previous time and labor. Gantry crane operators, who sit atop the large distinctive cranes that now grace port cities, can manually move a container from ship to truck or rail at a rate of one every minute or two. It is precisely the intermodal function of the container that has allowed logistics to be conceived and governed as a system rather than a series of disjoined movements. Indeed, while intermodality also relied on the deregulation and reregulation of the transport sector, the physical capacity for this networked infrastructure was entirely dependent on the container.

As Marx argued long ago, technologies are inextricably linked to the management of labor in production, both by directly replacing living labor and through the discipline that the threat of automation presents to workers. Yet technologies have arguably become ever more important, not only in speeding up production, reorganizing the nature of logistics labor, and undermining conditions of work. Over the course of the revolution in logistics, a series of new technologies have been crucial in constituting the very possibility for the transnational intermodal integration of diverse forms of work and infrastructures. In other words, automation in this sector has some particularly geographical implications in terms of the building of transnational sociotechnical systems through intermodal infrastructure. These technologies furthermore work to calibrate the worker's body to the "body" of the lively system. Global logistics relies on a postnational biopolitics of transnational sociotechnical systems.

Contesting Fast Flow

As in earlier moments, new technologies and managerial techniques "colonize" the subjectivities of workers today, producing work and worker anew. Yet the speeding up of supply chains and its effects on the nature of work is powerfully challenged by logistics labor. The sheer number of logistics labor actions that are taking place around the world is a testament to the profoundly contested nature of supply chain management. Figure 24 offers an informal survey of significant labor actions in the logistics sectors since 2007. Without even attempting a comprehensive inventory, what is notable here is the sheer number of events and their global distribution. It is also significant that there are common provocations

FIGURE 24. A survey of labor actions in logistics industries since 2007.

underpinning these struggles, as well as convergence in the nature and severity of state response. The common provocations include corporate attacks on conditions of work in the logistics sector or the privatization of infrastructure and employment. The latter is almost unavoidably an instance of the former, as the case of the Greek port of Piraeus revealed (Faiola 2010; Morris 2011), where despite major opposition from workers, China Ocean Shipping Company (COSCO) assumed control of formerly public container operations. COSCO's acquisition meant the extension of new labor practices and management, including no union recognition and cuts in industry standards in everything from wages to training and working hours (Morris 2011).

If demands for heightened productivity target the worker's body, it is also notable that resistance to these managerial strategies and tactics exposes the inescapable physicality of the conflict between logistics labor and capital. In sometimes breathtaking ways, the body of the port worker literally, physically, disrupts the workings of logistics systems through labor actions. In 2011, port welder and activist Kim Jin-Suk occupied a gantry crane in the port of Busan, Korea (Su Seol 2011a). Protesting Hanjin's plans to cut workers and wages, her occupation began on January 6, 2011, in tandem with a workers' wildcat strike on the ground. While the striking workers eventually accepted concessions on their contracts, Kim Jin-Suk held her position. A movement of thousands formed on the ground around her, dubbed the "hope riders," providing her with logistical and political support. *After 309 days*, Jin-Suk's occupation paid off; workers were rehired and compensated with back pay in what became the first labor victory in South Korea in fifteen years (Su Seol 2011b).

Ironically inverting the physicality of their work, transport workers use their bodies in labor actions to contest management and make circulation improbable or even impossible. Picket lines frequently take on the spirit of occupation; like the iconography that has long adorned transport union gear, labor actions are often marked by a deeply classed masculinity performed through muscled and bulky bodies. States are responding aggressively to logistics labor actions (as they are to many other disruptions to supply chains; see chapters 4 and 5) with massive physical force, and the force deployed is often explicitly militarized. When 1,500 dock workers in Bangladesh went on strike to protest the Chittagong Port Authority's privatization of container and bulk operations in October 2010, the government employed military force to contain the strike and coerce resumption of job duties ("Bangladesh Port" 2010). Just over a year later, the U.S. military intervened in a labor conflict in Washington State. After the transnational grain company EGT built a new processing facility in the port of Longview, they unlawfully contracted non-ILWU labor in contravention of the master grain agreement. This direct attack on the union's jurisdiction elicited a powerful response from the ILWU in the form of spirited pickets, blockades, and direct physical confrontation with police (Corvin and Harshman 2011; McEllrath 2011; Martin 2011; Rohar 2011b). The action eventually earned massive and very public support from the "Occupy" movement, as well as solidarity rallies from dock workers as far away as India and Korea.[2] Despite the unlawful actions of EGT, picketers were met with aggressive police actions (including 220 arrests), and President Obama eventually sanctioned the use of the Coast Guard to escort EGT's ships (Cordon 2012; Heyman 2012). The Coast Guard is a military organization, but because of its long history as an exceptional force that also protects domestic waters, it is not subject to the Posse Comitatus Act (1878), which prevents the use of the military on domestic soil.

This is by no means the first time that military force has been deployed in response to labor actions in the United States or elsewhere (Graham 2006; Lutz 2001; Markusen et al. 1991). And yet, these and other events do mark something significant: the increasingly common designation of logistics labor actions as matters of *national security*. Just a few years earlier and a thousand miles to the south, another ILWU local was deemed a threat to national security. In 2002, the ILWU began to protest a record-breaking number of workers' deaths on the docks (five deaths in six months). The union denied any organized work slowdown but also said, "The ILWU Negotiating Committee passed a resolution today, calling on members to redouble efforts to improve safety on the docks. The resolution, distributed to all locals, calls on longshore workers to follow all safety procedures, including speed limits, to refrain from working extended shifts, working through lunch hours, or doubling back" (Walker 2002a, 2002b). The Pacific Maritime Association (PMA)—the maritime employers' organization—insisted that the ILWU had orchestrated the slowdown and in response locked out workers. Acting in support of the employers, Vice President Dick Cheney declared ILWU actions a threat to national security. Following pressure from corporations such as Dell, Ford, and Boeing, who experienced shortages in their just-in-time supply chains, George W. Bush enacted the Taft-Hartley Act—America's notorious "slave labor law"—in the largest U.S. ports of LA/Long Beach. President Bush compelled workers to comply with PMA demands under threat of fines, criminal charges, and military deployment. These events were striking, not only because it was the first time in history that an employer lockout was used to implement the Taft-Hartley law. According to one union representative, "The message to employers is that you can create a crisis by locking out your workers and then get the government to intervene with Taft-Hartley that violates all the rights of workers to collective bargaining" (OWCW 2002). In other words, it establishes that ports are an exceptional space and time where the law can be used to undermine the law. Labor movement leaders were surprised by this aggressive attack. Ron Judd, American Federation of Labor and Congress of Industrial Organizations (AFL-CIO) western regional director, diagnosed it as "the most egregious attack on workers' rights in 50 years" (ibid.). Marking the seriousness of the event for the labor movement as a whole, Judd explained, "If they can do it to the ILWU, they can do it to any union." The events in LA/Long Beach also establish that the disruption of supply chains is understood as a matter of national security. This is precisely the logic of supply chain security. Trade disruption has moved from an economic cost to a security threat.

Securing Circulation: Transport Labor as Target

The architecture of global production and trade is built on the assumption of fast flows. Commodities need to remain in physical motion if capital will continue to circulate. Disruption to commodity flows exposes the vulnerability of just-in-time production systems and so too the centrality of logistics infrastructure and its protection to the politics of our present. As InterVISTAS Consulting recommends in a report to the Canadian federal government on the future of logistics gateways (quoted at the beginning of this chapter), the ideal target for labor management would be "zero work stoppages" (2007). The longstanding interest in speeding up production and distribution systems that we encountered with Marx and Taylor and that was given new importance with the revolution in logistics today melds powerfully with contemporary efforts to secure supply chains. The managerial desire for zero work stoppages is increasingly managed through securitization, where labor actions are understood to threaten the (national) security of (global) trade.

As we saw in chapter 2, the supply chain has an important spatiality, and this implicates questions of security directly. If the object of protection takes the form of a network or a chain, then "security in a 'chain' is only as good as the weakest link" (APF 2008, 10). This notion of weak links is a productive part of a political geographic imaginary that aims to identify threats so that they may be targeted and spatially contained. In a moment of convergence with broader managerial strategies of making the system visible in the interests of control through process mapping, efforts to secure the supply chain are provoking their own calls for mapping systems of supply so that risks and threats can be governed. The first strategy outlined as part of the Asia Pacific Gateway and Corridor Initiative (2009) for security is to "initiate a project to map and inventory the supply chain that comprises the Gateway, including the full scope of facilities and services that fall under a common security umbrella." The industry map of "supply chain risks" that appeared in chapter 2 marks global "chokepoints" and "threat zones" for trade, making them visible so they can be managed by security initiatives. One of the places these maps circulate is in a major industry report titled "Transportation & Logistics 2030 Volume 4: Securing the Supply Chain," which makes some intriguing connections between labor actions and terrorist events (PwC 2011). While the explicit focus of the report is on terrorism, it also draws some equivalence between the two by suggesting that labor actions in chokepoints provide a useful proxy for the effects of terror. "Attacks on supply chains are often looking for a big return on a small investment," meaning "logistics hubs like airports or ports offer the ideal target," PricewaterhouseCoopers (PwC 2011, 16) explains. The report continues by asserting, "Possible consequences of disrupting a logistics hub . . . can be seen by taking a look at the port strike in 2002, where 29 ports on the US West Coast were locked out due to a labor strike of 10,500 dockworkers." It proceeds to detail the impacts of the lockout, estimated to have cost $1 billion per day in trade.

Yet beyond indirect allusions to the common effects of labor actions and other forms of disruption, workers have been explicitly deemed a particular threat to the security of supply. Labor actions are frequently included in inventories of security threats: "labor strike," for instance, is included among the risks that threaten the security of supply chains in a recent book that has been influential across supply chain industry professionals (Lynch 2009). More important, logistics workers are centrally and directly implicated in a series of recent supply chain security initiatives. As chapter 2 explored in some detail, supply chain security has become a central pillar of post-2001 securitization in the United States. Direct pressure from the United States on the international community prompted the international shipping community (the governments and corporations that constitute it) to follow suit through an aggressive push for successive regulatory acts through a range of bodies of global governance, such as the United Nation's International Marine Organization. This securitization of supply chains directly targets transport workers. A central pillar of this initiative is a massive program designed to improve security in the transport sector, with a focus on maritime ports. The Transportation Worker Identification Credential (TWIC) presumes that targeting a key link in supply chains—the people handling cargo in ports—will preempt disruption. In order to access their work places, workers must undergo invasive security screenings. Those who are successful in obtaining clearance must carry security cards—biometric cards in the United States—that are linked to the newly created security perimeters surrounding ports. Workers can be deemed threats to national security by virtue of state suspicion of their own activities or those of their affiliates and thereby denied clearance and so too employment. These programs undermine collective agreements, privacy rights, and employment security for workers. Ironically, they also invest responsibility for national security in workers even as they criminalize this same group. The onus placed on workers to protect the nation even while constituting a likely threat to its security exceeds the bounds of neoliberalism and can perhaps only be explained as a deeply *neurotic* form of citizenship and governmentality (cf. Isin 2004).

The U.S. Transportation Worker Identification Credential (TWIC), a joint responsibility of the Transportation Security Administration within the Department of Homeland Security (DHS) and the U.S. Coast Guard, is in fact operated and maintained by Lockheed Martin. This private management of the TWIC program is another indication of the neoliberalization of national security; the government assumes the role of agenda setting, but implementation is assigned to the lowest bidder.

But perhaps most important for this investigation, port security programs have the effect of blurring the boundaries between crime and terror. The TWIC requires that workers undergo a security threat assessment, which includes criminal history records checks, immigration checks, and an intelligence/terrorism check. Workers are deemed to be a threat to national security and denied security clearance on a permanent basis for a range of crimes including the "attempt to improperly transport a hazardous material" or the "attempt to commit a crime involving a security transportation incident." Workers are denied clearance for seven years for a much longer list of crimes including "attempted dishonesty, fraud, or misrepresentation, including identity fraud and money laundering"; attempted immigration violations; and "attempted distribution, possession with intent to distribute, or importation of a controlled substance" ("TWIC Rules and Regulations" 2007).

The TWIC affects at least 1.5 million workers according to conservative estimates (Emsellem et al. 2009). Frustrated officials from the Port of Houston suggest DHS estimates are far off and that actual numbers should be ten times higher. Critical in all this, an estimated 30–50 percent of port truckers who are undocumented migrants will automatically be ineligible for the pass, suggesting an intensification of the territorial bounds on human mobility at the same time that those same boundaries are recast to facilitate the flow of goods. The TWIC both rewrites the limits of state surveillance and supplants labor protections, but it does so without presenting itself as labor law. Robert McEllrath (2011), international president of the ILWU, explains the effects of the TWIC on his members:

> The Transport Workers Identity Credential has been nothing short of a disaster. TSA sent letters to tens of thousands of individuals suggesting they may not be eligible for a TWIC because they may have been convicted of a crime. Then, TSA put the onus on the workers to prove they were never convicted. Under this twisted logic, workers were guilty until they could prove themselves innocent. TSA sat on these appeals for an average of 69 days. The result was thousands of workers left unemployed, unable to make house and car payments, or attend to their families' needs. According to a July 2009 National Employment Law Project report, African-Americans and Latinos waited even longer. On average, African Americans waited one month more than their white counterparts, which translated to one month more in lost wages. Latinos on average waited two months longer.

Much like the American TWIC program, Canada's Marine Transport Security Clearance Program (MTSCP) requires the creation of "secure areas" around maritime ports and limits access to the area to those with a valid security credential. As I have argued elsewhere (Cowen 2007), these programs cross long established lines of domestic state authority and mix technologies for fighting terror and crime, effectively suspending basic rights and protections. Like the U.S. TWIC, the Canadian MTSCP and the Australian Maritime Security Identity Card (MSIC) make crime, or even *potential crime,* a matter of national security. In this way, job security and even collective bargaining are supplanted; if a worker cannot attain clearance, he or she cannot be employed in the port. Tom Dufresne, president of ILWU-Canada, points out that "[unions and their members] would never agree to have a collective agreement with no grievance procedure in it, without some final arbitrator making the decision on whether or not a person is guilty of an offence or what the penalty should be. And yet, with the security regulation—the internal review they're proposing— there is no independent, transparent, affordable appeals process other than going to the federal court of Canada. And then all you might get is 'by the way, you were right.' Who do I go to for compensation? There is no compensation." The fact that these conditions would never pass a regular negotiation with port actors is exactly the point. Governments are able to implement the regulations specifically because they are not framed as labor law but rather as exceptional measures that respond to crises of national security. It is precisely through the mobilization of crisis that the foundations of territorially based national citizenship rights (the distinction between inside and outside national space) are undermined. As one joint report from Australia's transportation unions addressing the new Marine Security Identity Card asserts, "There is always the tendency for commentators to refer to issues of criminality as opposed to real terrorist activities. As the debate deepens there is a blurring between criminality or more specifically a history of criminal convictions and the deliberate risk of terrorism" (Maritime Union of Australia 2005, 8). This collapse of all criminal activity, and even *suspected* criminality, into threats to national security simultaneously undoes protections formerly associated with national status while reconstituting the very meaning of *in*security. The Maritime Union of Australia (2005, 8) suggests that "if the arguments around the introduction of the MSIC cards are allowed to broaden the scope to include the detection of criminals or reformed criminals in the transport chain then the effectiveness of any maritime security measures are diluted." However, we must consider the possibility that "security" actually means something significantly different in these new border programs; it is *recast rather than reduced* through this broadening sweep of threats, in ways that have serious implications for citizenship.

Both the U.S. and Canadian transportation authorities are reputed to have plans to extend these programs across the transport sector, potentially implicating several million workers. Labor leaders are convinced that the security clearance could also serve as the basis for a biometric national identity card. The TWIC, the MSIC, and the MTSCP are being introduced as exceptional measures targeted to a highly specialized group of workers, but they nevertheless establish precedents that may rework labor law and civil rights more broadly. Despite the dramatic precedents these programs set, few people beyond the bounds of the ports have ever even heard of their existence. Governments have deliberately kept them out of the public realm by treating them as highly technical regulations rather than fully political pieces of legislation. This is consistent with what Daiva Stasiulis and Darryl Ross (2006, 335) and others refer to as "securitization": "practices of governing that distinguish 'security' from politics, deploying the former in a general process whereby a policy issue is turned into a security issue, removing it from the realm of political contestation."

Boomerangs and Circuits

Securitization is also becoming more standardized across more sites and jurisdictions. Without a doubt, the United States has played a profound role in the global securitization of supply chains, demanding new security policies be implemented at the global scale while also designing programs that govern people and places well beyond U.S. territory (Boske 2006; Browning 2003; DHS 2009). Extraterritorial U.S. security programs like the Container Security Initiative (CSI) and the Customs-Trade Partnership against Terrorism (C-TPAT), discussed in chapter 2, explicitly extend U.S. authority "upstream" to include the cargo and people that circulate through the global logistics system and into American territory, making many national security policies effectively global in scope (Branch 2008; Browning 2003; CRS 2005; Mongelluzzo 2012). American officials have also pressured supranational governing bodies to develop new standards and policies where the noncompliance of member nations results in their isolation from global trade. The International Marine Organization's International Ship and Port Facility Security (ISPS) code is a prime example (Boske 2006). U.S. policies have also been extremely influential in other states' policy design—for instance, with the TWIC program and its close cousins in Canada and Australia. Despite powerful resistance to American global hegemony, very few states risk expulsion from trade in a U.S.-centered global factory.

While the United States is centrally implicated in global securitization in these ways, we can also trace a different movement in trade security where exceptional states—those whose practices in the realm of citizenship, labor, and security are ostensibly antithetical to the principles of freedom and democracy that the United States officially espouses—serve as models for the reorganization of American political rights and spaces through trade security. This "boomerang" effect—which Foucault ([1997] 2003, 103) describes as a haunting feature of colonial circulations where techniques of colonization and "its political and juridical weapons" were "brought back to the West"—has already been well documented in the contemporary politics of war and security (Graham 2004; Gregory 1994), and it is certainly a feature of the protection of supply chains.

The United Arab Emirates, and especially Dubai, is touted as a model for U.S. port security. The UAE may seem a world away from the United States, but Dubai's geographic resolution to the problem of containing disruption and supporting flows has been a model for port and infrastructure security in U.S. cities. A more thorough discussion of Dubai appears in chapter 5, but in a discussion about the intersections of trade security and logistics labor it is impossible not to briefly "visit" the place. Direct dealings between Dubai and U.S. ports were called to a halt in 2006 following public controversy in the United States about the potential "Arab operation" of American shipping terminals. Massive public outcry denounced a plan for Dubai Ports World (DP World), a UAE state-run firm with terminals in dozens of countries (including Vancouver, where this chapter began), to assume operation of twenty-two U.S. ports. Like the vast majority of terminals in the United States, those in question were already foreign owned and operated. But potential ownership by an "Arab state" provoked broad bipartisan Congressional opposition rooted in racist fears for national security (Friedman 2006; Gibson 2006; Kirchgaessner 2006; "Peter King" 2006; Overby 2006). The sale was approved by the executive branch of government and vigorously supported by the president, who even threatened to use his first-ever presidential veto to protect the deal (Sanger and Lipton 2006). Nevertheless, the scale of opposition, peppered with regular expressions of explicit racism, eventually led DP World to sell its interests ("Dubai Company" 2009). Serious concerns about labor practices and human and civil rights in Dubai occasionally infused the debate, but the vast majority of public discourse simply equated Arabs with terrorists, using stereotyped and racist imagery. Nevertheless, the failure of this deal should not blind us to the broader connections between these places and their ports. As chapter 5 explores in some more detail,

Dubai is heralded as a petri dish for practices of port security and the broader political logics of secure trade.

Like Dubai, U.S. ports have also become transnational logistic centers. Rapid movement from primary production sites (largely in China) across multiple modes of transport and through a series of transfer points in places like Dubai take commodities through U.S. ports and on to American consumers. Indeed, it is new security measures that are transforming U.S. ports into bounded spaces of exceptional government, inching them toward the Dubai model. Dubai was the first "Middle Eastern entity" to join the Container Security Initiative in 2005, and as a result, U.S. Customs and Border Protection (CBP) works especially close with Dubai Customs to screen containers destined for the United States. As the CBP (Dwyer 2006) reports, "Cooperation with Dubai officials has been outstanding and a model for other operation within CSI ports." Containing labor is furthermore a key realm of convergence between Dubai Logistics City and U.S. ports. A violent refusal of workers' rights in the interests of trade flows is crucial to the Dubai model, and the TWIC program can be understood as an attempt to institutionalize similar violence.

That Dubai has become a model for U.S. practice may be initially surprising given its particular regime of citizenship and labor. Strikes and trade unions are illegal in the UAE, and participation in either can result in permanent expulsion from the country (Al Tamimi n.d.; UAE Ministry of Labour 2001). The vast majority of workers are on temporary work permits without any formal citizenship. Noncitizens make up 99 percent of the private work force (two-thirds of whom are South Asian), making the very status of formal citizen exceptional (Kapiszewski 2006). While countries like the United States rely heavily on noncitizen labor, no place on earth matches the UAE in this regard. But it is precisely this emaciation of political rights in the face of trade flows that makes Dubai so appealing to the United States. Accumulation through dispossession of formal and substantive citizenship rights, managed through the production of securitized logistic space, is the ominous model that U.S. port cities are borrowing from Dubai. Indeed, the TWIC both rewrites the limits of state surveillance and supplants labor protections, but it does so without presenting itself as labor law. It undermines collective agreements and privacy rights and evacuates meaningful notions of employment security. Most important, the TWIC blurs the border between crime and terror and between police and military authority. The TWIC cannot single-handedly turn U.S. ports into the "Logistics City" on offer in Dubai, but as part of an ensemble of security policy, it makes deep and largely unnoticed attacks on labor and political rights that pull these worlds much closer together. If the logistics revolution has stretched the factory around the world, trade security works to "smooth" labor regimes, working to standardize the rights of the fast flows of stuff over the political rights of people.

It is not only parcels and policies that are circulating in contemporary supply chains; people are also on the move. This discussion has certainly touched on peoples' movements, though largely at the scale of the worker's body and its control. But of course, people move in many ways across vast distances through supply chains. The most obvious kinds of movements of people in supply chains would be those who move as workers alongside cargo, such as truckers, rail workers, pilots, and seafarers. Workers who move across transnational space—especially those who move on ships—face notorious working conditions, largely because of the challenge of regulation in the context of "flags of convenience." But the rise of global supply chains has much further reach than those immediately in the logistics sector. If the invention of the global supply chain stretched the factory around the world, it has done so precisely to incorporate, in spatially precise and strategic ways, uneven modalities of labor into the production process. Not only has this entailed the deindustrialization of many old industrial regions and the offshoring of production to lower-wage regions of the world, but it has also meant downward pressures on conditions of work in the global north (where many precarious workers are migrants from the global south) in relation to the hyperexploitation of workers in the global south, but within the same disaggregated production process (see Cowen 2009). Neilson and Rossiter (2010, 12) argue, "What needs to be emphasized is that logistics plays a role in controlling the movement of labor power as much as it applies to the passage of other commodities. It is thus a key technology to consider when examining the politics of border control, the reshaping of labor markets and the demise of the figure of the citizen-worker." This has painfully ironic implications for many of the world's people who move from the global south to the global north in search of better conditions of work and life but who find themselves incorporated into supply chains in forms and conditions of work that look much like those "back home."

The story of Ameera helps highlight the intimacies of this global scale story of logistics and supply chains. Her life is especially helpful to hear about if we remember that logistics has a powerful and persistent relationship to warfare. Ameera grew up in a cage and now works in a cage, halfway around the world from where she began. Her biography is filled with violence and irony; she spent much of her youth in a detention facility in northern Iraq that was "like an open warehouse." Ameera and several members of her family were put in detention in 1986 following a failed attempt to cross the border into Turkey as undocumented migrants. Today Ameera is a precarious, low-wage temp worker in a heavily securitized distribution center in New Jersey. While the detention center resembled a warehouse, Ameera and her coworkers are clear about the feeling of their workplace: "The cage—that's what we call it—the cage." She has good reason. Her work actually takes place in a caged-in section of a large warehouse. Two levels of security check must be passed in order to access her workstation, and security cameras follow her hands for the duration of her working day. This level of securitization would suggest that Ameera works with either sensitive or high-value materials, yet her job involves unpacking, tagging, and repacking mass-produced clothing for discount stores. Ameera suggests that there is thick tension between management and workers, with a general atmosphere of suspicion. Her account embraces the paradox of securitization; poor conditions of work fuel management's conviction that workers have no loyalty and will steal from the company, which they respond to with increased securitization, which further undermines the quality of work. Ameera works in a facility run by transnational logistics corporation DB Schencker, though her official employer is a temp agency housed inside the facility. DB Schencker operates 2,000 facilities in 130 countries, making it one of the largest globally integrated logistics providers in the world. In the United States, the company operates more than fifteen million square feet of space and is a member of the Customs-Trade Partnership against Terrorism. This means that the company that controls Ameera's cage is not only designated a "trusted trader" by the Department of Homeland Security and so delegated responsibility for monitoring its own compliance with supply chain security programs, but it is also invited to participate in defining those same policies through participation in the "trusted trader subcommittee" of the CBP's Advisory Committee on Commercial Operations.

Logistics Labor in the Global Factory

Logistics labor is at the center of the story of the global reorganization of trade of the past five decades. The movements of workers' bodies are what make the movement of global cargo possible, and yet workers' bodies are also often the cost of the high speed of commodity circulation in logistics space. All this attention to workers' bodies is a feature of the physicality and materiality of global logistics, but it is also a symptom of the active effort to integrate workers into the system and calibrate the rhythms of their movements with the needs of an automated system of stuff. Workers' bodies are implicated directly in techniques of managerial discipline and control both historically and in the present, in part because of fears of the unruly, undisciplined working-class body. The myriad forms of securitization also target workers' bodies, from the biometric data that underpins security credentialing and the surveillance of their movements through cameras and maps to the brute bodily injury that is invoked with military and civilian security force. Indeed, supply chain security has the goal of keeping workers aligned with logistics' systems yet prepares for the possibility of disruption as it also works to preempt that potentiality. If it is the security of efficient trade flows that animates maritime security today, then the interference that comes from "inefficiencies" like democracy and the actors that demand it may themselves be construed as security threats. Democracy of work in the crucial node of the ports is a barrier to current security projects that govern through exceptional means, suspending basic rights of citizenship and abolishing established barriers between crime and terror, all in the name of the security of supranational supply systems.

The revolution has left logistics labor incredibly dangerous, largely low wage, precarious, highly racialized (Bonacich and Wilson 2008), and now increasingly securitized. Yet things may be changing. Bonacich (2003) suggests, "Logistics workers are crucial local factors in global production and delivery systems . . . they cannot 'be moved offshore.'" Reifer (2011, 10) argues that the logistics revolution "arguably increased the power of workers in the global supply chain," suggesting that if "coalitions are able to capitalize on their strategic strengths as key nodal points in global trade and production and actively work on international solidarity across borders, the stage could be set for a radical revamping of the global system." Or in the simple words of Jo Ann Wypijewski, speaking at the 2010 Dockworkers Conference in Charleston, "The people who move the world can also stop it." Indeed, signs of this capacity are hidden in plain view in some dramatic though underreported recent events. On the one hand, gradual organizing efforts in sectors that have been notoriously difficult to organize, precisely by virtue of their global scale and strategic political geographies, are growing. We are seeing major global campaigns gaining steam in sectors like seafaring (led by the International Transport Federation and Save Our Seafarers) and courier services (Teamsters for a Democratic Union). Even more striking are recent actions in the two largest logistics chokepoints on the planet: the Suez and Panama Canals. Both sites appear on the previous map of labor actions, and both events mark labor movement strength and success, despite palpable odds and enormous pressure from corporate and state power. In Panama, expansion workers went on strike in January 2012 and were quickly met with a 13 percent wage increase and promises of back pay. The same workers struck again in April 2012 in response to the death of a worker and this time were successful in achieving forty-three demands for improvement in working conditions, industrial safety, and salaries (Radicella 2012; WSWS 2012). A year earlier and half a world away, as part of a definitive moment of the decade, canal workers were critical in the overthrow of Hosni Mubarak in Egypt. Supply chain management has long feared disruption to this crucial global chokepoint, and in 2011, this disruption took place with enormous implications. On February 8 of that year, some six thousand Suez Canal workers at five service companies initiated a wildcat strike in the cities of Suez, Port Said, and Ismailia. Dock workers stopped work at the key port of Ain Al Sokhna, disrupting Egypt's vital sea links to the Far East, and as Egypt's state-controlled newspaper *Ahram Online* and then the *New York Times* reported, "Disruptions to shipping movements, as well as disastrous economic losses, are expected if the strike continues" (Mackey 2011; Rohar 2011a). Needless to say, this became a definitive action in the mass mobilization for regime change. The stakes are high for labor in the industry and era of global logistics, but these are no doubt signs that the winds could be changing.

CHAPTER FOUR

The Geo-Economics of Piracy

The "Somali Pirate" and the
Remaking of International Law

Since antiquity, different legal concepts of "piracy" were
repeatedly adjusted by Europeans to suit their immediate aims,
such as legitimizing imperial politics.

—Michael Kempe,
"Even in the Remotest Corners of the World"

Supply chains must be secured against any form of man-made
and natural disruption. This certainly isn't a new revelation.
Some hundred years ago commercial shipping was threatened by
pirates and renegades like Anne Bonny, Sir Francis Drake or Klaus
Störtebeker, and so transport ships were equipped with cannons
and crews ready for a fight. Today piracy as a "business model"
is enjoying a remarkable renaissance. It's but one of many threats
facing international logistics.

—PwC, "Securing the Supply Chain"

Denying Somali pirates the benefit of context is not simply an act
of ignorance; it is in act of imperialism.

—Muna Ali and Zahra Murad,
"Unravelling Narratives of Piracy"

The diagram in Figure 25 marks the constitution of a new space: the
International Recommended Transit Corridor (IRTC). This space cannot

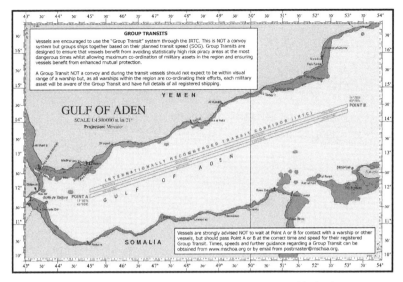

FIGURE 25. International Recommended Transit Corridor, Gulf of Aden. Source: IMO 2009a.

be seen on the open waters; there are no flags, checkpoints, or other markers of territorial authority on display. Yet the IRTC—a special zone for commercial ship traffic now subject to intensive multinational naval policing in the Gulf of Aden—is a key element in a dramatic experiment in the recasting of political space, international law, and imperial violence. The IRTC is part of an ensemble of legal experiments to assert geo-economic imperial authority in the area. Faced with a growing number of attacks on ships in this critical transit way to the Suez Canal, transnational corporations, national states, and supranational governing bodies have all intensified efforts to protect the global circulation of stuff (Intertanko 2009; Stockbruegger 2010). But the IRTC is not simply an element in a growing *number* of security plans and programs; it is also a part of a profound reworking of the way law governs space. A series of UN Security Council resolutions in 2008 authorized the use of military force within sovereign Somali waters and inland territory.[1] Multiple security forces are now active in the area operating under wildly varying frameworks of legality and authority. Shipping companies contract private militaries to provide onboard armed escorts through the region, provoking complex negotiations around state sovereignty in the Suez Canal. Multinational military forces have coordinated increased patrols in order to "police" the waters, but with tremendous national variation in the use of force, detention, and prosecution (MSCHOA n.d.; Stockbruegger 2010).

Precisely because piracy is a crime that occurs outside the authority and territory of any singular national authority, the pirate has long been a figure that is constituted by the geographies of (national) sovereignty but also fundamentally troubles them (Cordingly 1996; Sutton 2009; Thomson 1994). Until 1858, international law recognized two legal entities: the individual and the state. The invention of the pirate as universal criminal at that time created a third entity, defined by criminal action not simply outside a state but outside *all* states and subject to persecution by all states (Benton 2010; Rediker 2004). Operating in the constitutive outside of state space, the pirate has thus long been a figure that both stabilizes and undermines binary geopolitical categories of inside/outside, and the "legal labeling" of piracy has offered a favored means for empires to disguise the "political use of violence" (Kempe 2010, 36).

In an era of supply chain security where authority is reconstituted to protect corridors of corporate commerce, the particular dangers posed by piracy have shifted, and so too have strategies and spaces for managing them. Indeed, security agencies question whether Somali pirates are in fact terrorists, with an entire arsenal of legality dependent on the answer. Ironically, the entanglement of militaries and markets through the project of supply chain security in the Gulf of Aden relies on an absolute yet fundamentally tenuous distinction between the economic and the political. For piracy to be managed by this diversity of unregulated violence, it cannot become an object of outright warfare; the pirate must remain conceptually and legally distinct from the figure of the terrorist. If Somali pirates are "people who have consistently identified themselves as Somalia's Coast Guard" (Ali and Murad 2009, 91) and who thus claim an explicitly political position for their actions, the distinction would seem to dissolve. The political dimensions of Somali actions are thus denied at the same time as the state military interests in transnational corporate trade are asserted.

This chapter investigates the recasting of political and legal authority currently under way in efforts to secure supply chains and manage the problem of the Somali pirate in this critical shipping corridor. It explores the mutual constitution of legal categories, subjects, and spaces in the making of new imperial forms through the politics of circulation and security. The IRTC reveals how the production of new kinds of political space is vital to the assemblage of supply chain security and suggests that historically and in the present, efforts to govern piracy are diagnostic of the broader organization of imperialism.

"Hunting the Somali Scourge"

On May 14, 2012, European Union Security and Defense published a video online called "EU Naval Force (EU NAVFOR) - Operation ATALANTA" about the EU Naval Forces operation in Somalia. The video opens to the ominous sound of a military drumbeat. Images of navy ships intercepting Somali pirates at sea fill the screen as a middle-aged male voice with a British accent tells the viewer in a serious tone, "The threat of piracy to WFP [UN World Food Programme] shipments is *very* real. EU NAVFOR escorts are critically important to the security of the food shipments to reach the people of Somalia." The image shifts to footage of emaciated African children—still, glassy-eyed, with flies in mouths—warning of the crisis of mass starvation that looms. The camera then cuts to an interview with British Rear Admiral Duncan Potts, operational commander of Atalanta, who explains, "It's important that we use every means and lever available to us to combat piracy . . . we try and locate them where we can . . . we try to use every means, every *legal* means within our capability" (emphasis his). Following Potts, we meet a stylish young white-skinned European woman—Ifigenia Metaxa, the shipping logistics officer for World Food Programme Somalia. Hopeful and smiling, she explains that shipments are now "uninterrupted . . . continuous, timely, safe . . . thanks to EU NAVFOR." The voiceover then resumes, now with images of healthier Somali children eating WFP aid meals: "Counter piracy remains the day to day bread and butter task of EU NAVFOR, while on a humanitarian front Operation Atalanta continues to ensure that the people of the horn of Africa receive the much needed food and help through this difficult time."

The day after this video was published online, the European Union bombed Somalia. In the early morning hours of May 15, 2012, maritime aircraft and attack helicopters bombed the Handulle village in the Mudug region of Somalia's central coastline, which the EU identified as a "pirate den." Despite the fact that "pirates" and local fisher folk are often the same people in present-day Somalia (Ali and Murad 2009) and that Operation Atalanta is represented as a *humanitarian* mission, the EU hardly hesitated in engaging in armed combat against civilians. "What we want to do is make life more difficult for these guys," said Lieutenant Commander Jacqueline Sherriff, a spokeswoman for the European Union's antipiracy force. "This is a fantastic opportunity" (quoted in Gettlemen 2012). The attack was widely described in media as a strike "against the scourge of Somali piracy" (ibid.). While no casualties were reported from the attack, the "Somali logistics infrastructure" was compromised. "They destroyed our equipment to ashes. It was a key supplies center for us," Bile Hussein, a purported "pirate commander," explained in an article that appeared in newspapers around the world. "Nothing was spared" (Guled 2012). The EU is one of several multinational forces conducting antipiracy operations in the region alongside NATO and the U.S.-led Combined Task Force (CTF) 151. With as many as ten warships off the coast of Somalia, the European Union Naval Force (EU NAVFOR) is responsible for protecting ships carrying aid to the country, but it also provides the logistical support vessels for African Union troops deployed within ("EU Forces" 2012). The EU is the main financial sponsor of the Somali Transitional Federal Government—a body about which skepticism abounds. Mohamed Hassan (2010) argues that the transitional government "has no social base or authority in Somalia. It only exists on the international level because the imperialist forces support it." The EU trains the transitional government's army troops and provides reinforcement to the navies of five neighboring countries toward antipiracy efforts.

The EU authorized the attacks on land in March 2012 following a series of meetings in London during February of the same year. The outcome of debates between European nations was that airpower could be mobilized to follow pirates on land but that the risk to European lives should be limited by avoiding ground combat (Dempsey 2012). EU public statements after the attack repeatedly emphasized that "at no point did E.U. Naval Force 'boots' go ashore" (Gettlemen 2012), as if to suggest that airpower entailed a lesser violence or trespass of Somali sovereignty. This claim, however, did not stop the London group Hands off Somalia (2012) from asserting that the attack "could be the first direct attack on Somalia by European imperialists since colonial times."

No doubt, the colonial ripples of the attack are acute. It was on this very same land that the British first experimented with the doctrine of airpower in military campaigns nearly a century ago; the entire disastrous history of airpower began with the British bombing of Somaliland in 1920 (Omissi 1990). The Royal Air Force bombed the northern region of what is currently Somalia for twenty-one days, abruptly concluding more than two decades of failed ground operations. Airpower was critically important to the persistence of British imperialism in the wake of World War I; it allowed for the exhausted empire to maintain rule with an economy of force. As Anthony Clayton (1986, 11) argues on the exercise of "power" over "force," "Power, then, with the minimum actual use of force, was to be the keynote [of colonial rule] . . . power was economical, since the use of raw force quickly led to its attrition. Further, force used in one place could not simultaneously be used elsewhere, while the weight of power could be felt in many places at once."

If the 2011 bombing of Somalia marks a revival of European imperialism in this region, the EU video is a critical element of its architecture. EU NAVFOR reproduces a series of well-worn tropes of colonial cinema—most obviously the image of Africa as helpless child. The video sets a scene where infantilized Africans are in dire need of white European care. The young Somalis are not only helpless and suffering; they are also threatened and in need of protection. Thus, in a second maneuver, the adult Somalis who appear on screen—the pirates—figure as a grave threat to the Somali children. The video shows us that Europeans must save Somali children from Somali men. The context of its production shatters any illusion that this video is anything other than a visual score for imperial violence. With the video officially circulated on the eve of the bombing mission, its instrumental aims are difficult to deny (Landman 2009; Carter 2010). In a striking episode of what Teju Cole (2012) has termed the "white savior industrial complex," the hunt for the Somali pirate figures centrally in a series of legal, political, and military experiments in contemporary imperial rule. This complex is certainly not new; its sentimentality emerges out of long histories of colonial rule. Indeed, as Lynn Festa (2006, 8) argues, "Sentimentality fashions the tropes that render relations with distant others thinkable."

With a "new scramble for Africa" (Carmody 2012; Hallinan 2011) and its maritime borders under way, so too we see the circulation of new sentimental forms. The debate about this "new scramble" focuses largely on American and Chinese interventions on the continent in the interests of resource extraction and geopolitical rule, but it also marks shifting geographies and logics of imperial power. References to this colonial scramble are sometimes paired with descriptions of a "new spice road," which helpfully highlight the infrastructure of trade and circulation. Nick Turse (2012) explains that today's "'spice road' has nothing to do with cinnamon, cloves, or silks. Instead, it's a superpower's superhighway, on which trucks and ships shuttle fuel, food, and military equipment through a growing maritime and ground transportation infrastructure to a network of supply depots, tiny camps, and airfields meant to service a fast-growing U.S. military presence in Africa." Humanitarian affect is a powerful feature of contemporary military missions. Debates about the blurring borders between warfare and development have also been energetic in recent years in an era of "unending warfare" (Duffield 2007). Cole (2012) is attentive to the pivotal role of humanitarianism within this complex (see also Holzgrefe and Keohane 2003). He asserts, "The white savior supports brutal policies in the morning, founds charities in the afternoon, and receives awards in the evening." He further suggests, "The banality of evil transmutes into the banality of sentimentality."

Likewise, piracy around the Horn of Africa has been repeatedly identified as not simply a problem for Somali food security, as in the EU video, but fundamentally a problem for *supply chain security* by national militaries, transnational governing bodies like the EU, and the shipping industry. If geo-economics animates the contemporary logic of imperial intervention on the continent, then it is the protection of supply chains that organizes the use of force in the Gulf of Aden and the Horn of Africa. The debate about how to manage the problem of Somali piracy exposes how vital the issue of goods circulation has become. In his statement to a U.S. House of Representatives subcommittee in April 2009 on "International Efforts to Combat Piracy," Rear Admiral William Baumgartner of the U.S. Coast Guard explained, "The unimpeded flow of maritime commerce is the lifeblood of the global economy." Not surprising given the United Kingdom's central role in the shipping industry since the height of its imperial power and its longstanding imperial relationship to Somalia specifically, the UK Parliamentary Foreign Affairs Committee (2011) exclaims how "the particular importance of the global maritime industry to the UK economy" means that "combating piracy should be a major priority for the UK Government. The UK sits at the centre of the global shipping trade . . . Piracy is therefore very much a British problem." It is not only states but also corporations that assert that Somali pirates threaten the global economy. In a joint public statement in 2008, the international shipping community, led by the International Chamber of Shipping (ICS), asserted, "Pirates in Somalia threaten lives of seafarers and the security of world trade."

A focus on the question of piracy, which prompted the EU violence, exposes some particularly crucial dimensions of contemporary imperialism that highlight the remaking of territory and sovereignty in the service of the protection of trade flows. The pirate is portrayed not simply as the enemy of Somali people; rather, the threat they pose to the lives of starving children makes them monstrous. The pirate is not simply the enemy of particular humans but rather an enemy to *our common humanity*. This is precisely the role that the pirate has played historically—"hostis humani generis" (Benton 2010; Cordingly 1996; Poier 2009; Rediker 2004). As in the early colonial era when the figure of the pirate played a pivotal but largely overlooked role in the making of the laws of nations, today the pirate once again plays a key role in remaking norms of global governance. At stake in contemporary antipiracy initiatives is the remaking of legal and sovereign space and imperial (geo-economic) global government.

What Is Piracy?

It is impossible to embark on a discussion of piracy without immediately encountering popular culture images of the rough and tumble hard man with eye patch, tricorner captain's hat, skull and crossbones, striped shirt, and parrot perched on the shoulder uttering the notorious "arrghh." This cartoonish image circulates in films, comic books, children's stories, and beyond, and it derives from the high time of European piracy in the seventeenth and eighteenth centuries. Yet piracy has a much longer history—a global one—and lives on in the present in ways that look very different yet remain somehow recognizable (Ali and Murad 2009; Benton 2010; Cordingly 1996; Konstam 2008; Sutton 2009; Thomson 1994). Unlike these cartoonish images, in the global history and contemporary geography of piracy the figure is only occasionally white and certainly dons a different wardrobe. This gap between the pirate of pop culture and the pirate of so much maritime conflict both marks and masks the imperial politics at play. But alongside the differences in the actual and imagined aesthetics of piracy, there are also important continuities. In Salvatore Poier's (2009) words, "Even if the word 'piracy' had been applied to many different activities in totally different contexts, the social and political core of its meaning has been unchanged since the very beginning." Across time, the pirate is cast as both villain and hero. Then and now, the figure of the pirate is both revered and reviled. As Poier writes, "Pirates have also been seen—and still they are . . . as bloodthirsty but also romantic heroes." What makes the pirate distinct is precisely his undecidability; he is outside the either/or of any binary system of affect and, importantly, of Western law. Popular narratives of piracy often implicitly recognize or even embrace the arbitrary nature of national authority that casts a mariner as a defender of the crown at one moment and an enemy of humankind in the next. The popular love affair with the pirate persists not despite but *because* of the figure's "transness"—his home on both sides of the law.

The most powerful historical continuity in the social life of the pirate is not aesthetic or cultural but political. While pop culture may offer glimpses of the trouble that the pirate causes to our categories, popular intrigue in fact largely distracts attention from the momentous political stakes at play in his deployment. At key moments in the past, the figure of the pirate plays a critical role in remaking geographies of violence and sovereignty (Benton 2010; Thomson 1994), and the figure does so again today. Alongside popular and playful images of the pirate, we can also trace a profoundly serious role for this figure, at least since antiquity. Piracy was a formidable issue for the ancient world. Cicero famously described pirates as "hostis humani generis," the enemy of humankind. Michael Kempe (2010, 356) emphasizes the non- or subhumanity of pirates in Cicero's work, suggesting that "pirates were placed outside humanity, in a realm otherwise reserved for wild animals." Piracy thus marked not simply an exceptional legal status; located outside the law, those labeled as such also lost their humanity. For Cicero ([44 BC] 1887, 107), the pirate is a special kind of enemy, "not included in the list of lawful enemies, but is the common enemy of all; among pirates and other men there ought be neither mutual faith nor binding oath." Two thousand years ago Cicero placed the pirate outside the realm of normal law—in the complicated position of a criminal beyond criminality. In this way, long predating any meaningful conception of human rights, Roman statesmen conceived the pirate outside of the human by virtue of the threat they posed to humanity (Heller-Roazen 2009, 9).

Cicero's words directly influenced the sixteenth-century jurist Alberico Gentili, who described pirates in 1589 as "common enemies" who "are attacked with impunity by all, because they are without the pale of the law. They are scorners of the law of nations; hence they find no protection in that law." The idea of pirates as outside the law was thus imported into early modern European thought through Gentili and was then eventually codified into legal statute in the nineteenth century. In his 1755 work *Commentaries on the Laws of England*, English jurist William Blackstone reiterates this exceptional status of the pirate vis-à-vis international law while also casting the pirate as a savage in relation to imperial notions of "civilization." In a chapter titled "Of Offences against the Law of Nations," he repeats the definition of the pirate as "enemy of mankind." On this basis he asserts, "[The pirate] has renounced all the benefits of society and government, and has reduced himself afresh to the savage state of nature, by declaring war against all mankind, all mankind must declare war against him" (Blackstone [1755] 1922, 51).

The exceptional legal status of the pirate as marked by his "location" beyond the reach of the law was not simply a matter of metaphor; rather, it exposes the *legal geographies* that are centrally at play. The high seas have long been envisioned as the natural home to pirates, and this association of the figure with the oceans is still immediately conjured in popular culture. Blackstone, like many writers before him, defined the "offense of piracy" in firm relation to the maritime *space* in which the act is committed. Piracy, he expounds, "consists in committing those acts of robbery and depredation upon the high seas, which, if committed upon land, would have amounted to felony there." Thus the crime takes on its seriousness by virtue of its *location,* its geography.

For millennia, writers have detailed the heinous nature of attacks at sea in their discussions of piracy. Yet even as things maritime have played a crucially important role in the historical geographies and iconographies of piracy, it is not exactly the maritime qualities that constitute the pirate but rather the exceptional status of the high seas in the realm of law and politics that are definitive (Benton 2010; Kempe 2010; Perotin-Dumon 1991). The fact that we have come to know forms of piracy more recently that are defined in relation to other seemingly ungovernable spaces—the skies in the twentieth century and the Internet more recently—highlights that it is this seeming ungovernability of the oceans that has made them the iconic space of piracy.

This historical emphasis on the exceptional nature and space of piratical acts was thus well established in Western philosophical and legal writing well before the modern era of nation-states and international law. These are the two key features of what Daniel Heller-Roazen (2009, 10) defines as the "piratical paradigm," which constitutes something of a malleable essence that persists in the government of piracy in the present and that makes the pirate such a powerful figure. The first characteristic, he suggests, is that this paradigm "involves a region in which exceptional legal rules apply." In other words, as we have seen in the work of Cicero, Gentili, and Blackstone, the act of piracy is largely defined by its location outside the geographic authority of law, most commonly on the high seas. Second, Heller-Roazen explains that this piratical paradigm "involves an agent who, committing deeds in such an unusual legal space, displays an antagonism that cannot be defined as that of one individual with respect to another or one political association with respect to another." This explains the pirate's status from antiquity through the present as a "universal criminal," understood as a threat to the whole of humanity and thus prosecutable by all. In a sense then, Heller-Roazen's first two traits of the piratical paradigm imply each other, and thinking them separately is necessary in part because of the common neglect of space in our political imaginaries. Yet it is when we engage the last two features of his paradigm (already implied in the first pair) that the stakes in debates about piracy are revealed. This exposes, first and foremost, the extent to which the politics of space are at the core of the issue.

Heller-Roazen (ibid.) asserts that these first two characteristics (the exceptional space of piracy and thus the exceptional legal status of piracy) entail a third: the "confusion or collapse of criminal and political categories." This third feature of the piratical paradigm also implies a fourth characteristic: "Piracy entails a transformation of the concept of war." In other words, because pirates are constituted as criminals outside the authority of the law, "operations carried out against them" involve "procedures of external relations and internal security—technologies of politics and police." In a sense then, Heller-Roazen's entire paradigm rests upon the first feature—*the problem of legal space*. The troubling of warfare, criminality, and sovereignty all follow from the attempt to govern beyond the geographic authority of government.

This distinction between external and internal security became ever more important with the rise of the system of nation-states, thus making the pirate an even more pivotal figure in the modern era as the figure that both undermines and stabilizes international law. Kempe (2009) makes a parallel set of claims. He argues that piracy has a very long history on the oceans and in legal debate, but it is the period between the sixteenth and nineteenth centuries that becomes of "salient interest" if we take a global perspective on the relationships between piracy, transnational relations, and international law. This is precisely the time when the European system of nation-states was assembled, and piracy played a profoundly important, though frequently overlooked, role in that process. In a momentous work that is centrally concerned with the government of piracy, Janice Thomson (1994, xvii) writes that violence in the contemporary world is both "statist and territorial." While these features of political geography are often naturalized, she reminds us that they in fact "distinguish the twentieth century state system from prior world political orders and their institutions of governance" in a manner that is "stunningly unique." Following Max Weber (1978, 54), who defines the modern state as a "compulsory political organization with continuous operations" whose "administrative staff successfully upholds the claim to the monopoly of the legitimate use of physical force in the enforcement of its order," Thomson traces how that organization established itself. Concerned with the logistics of these maneuvers, she asks, "How did the state achieve a monopoly on violence beyond its borders that emanates from its territory?" (3). For this strange system to emerge, the state's monopoly on legitimate violence had to be built, and this was far from a peaceful process. The rise of the nation-state system was not natural or organic fact, and the authority of state actors did not go unchallenged by other formations. Thomson argues that "the disarming of nonstate transnational activities marked the transition from heteronomy to sovereignty and the transformation of states into the national state system" (4). In other words, as national states assumed a monopoly on political authority, so too was violence "shifted from the nonstate, economic and international realms of authority into the state, political and domestic realms of authority. It was dedemocratized, demarketized, and territorialized."

This begs the question of why piracy might be considered so critical to this reordering of power and violence. It may be counterintuitive that a problem of law on the open seas would matter so centrally to a system rooted in territoriality on land. But as Lauren Benton (2005, 702) asserts, international norms take shape not in Westphalia but at the edges of the Indian Ocean. Kempe (2009, 354) echoes this claim when he asserts, "In the international confrontation with 'piracy' we can observe the formation of central features and basic structures of modern interstate relations and international law." It is precisely because the international state system is premised on the division of absolute space into mutually exclusive sovereign "puzzle pieces" that the figure beyond its reach became so pivotal. The image of the puzzle pieces is of course incomplete, as European states were actively involved in colonizing whole regions of the world. Thus the authority of the state system was profoundly reliant on imperial geographies. The state system requires an outside but also asserts authority over its exterior. The pirate (as the figure that is paradoxically outside the authority of the system that governs him) is an effect of these fundamental tensions in modern sovereignty. The problematization of piracy during this period, and the emergence of a supranational paradigm for governing piracy, is a feature of the struggle between different European empires. In Kempe's (2009, 369) words, "The exercise of maritime policing functions was here inseparable from the effort to gain political hegemony." This political hegemony was an imperial one. This exercise in maritime policing through combating piracy "enabled the British navy to raise its flag in the Persian Gulf" under the official banner of "safeguarding international trading routes."

Another way of questioning the role of piracy in the assemblage of the system of nation-states is to ask *how* (as opposed to why) piracy contributed to the crystallization of that system. It is no accident that the period of nation-state formation was also the period when piracy was defined in international law. The latter was contingent on the former. Thomson (1994, 101) explains, "There is simply no question that piracy was a legitimate practice in the early European state system . . . by the early 18th century, however, pirates were being hanged on masse in public executions." Kempe (2009) goes a step further and suggests that it was the very practice of issuing letters of marque that helped *produce* the problem of piracy. Letters of marque were issued by nations active in maritime trade to private vessels. They allowed privateers to act on behalf of the state issuing the letters and often became an excuse for plunder. The word *marque* derives from Old English *mearc,* the Germanic *mark,* and the Proto-Indo-European *merg̑,* all of which signify "boundary" and "border." Indeed, the letter of marque acted as a kind of portable border, reassigning sovereignty by decree. Letters of marque allowed captains to legitimize what Kempe terms "maritime shopping": "As agents of sovereign states, these captains carried law across the sea in imagined corridors that corresponded to areas of spectacular, if sporadic, sea raiding" (354–55). And yet this system became untenable. Kempe (2009, 362) writes, "The emergence of piracy proper was partly due to the legal system of letters of marque and reprisal having reached truly inflationary proportions . . . sea robbers of this kind were so dangerous precisely because they always found the support of some nation or other, and were never the enemies of all nations at once." Kempe (2009), Thomson (1994), and Poier (2009) concur that the efforts to govern piracy under international law emerge immediately out of this context of competing imperial powers. Thomson (1994, 109) offers the most careful engagement with this moment and dilemma. She frames the problem encountered by emerging states in this way: "If no state is sovereign—that is, exerts authority—over the high seas, who is responsible for individual acts of violence launched from the sea?" By the early nineteenth century, Thomson argues that three possible responses emerged to the growing problem of piracy, which was increasingly threatening imperial commerce. A first response was for singular states to claim sovereignty over large areas of open water. She explains that Spain actually attempted this, but the sheer size of the sea and its uninhabitability made enforcement impossible (Thomson 1994, 111). A second strategy was for states to be held internationally accountable for acts of piracy committed by their own citizens—an approach that Britain took in their colonial trade with India. However, this approach also failed to provide the viable basis for a legal system; like today's system of flags of convenience, it was common that the nationality of a crew would differ from the letter of marque that gave the ship authority. The "solution" to the problem of piracy for imperial states was therefore to designate them as universal criminals in international law—meaning that any state could prosecute pirates, while no state was obligated to do so (Kontorovich 2009). Paradoxically, Thomson (1994, 111) argues, "According to the norm that did develop, pirates are stateless individuals and therefore, in an international legal sense, do not exist." In fact, until the 1856 Treaty of Paris, the emergent system of international law recognized only two legal entities: the individual and the state. Before then, a handful of states had national laws against piracy that were administered domestically, but there was no such thing as an international or universal approach. Thomson (1994, 111–12) is clear that this global norm "could not develop much less be universalized, until the state system produced a clear definition of what constituted piracy. And this was impossible so long as states continued to regard individual violence as an exploitable resource." In other words, "piracy could not be expunged until it was defined, and it could not be defined until it was distinguished from state-sponsored or sanctioned individual violence." The invention of the pirate as universal criminal entailed a wholly new, third entity in international law defined by criminal action not simply outside a state but outside *all* states and subject to persecution by all states.

Thus piracy became a matter for the law not in its challenge to specific rules but in its challenge to the law itself. As Walter Benjamin argues (1978, 277), the law's interest in a monopoly of violence "is not explained by the intention of preserving legal ends but, rather, by that of preserving the law itself; that violence, when not in the hands of the law, threatens it not by the ends that it may pursue but by its mere existence outside the law." What makes piracy unique is in the challenge it poses to the sovereignty of sovereignty. Whereas many forms of insurgency challenge the rule of law or even the authority of the system of law, it is piracy alone that challenges law's authority from outside the space of authority. Thus the concept of piracy is best understood "as a legal strategy" of imperial states (Kempe 2010, 354) where pirates are "not simply criminals who were attacking and plundering ships and rich ports" but "seamen and entrepreneurs who were immersed in a network of people, deals, traffics, and political struggles" (Poier 2009) that cannot be understood outside of the broader context of European imperialism.

Supply Chains and the Somali Pirate

Despite the recent flurry of interest and interventions, the issue of piracy is not new to the Gulf of Aden. Episodes of maritime theft have long been a feature of the waters off the coast of Somalia as they are in any area with an active maritime history. The Gulf of Aden is a necessary gateway for all transits through the Suez Canal, linking Europe with the Middle East, East Africa, and South and East Asia. Along with the Panama Canal, the Suez is a key link in the chain of global trade—and so too a chokepoint in the circulation of stuff. The very existence of the canal is a reminder that individual acts of piracy have no monopoly on maritime violence in this region. The physical infrastructure is a material marker of the deeply entangled histories of imperial trade and violence and a testament to a past filled with violent contests for control over this critical shipping corridor (Harlow and Carter 2003; Wallach 2005). The first canal on this site was built under Egyptian authority in the second century BC, with the current architecture dating back to the era of European colonial power in the nineteenth century. The canal sculpts global flows of maritime commerce, currently drawing more than twenty thousand ships into the Gulf of Aden every year (Chalk 2010, 94). This amounts to an astonishing daily average of fifty-eight ships transiting through these waters and constitutes 95 percent of European member states' trade by volume (MSCHOA n.d.). Charles Bumstead (2010, 148) asserts that the Gulf of Aden "is one of the most, if not the most, traveled sea routes in the world." Even as maritime violence of both the singular and state-led varieties is an old story in the area, there has nevertheless been a dramatic increase in both piratical acts and naval interventions over the last decade that pivot around a new figure in global politics: the Somali pirate.

It is widely noted that piracy has been increasing globally since the 1980s. According to Bumstead (2010, 145), pirate attacks in the 1990s "increased threefold, while the increase in the 2000s has more than tripled again." But amid this general increase in piracy around the world, there has been a particularly marked growth around the Horn of Africa and particularly in the first decade of the twenty-first century. The International Maritime Bureau (IMB) reported in 2009 that there had been a stunning 11 percent worldwide increase in incidents of piracy or armed robbery in the previous year, and well over a third took place off the coast of Somalia. The report notes that this entailed a 200 percent jump in incidents in the corridor linking the Suez Canal and the Indian Ocean (IMB 2009, 1–2). In what was the busiest year in recent history, 322 actual or attempted pirate attacks were reported in the area between 2008 and 2009, making up almost half of all global incidents (Chalk 2010, 90). Recent debates at the UN Security Council confirm that incidents in the area are reported at a rate of two every three days (2012a).

Piracy in the Gulf of Aden is a concern because it disrupts the circulation of goods and capital, but it is also a rapidly growing direct cost for the global shipping industry. All this explains the mounting concern about supply chain security from industry lobby groups and states that dominate global trade. If it is possible to measure an average ransom, Peter Chalk (2010, 93) places it at around $5 million in 2011, up from $4 million in 2010. The U.S. Kirk Report estimates that between 2008 and 2010 the average ransom increased thirty-six times, from $1.3 million to $5.4 million per ship (Kirk 2011). There is some variation in the precise figures, but there is consensus about the range and trajectory of demands. Even without accounting for the growing cost of ransoms to shippers, the rising costs of insurance, protective measures, and even rerouting ships away from the area are regularly estimated to be as much as $5.5 billion per year (Gettlemen 2012). Central in this growing cost are the rising rates of insurance for ships that transit the Gulf. Chalk (2010, 93) notes that the cost of a binder[2] for vessels transiting the Gulf of Aden has reached $20,000 per voyage, *excluding* injury, liability, and ransom coverage. He furthermore highlights that the U.S. Department of Transportation estimates a rate of $500 for coverage for the same journey in 2007 and early 2008, thus marking a fortyfold jump in cost. These costs are being passed on from shipping companies to those who contract them, with surcharges on container rates doubling for passage through the Gulf (Chalk 2010, 93). In comments to the UN Security Council, the Russian Federation estimated that the costs of ransoms and other losses due to piracy were amounting to $12 billion per year (2012a).

This recent growth of piracy begs the question of its causes. Why has there been such fast and furious rise in the number of attacks? Predictably, there is a range of answers on offer to these questions. It is telling that the simplest answers emerge from the states and organizations most active in military operations in the area. There are a number of transnational forces with active antipiracy operations in addition to the European Union; NATO is there in force, as is the U.S.-led CTF 151. Somali piracy, according to these organizations, is actually a land-based problem of "failed states." Over and over again, we are told a Hobbesian tale of a vacuum of state power in Somalia following two decades of civil war giving rise to lawless violence, including the growing number of attacks at sea. CTF 151, a U.S.-led multinational naval force comprising twenty-six countries charged with antipiracy operations in the Gulf of Aden, defines the problem in this way on the Combined Maritime Forces website: "Somalia has been identified as the source of the modern day piracy in this region that has grown from the economic, social and political strife that has gripped the country since the mid-1990s. The rise of piracy in the region can be directly linked with the fall of the stable government and breakdown of law and order in Somalia in 1991. Gangs formed under local clan loyalty and warlord leadership and developed into the piracy groups of today." While the rise of violence in the context of civil war is difficult to deny, this is far from a complete account. Most notable here is the utter absence of foreign intervention in explaining the rise in maritime attacks; what is happening in Somalia is explained only with reference to the problems of Somalis. This is in profound conflict with the explanations emanating from the pirates themselves, from activists and organizations within the Somali Diaspora (such as London-based Hands off Somalia or recording artist K'naan), and increasingly from critical scholars (Ali and Murad 2009; Poier 2009; Salopek 2008). No doubt, Somalia has been in a state of brutal civil war since 1991, and the violence has pushed nearly 678,000 Somalis into the hands of the UN Refugee Agency. Somalis are at present the third-largest refugee group in the world after those from the official war zones of Iraq and Afghanistan. More than twenty years of violence has indeed created conditions for further violence. However, any account of this violence that focuses only on the problems of Somalia and Somalis brackets the imperial violence that crafts these conditions. On the one hand, this narrative doesn't recognize the persistent foreign intervention that has produced the current situation on land. Second and even more immediate, this account ignores the central fact of foreign intervention in Somali waters that is the centerpiece of the accounts provided by Somalis to explain the rash of so-called piracy. Official accounts of the causes of piracy are not only directly connected to contemporary imperial violence, but according to Ali and Murad (2009), the denial of context for the rise in piracy at work in international governing bodies accounts is itself "an act of imperialism."

Alternative accounts for the rise of piracy in the Gulf of Aden emphasize both the long and recent history of Western intervention in Somalia, which saw not only the British create the "postcolonial" territorial partitions in 1960 that are still disputed today but the first-ever U.S. ground war in Africa in the early 1990s and the violence of UN interventions (e.g., with Canada's murderous "peace-keeping" operations there; Razack 2004). The complex form this intervention has taken is increasingly exposed to broader public scrutiny; scholars are questioning the effects that Western powers had when they contracted private companies to "secure Somalia" in the 1990s in terms of the formation of armed insurgent groups. Most important, explanations for the rise of Somali piracy that emerge from Somalis repeatedly highlight the maritime violence of foreign powers at the close of the twentieth century and in the opening of the twenty-first. The primary motivating event for the rise in piracy was illegal overfishing and illegal dumping of toxic waste. Combined, this devastated Somali fishing and removed a significant source of livelihood for those living in coastal communities. The "pirates" assembled as a volunteer coastguard. As internationally celebrated Somali recording artist K'naan (in Smith 2009) reports, "The pirates are in the water because there is a nationwide complaint about the illegal mass fishing going on in Somali waters. And nuclear toxic waste is illegally being dumped on our shores. People in Somalia know about this." Claims about the role of foreign ships depositing and withdrawing illegally from Somali waters are sometimes echoed in mainstream media. Writing for the *Chicago Tribune*, Paul Salopek (2008) reports on the dumping of industrial waste that has been taking place since the 1990s, when "Somalia's unpatrolled waters became a cost-free dumping ground for industrial waste from Europe." He specifically mentioned the role of "boats from Italy" that "were reported to have ferried barrels of toxic materials to Somalia's shores and then returned home laden with illicit catches of fish." With 3,330 kilometers of coastline with a narrow continental shelf, Somalia not only has the largest coastline of all continental Africa but also is one of the most important marine habitats of the Indian Ocean (UN 2011). Salopek (2008) marks an important socionatural event that exposed these illegal practices and propelled rapid growth in the number of Somalis patrolling their shores: a tsunami in 2005 that left rusting containers of hazardous waste on Somali beaches. The logic is financial. Citing a UN report, Salopek outlines that it costs $2.50 per ton for a European company to dump uranium off the Horn of Africa, a hundredth of the cost to dispose of the material in Europe cleanly. Without a political authority to enforce protection of the waters or the fish stock, the Somali coast became a low-cost dumping ground for the same nations that now lead the "antipiracy" initiatives. Indeed, Italy is accused of playing a pivotal role in these illegal activities that have damaged fish stocks and contaminated waters; it also happened to be the other original colonial power in the southern parts of Somalia alongside the British colony to the north. Italy and the United Kingdom now head two of the five working groups of the Contact Group on Piracy off the Coast of Somalia.

A growing number of these media reports of illegal dumping and fishing appear to have compelled the UN to address the longstanding complaints of the Somali people. Before 2010, UN documents made no mention of these events; they echoed the narratives of the EU, NATO, and CTF 151 and focused exclusively on the problem of the failed state and the ungovernability of Somalia (see UN Security Council 2008). However, since 2010, UN reports on the state of piracy in Somalia quietly began to echo concerns about foreign intervention. Resolution 1950, passed in November 2010, includes the following statement, which begins to acknowledge the issue of illegal activities yet frames it with suspicion: "Recalling the importance of preventing, in accordance with international law, illegal fishing and illegal dumping, including of toxic substances, and stressing the need to investigate allegations of such illegal fishing and dumping, being concerned at the same time that allegations of illegal fishing and dumping of toxic waste in Somali waters have been used by pirates in an attempt to justify their criminal activities." By October 2011, the UN had undertaken research on the alleged activities and produced the "Report of the Secretary-General on the Protection of Somali Natural Resources and Waters." The report outlines how since the 1991 fall of the Siad Barre regime, foreign-flagged industrial fishing trawlers have encroached into Somali waters (UN Security Council 2011a, 10). The report recounts how these trawlers working illegally not only were pulling in more than 50 percent of the overall catch in the area but were reported to be "frequently engaged in intentional collisions with local fishermen in Somali waters, leading to the destruction of fishing gear, injuries and even deaths of local subsistence fishers." Citing evidence from a 2005 UN Food and Agricultural Organization report, the report estimates that "approximately 700 foreign flagged trawlers were engaged in illegal, unreported and unregulated fishing in and around Somali waters." The report conservatively suggests that "the socio-economic and ecological damage caused by the alleged illegal exploitation of Somalia's marine resources over the past two decades could be considerable."

The report also provides some stunning support for the longstanding claims about illegal toxic dumping in Somali coastal waters. "In the past few decades," it reads, "multiple cases of illegal dumping have been documented in Africa." It describes two prominent incidents, the first from 1987 when ships transported eighteen thousand barrels of hazardous waste from Italy to Nigeria, where a farmer was paid $100 monthly rent for dumping on his land. A second high-profile incident occurred in August 2006, when a ship chartered by the Swiss shipping company Trafigura Beheer BV transported and dumped toxic waste in the Côte d'Ivoire. The report proceeds to consider the case of Somalia specifically, citing allegations of illegal dumping that "have been made for almost 20 years" (12). The report suggests that evidence is "circumstantial" and that verification has not been possible due, with bitter irony, to the "security situation in Somalia." And yet, the report assembles a raft of research that clearly corroborates local peoples' accounts. It cites the UN organization's own research, including a 1997 report of the United Nations Environment Programme (UNEP) / Office for the Coordination of Humanitarian Affairs Environment Unit and the United Nations Coordination Unit for Somalia, which "noted that marine vessels normally dispose of waste at ports, but since Somali ports lack both security and services, ships dispose of their waste offshore while at sea, with annual discharges." The report cites another piece of UNEP research: this one from 2004 following the tsunami mentioned in the aforementioned media reports. While the team from UNEP could not access much of the Somali coastline to complete a proper investigation, once again because of "security concerns," they assert an "urgent need for comprehensive assessment of alleged dumping of illegal toxic waste in Somalia both on land and at sea." The UN reports that INTERPOL has received repeated complaints regarding both illegal fishing and illegal waste dumping off the Somali coast. Finally, it considers a recent Greenpeace report that provides a mountain of evidence about the networks of trade, largely operating out of Italy but involving a number of countries and corporations, dumping toxic waste in the waters of Somalia. The UN highlights the range of evidence that Greenpeace offers, including "testimony from an Italian parliamentary commission; documentation from 1996 purportedly authorizing a waste treatment facility; evidence uncovered by an Italian prosecutor, including wiretapped conversations with alleged offenders; and warnings by the Special Representative of the Secretary-General for Somalia in 2008 of possible illegal fishing and illegal dumping in Somalia." In addition the Greenpeace report "included photos dated 1997 of an alleged dumping site, and estimated that thousands of barrels constituting millions of tons of toxic waste had allegedly been moved to Somalia in the 1990s." Indeed, Greenpeace (2010, 22) asserts that UN representatives have corroborated many of these accounts of dumping firsthand. They quote Nick Nuttal, the UNEP spokesman who confirmed that the 2004 tsunami did indeed wash containers full of toxic waste onto the Somali shore. "We are talking about everything from medical waste to chemical waste products," he explained. They also quote the UN special envoy for Somalia, Ahmedou Ould Abdallah, who in 2008 "repeatedly sounded the alarm about illegal fishing and toxic dumping off Somalia by European firms." Despite reliable evidence that European, American, and Asian companies were dumping toxic, even nuclear waste in the region, the "European Union has responded to these allegations with silence."

The UN would not ignore their own report on these matters, and indeed, its release changed the way in which UN resolutions framed the issue. From entirely ignoring the question of dumping and fishing to mentioning it cynically and in passing in 2010, by late 2011 a different tone was evident. Since that time, the UN Security Council (2012b) declares it is "stressing the need to investigate allegations of such illegal fishing and dumping, and noting with appreciation in this respect the report of the Secretary-General on the protection of Somali natural resources and water." And yet, the repeat endorsement for and investment in militarized antipiracy operations suggests that the attention goes only skin deep. The hypocrisy of the combined acknowledgment of the role of illegal dumping and fishing in the rise of piracy alongside the active UN role in military intervention is particularly striking in light of a key passage of the UN report. In what is perhaps the most revealing set of comments in the entire document, the UN report (UN Security Council 2011a, 12) asserts, "It was widely reported that the surge of piracy since 2004 led to decreased illegal fishing off the Somali coast. Today, some observers claim that the international naval presence to suppress piracy, authorized by the Security Council, has in fact inadvertently facilitated a resurgence of illegal fishing in Somali waters." It is hard to find more practical support for the claims of the so-called Somali pirates, "people who have consistently identified themselves as Somalia's Coast Guard" (Ali and Murad 2009, 91). This is increasingly what a number of critical scholars are arguing. Peter Lehr, a British scholar of piracy, argued that the effect of the pirates is "almost like a resource swap." He explains how "Somalis collect up to $100 million a year from pirate ransoms off their coasts" yet emphasizes that this is in the context of European and Asian poaching valued at "around $300 million a year in fish from Somali waters" (quoted in Salopek 2008). Thus despite the superficial acknowledgement, K'naan (in Smith 2009) is right when he says that "the west is completely ignoring the basis for piracy in Somalia."

New Spatialities / Shifting Legalities

Both continuity and change are striking in the imperial logics of contemporary efforts to govern maritime piracy. In the present as in the past, the politics of piracy are crucial to the remaking of systems of global governance, and the pirate remains important precisely because of his exceptional legal status across time, within global legal space. We can trace the logics and logistics of this contemporary recasting of authority by looking more carefully at current efforts to govern the Somali pirate.

Somalia is a war zone, though it is not officially declared as such by those undertaking military operations there. Naval, aerial, and ground operations are all under way by foreign states and corporations working in various multinational and cross-sectorial alliances. The different forces that are active in the area operate under wildly varying frameworks of law and authority, guided by successive resolutions from international governing bodies, diverse national legal codes, and corporate "best practice" in antipiracy. As part of the legacy of the international laws of piracy, the prosecution of pirates is sanctioned for all states, but the specific legalities around detention, trial, and punishment are left to national courts to define. This helps explain the deeply ironic use of frontier metaphors by leading members of the shipping industry to describe the current status of the Gulf of Aden. Peter Hinchliffe, secretary-general of the International Chamber of Shipping, refers to the region as resembling the "wild west" (Odell 2011). While intending to describe the seeming lawlessness evident in the area, Hinchliffe's comments also betray the exceptional legalities of colonial violence deployed in spaces beyond the authority of national law. The International Maritime Organization (IMO) has been intensely involved in antipiracy work globally since 1998, though they were also actively involved in the issue earlier (see Hesse and Charalambous 2004), and the specific focus on the Gulf of Aden came later. The first recent multinational naval operation in the Gulf of Aden is CTF 150, which has been in the region since 2002. Initially a U.S. Navy formation and part of U.S. Central Command, CTF 150 was transformed into a multinational maritime security force with rotating leadership drawn from more than a dozen participating countries. CTF 150 was tasked with maritime security operations and is still active in the area, but a growing desire to separate "security" and "law enforcement" operations prompted the creation of a new combined task force in 2009—CTF 151—with a specific antipiracy mandate. Since 2008, the European Union's Operation Atalanta—the first-ever maritime operation conducted within the framework of the EU Security and Defence Policy—has been active in the region, acutely so in the spring of 2012, as already discussed. Also in 2008, NATO launched Operation Allied Provider to provide escorts to the WFP, which was quickly succeeded by Operation Allied Protector with a broader mandate to protect commercial maritime routes, itself succeeded by Operation Ocean Shield in 2009 with a specific counterpiracy mandate.

These operations have become increasingly coordinated over time through changes in the international legal regulation of piracy and a growing emphasis on private-, regional-, and global-scale governance of antipiracy initiatives. Increasing coordination of transnational security initiatives marks the post-2001 period, and maritime security is no exception. International securitization since 2001 (as explored in chapter 2) has given rise to a whole new era of maritime security. The 2004 International Ship and Port Facility Security (ISPS) code is particularly prominent within that shift and has entailed new forms of surveillance of ports, ships, and the people that labor in those places (Boske 2006). The ISPS code has also prompted new forms of cooperation and information sharing between organizations like the World Customs Operation and the International Maritime Organization (Hesse and Charalambous 2004). Changes in the regulation of maritime security since 2001 are provoking fundamental changes in the scope and scale of authority at sea. For the UN, 2008 was a particularly busy year, with a series of resolutions passed that hold profound significance for international law and politics. UN Security Council Resolutions 1816 and 1846 sanction states to "take all necessary measures that are deemed appropriate to suppress Somali-sourced piracy and armed robbery at sea" (Chalk 2010, 97). Together these resolutions authorize search and interdiction of suspect vessels in Somalia's coastal waters. The significance of this shift is palpable if we recall the first basic tenant of Heller-Roazen's "piratical paradigm," or countless other popular, philosophical, and juridical definitions of piracy, including the Geneva Convention (UN 1958) and the UN Convention on the Laws of the Sea (UN 1982). Piracy has historically been defined first and foremost by its location in the exceptional space of the high seas. Even as the concept of piracy has been extended to aerial and virtual space, constant has been the location of the acts beyond the territory of any sovereign state authority. And yet with United Nations Security Council Resolutions (UNSCR) 1816 and 1846, Somalia's sovereign maritime space is in effect transformed into exceptional space by decree.

If UNSCR 1816 and 1846 changed the game in profound ways, it was another resolution—UNSCR 1851—that provoked a whole new scale of concern for the rapidly changing nature of antipiracy operations in this region. The resolution sanctions member states to "undertake all necessary measures that are appropriate in Somalia, for the purpose of suppressing acts of piracy and armed robbery at sea," but what this means in practice, as the bold heading of the resolution indicates, is that the council "authorizes states to use land-based operations in Somalia" (UN Security Council 2008). These resolutions are "unprecedented in the level of authority they grant the international community to counter threats in the maritime realm." Chalk (2010, 97) explains that they extend, "in principle, to the use of armed force on land." Of course, we know that this potential principle has become actual practice. Indeed, it took another four years until the EU "toughened" its antipiracy mandate "to allow forces patrolling the Indian Ocean to attack bases on Somali land. Before that, the forces were allowed to pursue pirates only at sea" (Gettlemen 2012). UN Security Council Resolution 1851 was a major and shocking regulatory change that prompted the formation of a wholly new body in 2009—the Contact Group on Piracy off the Coast of Somalia (CGPCS)—to facilitate coordination among more than sixty states and organizations. The CGPCS coordinates military operations, develops "best practices" in security for the shipping industry, and has created trust funds for countries participating in another new governing body: the "Djibouti Code countries." Drafted in January 2009 in response to UNSCR 1851, the "Djibouti Code of Conduct Concerning the Repression of Piracy and Armed Robbery against Ships in the Western Ocean and the Gulf of Aden," or simply the Djibouti Code, has now been signed by twenty countries in the region.[3] The Djibouti meeting was convened by the IMO—the organization that has been pivotal in lobbying the UN Security Council for the new regulations for Somalia and the Gulf of Aden. The IMO began this lobbying in 2005 and takes large credit for the drafting of resolutions 1816, 1846, and 1851 (IMO 2009b; see also PMAESA 2008a). The problem of piracy in the Gulf of Aden is thus provoking profound change in who governs, where, and how. Naming the complex contestations in the Gulf of Aden a problem of piracy enables massive legal change in the authority of foreign national and multinational powers to govern Somali sovereign maritime and territorial space. What is being worked out in response to piracy is thus momentous and unprecedented and has implications for global government well beyond the domain of piracy. As Chalk (2010, 99) writes,

> The international response represents an unprecedented level of intergovernmental cooperation that has been achieved in a remarkably short period of time—frequently between sovereign entities that have rarely, if ever, operated on a common footing. This collaborative action not only gives concrete expression to the reality that maintenance and regulation of the seas ultimately relies on joint interstate and agreement and enforcement, but it also provides the U.S. Navy and partner nations a unique opportunity to engage one another and work out issues of interoperability and coordination. Properly developed, this could lay the foundation for an effective regime of maritime order that is able to address piracy and other transnational threats, such as illegal fishing, drug trafficking, and environmental degradation.

The legal experimentation under way in contemporary antipiracy initiatives is not only unprecedented but also profoundly a form of experimentation with *space*. In an era of supply chain security when authority is reconstituted to protect corridors of commerce, the particular dangers posed by piracy have shifted, and so too have the strategies and spaces for managing them. This is stark not only in the dramatic recasting of the geographies of sovereignty exacted by UNSCR 1816, 1838, and 1851 but also in multinational and corporate efforts to directly protect shipping corridors and prosecute pirates. If piracy has always been a problem of space, law, and power, whereby the category of the pirate provides imperial powers with a means to govern beyond their formal (territorial) jurisdiction, then the particular geographies of piracy and its government also change alongside new cartographies of power.

There is no better way to examine the centrality of space in efforts to govern the problem of Somali piracy than by looking to the IRTC, where this chapter started. The creation of this corridor is literally the production of a new political space. First dubbed the Maritime Security Patrol Area (MSPA), the corridor was created in 2008 by the U.S. Naval Central Command and patrolled by a coalition of navy warships and aerial patrols led by Commodore Davidson of the Canadian Navy, then commander of CTF 150 (CENTCOM 2008). With the creation of the MSPA, naval ships that were already patrolling the region targeted their efforts in this designated corridor. Indeed, the security corridor is constituted by political agreements between states, shipping companies, and transnational organizations like the IMO. This space is not visible on the open waters; there are no flags marking the lanes and no other signs that any kind of border has been breached. Yet while the space is not marked by the symbols of national territory that have come to represent sovereignty in the modern era, it exists as a zone of intensive naval policing with clear boundaries that are marked in practice and recognized by the UN, the EU, the IMO, and the transnational shipping industry represented through the International Maritime Bureau (IMB), a division of the International Chamber of Commerce. Following adjustments made in February 2009, the eastbound corridor begins at 45°E between 11°53' and 11°48'N and ends at 53°E between 14°23' and 14°18'N. The westbound corridor starts at 53°E between 14°30' and 14°25'N and ends at 45°E between 12°00' and 11°55'N. The MSPA was established in support of the IMO's antipiracy efforts, and the corridor was taken over by and renamed the IRTC by the IMO later in the same year. Perhaps it is not surprising, given the country's longstanding and still powerful stake in international shipping, that it was the United

Kingdom's Hydrographic Office that published the standard map of the IRTC and makes it available to the maritime community online without fee as navigational chart Q6099 (Intertanko 2009; MSCHOA n.d.; Stockbruegger 2010).

The IRTC is part of an ensemble of efforts to assert geo-economic imperial authority in the area, which throw geographies of sovereignty into question. Indeed, if we place the IRTC within the broader global architecture of supply chain security, we see that it fits quite "seamlessly." If the rise of supply chain security entails a move away from territorial models of security in order to protect the transnational material and informational networks of global trade, as argued in chapter 2, then the IRTC can be understood as a specific piece of that system in a zone that poses acute challenges of disruption. Indeed, Commander Steve Waddell (2010) explains the Canadian naval presence in the Gulf of Aden by highlighting two defining features of supply chain security. First, he describes the global geography of supply chains, which creates particular relationships between places, and second, he marks the importance of trade to national security: "Why are we there? Merchant ships carry all kinds of commodities, which are imported into North American and Europe. You take for granted all these products. They're rarely made in Canada or the U.S., and so they have to come from somewhere. 90 percent of imports to Canada come by sea. There's no piracy off the coasts of North America, but lots of North America–bound ships travel through this area, known as 'pirate alley.' We're trying to stop piracy at the source. Globalization makes events in Africa important." Indeed, Waddell signals the ways in which supply chains sustain particular kinds of relations between places through maritime shipping corridors. While this strategy of creating intensely policed naval corridors for managing cargo movement through the Gulf of Aden is recent, the broader project of protecting specific maritime passageways has a long history. Kempe (2010, 359) cites the work of historian Lauren Benton to describe maritime passageways: "Like 'vectors,' they crossed the maritime sphere, and thus transformed the ocean into a 'legal space' characterized as a complex tangle of such strategies." Indeed, Benton (2005, 2) challenges the image of the high seas as unregulated spaces and argues that historically "empires did lay claim to vast stretches of territory, the nature of such claims was tempered by control that was exercised mainly over narrow bands, or corridors and over enclaves and irregular zones around them." Today we see these strategies again taking center stage.

Like the protected trade corridors explored in chapter 2, maritime security corridors help to forge a networked space of transnational supply chain security. Also like other projects of supply chain security, the IRTC relies on a public–private security partnership of national force, transnational regulation, and corporate practice. Indeed, like other supply chain security initiatives, in the Gulf of Aden states create the legal and regulatory frameworks for trade security, while industry is expected to manage the day-to-day practice through private means and support the development of corporate best practice. EU NAVFOR Somalia, NATO, and a long list of private shipping companies have together produced the document series "Best Management Practices for Protection against Somalia Based Piracy." The most recent release, BMP4, of August 2011 outlines the "presence of Naval/Military forces in the Gulf of Aden, concentrated on the Internationally Recommended Transit Corridor (IRTC)," which has "significantly reduced the incidence of piracy attack in this area," with the effect of forcing it out "into the Arabian Sea and beyond" (BMP4 2011, 3). BMP4 quickly establishes that the presence of naval patrol offers no guarantee of protection, suggesting that "there remains a serious and continuing threat from piracy in the Gulf of Aden," which remains the responsibility of the shipping company, the captain, and the crew. The report proceeds to recommend a range of protective measures that ships should adopt, focused centrally on the physical security of the vessel through fencing, barricading, and surveillance. The report even provides signage for ships to reproduce and attach as warnings to Somalis. These "best practices" are not only supported by transnational bodies like the CGPCS but developed as part of their broader antipiracy work, and according to Chalk (2010, 97), the BMPs have "full industry backing."

While a few states provide dedicated military escort through the Gulf of Aden to protect their own flagged ships, most do not. The common response has been to pool military force through the kinds of multinational initiatives discussed previously. However, these are increasingly paired with a new emphasis on the private sector in antipiracy (Isenberg 2012). The United States has led the way in encouraging their merchant marine to contract private companies to provide onboard armed escorts. Since 2011, a large number of other countries have made domestic policy changes to permit the use of armed guards on ships, including the United Kingdom, Germany, Malta, Cyprus, and India. William Marmon (2011) suggests not only that the policy change was a response to the growing number of attacks in the Gulf of Aden but more specifically that it was "spurred by an action earlier this year by the International Chamber of Shipping, the world's main trade organization for shipping," which "recognized officially that arms were effective when used off Somalia." Italy has taken a novel approach of providing "public" security (stationing military forces directly on their merchant vessels) and then recovering costs from shippers. Contracting private security companies to provide onboard armed protection has become "industry best practice," as the chief of the U.S. Coast Guard's Maritime and International Law Division, Captain Steve Poulin,[4] explained to me: "Most U.S. flagged vessels, after going through risk assessments, have decided that armed security is appropriate." In fact, U.S. flagged ships traveling in hazardous waters are now required to carry armed guards. Indeed, a number of large shipping companies have recently announced that they would begin contracting armed guards to ride ships, including China Ocean Shipping Company, Wallenius, Torm A/S, and the world's largest shipper, Maersk (Marmon 2011). As Jonathan Manthorpe (2012) explains, there was a direct economic incentive for industry: "Shipowners swallowed their traditional reluctance to take this step when insurance companies started offering cuts in premiums by as much as 40 per cent for ships carrying the mercenaries."

Yet this approach is by no means simple but rather provokes a host of questions of international law and politics. As Poulin suggested, when private security is contracted, "How do you get weapons through Egypt . . . when you are transiting the Suez Canal? How do you do that? . . . Then when you put armed security on board, the next question is: what is the legal authority of these individuals to use force? And that's an interesting legal discussion." The arming of the merchant marine with private security raises a bundle of profound questions about the jurisdiction of public law and private security, not only in the canal and in open waters, but also when armed merchant ships make calls at foreign ports. Under the British plan drafted in 2011, the Home Secretary is able to license guards for ships, but this move provoked some similar reflection. Harking back to old debates about the validity of national sovereignty on vessels in the high seas, the Home Office looked at "how to apply UK firearms legislation on board UK ships, and whether it was feasible to authorise and monitor the possession of 'prohibited' firearms at sea" ("Somali Piracy" 2011). Indeed, Heller-Roazen (2009, 126–27) recalls the debates between legal scholars of the nineteenth and twentieth centuries, who defined the ship, "with increased juridical exactitude, as 'floating territory' or 'swimming land.'" He proceeds to suggest that these terms "involve a curious, if decisive, juridical operation . . . they imply the legal procedure the Romans long ago named 'the fiction of the law': that device by which, for the purposes of reaching a judgment in court, 'the false' as Baldus explained, 'may be accepted as truth.'" Emphasizing even more clearly the geographic dimensions of this legal fiction, Heller-Roazen (2009, 127) explains, "The mechanism of confabulation is flagrant: that which is, in fact in motion and at sea is considered as if it were, by law, immobile and inseparable from land."

These questions have taken on ever more force in the wake of a 2012 incident that saw an armed Italian vessel shoot and kill two Indian mariners, leaving two Italians on trial for murder and sharp diplomatic tensions between India and Italy. According to Poulin, the United States believes its vessels have an inherent right to self-defense that includes the use of force. "We believe that is an international recognized principle," he stated. However, conceding that this *belief* might not hold in the context of international law, he continued, "Other nations might disagree and have a different view on the use of force. But there is express U.S. law that authorizes those on board a U.S. flag vessel to repel piracy attacks . . . and we have supporting legal authority beyond just the inherent right of self-defense . . . Congress, through the [2010] Coast Guard Authorization Act passed law to insulate members on board who use force, from liability." As countless critics have observed, the private industry in maritime security has exploded alongside the growth in counterpiracy initiatives. Yet a specific landmark event in 2011 reveals the rise of not only private guards for hire but a full-fledged private navy operating entirely according to market logics. Marmon (2011) reports on the establishment of the "Convoy Escort Programme Ltd, flying the Cypriot flag, to escort ships across through the Gulf of Aden—for a fee of $30,000 per ship." According to DefenceWeb (2011), the initiative is "backed by UK insurance and reinsurance broker Jardine Lloyd Thompson Group" and uses "seven ex-navy patrol boats, each with eight armed guards, costing US$30 million." The company has plans to expand to eleven boats. The Convoy Escort Programme website explains that it "is an initiative of the insurance industry . . . designed to protect the lives of seafarers, ships, cargo and the environment by keeping the threat of piracy, and the risks of armed conflict, away from ships engaged in innocent passage through this key trade route."

Current efforts to police piracy in the Gulf of Aden challenge established relationships between space and state sovereignty by bringing mercenaries centrally into the political realm. So too, contemporary practices of trial and detention are a domain of significant experimentation. Because of the precarious interplay of national and international authority at play in the prosecution of the exceptional figure of the pirate, approaches to trial and detention vary entirely according to the domestic laws of the prosecuting state (cf. Gavouneli 2007; Keyuan 2000, 2005). This prompts C. J. Chivers (2012) to exclaim, "Behold a seam in international law enforcement, and a case of high-seas legal limbo . . . what to do with the pirates that foreign ships detain? No system has been developed for prosecuting their cases." Some states capture and release suspected pirates, while others detain them and eventually bring them to trial on domestic soil. There are rumors that other states simply kill them at the site of encounter without any accountability. Likewise, when it comes to incarceration, there is a range of different practices (Kontorovich 2009). Perhaps most striking and increasingly common, poor *states* neighboring Somalia are being transformed into mercenary legal and carceral spaces for imperial powers. Indeed, it is not only armed guards that are increasingly contracted to police piracy in the Gulf of Aden; national court and prison systems are also contracted to provide a "regional solution" to the problem. Chalk (2010, 54) reports, "The United States, United Kingdom, and European Union have all entered into agreements with Kenya whereby Kenya will act as a third-party to prosecute individuals suspected of engaging in armed maritime crimes." He explains the emergence of this relationship as a feature of the close proximity of Kenya to Somalia, the friendly relationship already established between these countries in antiterror efforts, and the established legal infrastructure for prosecuting pirates, but Chalk is also clear that the Kenyan government's "willingness to take in suspects in exchange for Western development assistance dollars" is also key. Between 2006 and 2011, twenty states prosecuted 1,063 Somali pirates, with the vast majority (more than 900 suspects) prosecuted in eleven states within the region, five of which were prosecuting pirates with UN financial assistance (UN Security Council 2012a). Dwyer Arce (2010) reports that the Seychelles has become a focal point of these efforts, with the construction of entirely new state-of-the-art high-security cells in 2011 paid for by the UN Office of Drugs and Crimes. Britain has developed a particularly close connection with Seychelles and is spending close to a million pounds to create a Regional Anti-Piracy Prosecution and Intelligence Coordination Center (UN Security Council 2012a). Comments from the South African delegate to the UN Security Council suggest some of the problems of this approach. The delegate expressed the concerns of "a number of national authorities about the creation of new specialized anti-piracy courts with jurisdiction limited exclusively to piracy." He explained that "South Africa was concerned that such a move could serve to redirect limited prosecutorial and judicial resources from other crimes of equal importance to those countries to piracy issues—which in some instances would not be the most serious issue facing those countries" (ibid.). Indeed, the "renting out" of the legal infrastructure of neighboring states to foreign powers sets in motion some deeply troubling trajectories that mark some of the strange new cartographies of a geo-economic imperialism.

Military or Police? Public or Private? Political or Economic?

The growing reliance on private security not only provokes conflicts regarding what officially counts as violence, who can legally kill whom, and who can be armed where; it is also a central pillar in a broader recasting of the relationships between space, law, and state sovereignty. Between national courts, corporate best practice, and geopolitical force, a framework of law and set of norms are emerging out of these experiments in "counterpiracy" to govern a future of public–private partnership warfare. National states and organizations of national states have made significant forays into regulating the security of global trade, changing the very nature of sovereignty vis-à-vis the Somali pirate in order to do so. The shipping industry has nevertheless repeatedly and forcefully criticized governments and governing bodies for not doing enough. "Whilst we welcome [private security on board ships], it is a short-term palliative measure," ICS Secretary-General Peter Hinchliffe explained. Hinchliffe indicated that the ICS wanted to see "more arrests of suspected pirates, military attacks on pirates' Somali supply bases and a naval blockade 12 miles off the country's coast" (DefenceWeb 2011). The IMB has also publicly insisted, "It is vital that this naval presence be sustained or increased" (ibid.). Poulin confirmed these sentiments when he explained, "Industry would like [having naval guards on board]. Industry sees that it's a governmental responsibility to ensure maritime security . . . it's a governmental responsibility to use force . . . ah . . . it's a governmental responsibility to enforce the law. So I think it's fair to say that industry's preference—generally— would be if we had military teams. We obviously see it differently. We see that they have the inherent right of self-defense. We're putting naval combatants in the area including coast guard cutters . . . we're taking action with the means appropriate. We don't think that it requires armed military teams on board." This is in part a question of the impossibility—now as in the past—of effectively policing such a vast space. As Poulin suggested, "There is a capacity issue as well." Yet the resistance to provide "public" security in this way is not simply about cost or capacity. Rather, it goes right to the core contradictions of piracy and international law.

The state cannot declare war on the pirate if he is to remain an exceptional figure in the law. In order for piracy to resist sliding into the category of simple domestic criminal or enemy of a single state, the pirate's crimes cannot be conceived of as political. The entire framework for governing Somali attacks as instances of piracy is contingent on an outright denial of the politics of their actions and claims. This is the case, even as we have seen repeatedly that the boundary between privateer and pirate can be as slim as a piece of paper and as arbitrary as the mobile and instrumental interests of states. It is deeply ironic, though perhaps fitting, that the imperial logics of antipiracy efforts in the Gulf of Aden rely on an absolute yet fundamentally tenuous distinction between the economic and the political.

The insistence on the exclusively economic and apolitical acts of the pirates produces some fascinating reflections on the distinction between pirates and terrorists. For piracy to be governed so lawlessly, it cannot become an object of outright warfare—the pirate must remain legally distinct from the terrorist. Taking this approach, a 2009 RAND report asks, "Are pirates terrorists?" as if it were an empirical question to be answered through field research. The report reassures readers, "To date, there has been no credible evidence to support speculation about a [terrorism-piracy] nexus emerging. Just as importantly, the objectives of the two actors remain entirely distinct." This claim appears absurd in the face of voluminous historical research that traces the shifting and strategic legal boundaries defining each kind of actor. It is perhaps even more troubling to see this strategic legal distinction of the two figures as a means of denying the political claims of the Somalis. Yet the absurdity does not disqualify its underpinning an entire arsenal of law and violence.

It is clear that piracy has historically been a crucial legal technology for managing the contradictory geographies that define the system of national sovereignty. The rise of the nation-state system, organized through an absolute geography of territorial sovereignty, at once created the problem of the oceans. Because of the ungovernability of ocean space within the national-territorial model, oceans were deemed beyond the reach of the system (cf. Thomson 1994). And yet, the imperial basis for the nation-state system also meant that the oceans are integral to that system. Maritime space could not be governed, but it had to be traversed. It was outside the system of territorial authority but well within the geographies of the imperial nation-states. This is precisely why the pirate emerged as such a crucial *and* exceptional figure; the pirate was the criminal literally outside the space of the system of national sovereignty but legally within the authority of international law. The pirate was a means of managing the fundamental spatial contradiction of absolute space in a world of relations and circulations.

Something parallel but different is under way today. Poier (2009) asserts that "if the word 'piracy' had been applied to many different activities in totally different contexts, the social and political core of its meaning has been unchanged since the very beginning." But some things have changed, even if the profoundly imperial nature of antipiracy has not. As this chapter has demonstrated, in an era of supply chain security where authority is reconstituted to protect corridors of commerce, the particular dangers posed by piracy have shifted, and so too have the strategies and spaces for managing them. If, as Kempe (2010, 255) argues, "basic elements" of the "modern transnational order" arose "from the confrontation with privateering and piracy on the high seas and along various coasts," I argue here that the attempt to govern through piracy is playing a parallel role today in sculpting the postmodern transnational order. This order is not the law of nations but the transnational and corporate "P3" imperial warfare of logistics space.

CHAPTER FIVE

Logistics Cities

The "Urban Heart" of Empire

A world-economy always has an urban centre of gravity, a city as the logistic heart of its activity.

—Fernand Braudel, *The Perspective of the World*

The invention of the city as such lies in logistical preparation for war.

—Paul Virilio, *Speed and Politics*

Every city and its sister want to be the next logistics gateway. But some have nicer gates than others.

—Adam Bruns, "Emerging Logistics Hubs"

The illustration in Figure 26 is one in a series of designs for the dramatic transformation of a place that became globally notorious in the early years of the twenty-first century. While Basra Logistics City might not be familiar to many, the site's former identity marks it as one of the world's most violent and contested places in contemporary cartographies of warfare. Basra Logistics City is located in southern Iraq, near Umm Qasr—the country's only deepwater port. As Iraq's single maritime connection to the Persian Gulf, the port and surrounding area have for centuries been a busy trade and naval base. But in this geopolitically fraught region, Basra Logistics City occupies a particularly haunted space. Until January 2011, the site was known as Camp Bucca, the largest U.S. military detention facility in occupied Iraq (Al Mashni 2011; "US Jail Guards" 2008; DeMello 2011).

FIGURE 26. Basra Logistics City corporate offices, 2013. Source: Kufan Group.

FIGURE 27. Containers on the move at Basra Logistics City, 2013. Source: Kufan Group.

This chapter explores the politics of a new global urban form: the logistics city. On the one hand it interrogates the old and new imperial logics that permeate these centers of circulation, and on the other hand it explores the role of maps and plans in the production of logistics city space. The chapter opens with an investigation of the Basra Logistics City and the preceding illustration. It explores the January 2011 transformation of a notoriously violent Iraqi detention camp into a logistics city dedicated to processing goods and oil for transnational corporations. Despite its long life as an imperial military facility (first as a camp for the British and then for the Americans), the repurposing of the site as a logistics city was "seamless." In fact, it is not *despite* its military past that the site is so well suited to become a logistics city but *because* of it. In addition to the infrastructure invested in the site, Bucca also boasts an extensive system of physical security; features that were once essential to keeping Iraqis in will now serve the logistics cities' efforts to maintain a secure facility by keeping Iraqis out.

Basra Logistics City is one particularly striking example of a former military facility converted into a logistics city, and it opens an avenue to explore the broader relationship between militaries and markets in and through the city. This chapter follows networks of private logistics companies from Iraq to the Philippines, where Clark Air Force Base—formerly the largest U.S. military base abroad and the center for military logistics during the Vietnam war—is undergoing its own transformation into the Global Gateway Logistics City by some of the same companies that are

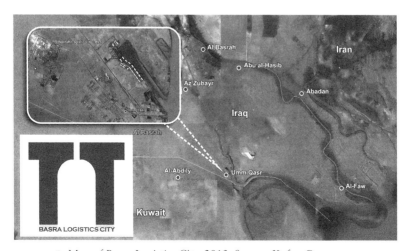

FIGURE 28. Map of Basra Logistics City, 2013. Source: Kufan Group.

FIGURE 29. Advertisement for Basra Logistics City highlighting security features onsite, 2013. Source: Kufan Group.

active in Iraq (Muñoz 2009). The chapter then moves to Dubai, the "pioneer" logistics city and also a financier for the redevelopment of the Clark base redevelopment. In a moment at once defined by national securitization and global trade intensification, the extreme means of managing this critical dilemma of flow and containment in Dubai Logistics City (DLC) has become a model incrementally replicated around the world. While DLC may be exceptional in its particular coupling of frenzied economic activity and anemic political rights, it is precisely this exceptional form that is serving as the model for the protection of infrastructure and trade flows and reshaping of ports across the global north (Fattah and Lipton 2006; Flynn 2006; Jacobs and Hall 2007). Indeed, the chapter follows this transnational policy transfer back to North America to dwell on Tsawwassen, British Columbia, where old and new colonial politics are at play in the struggles over land and rights that surround the building of a logistics city.

An investigation of the current entanglement of corporate and military logistics exposes military forces clearing way for private logistics companies, but the latter actively supporting the former as well. Indeed, logistics is the most heavily privatized area of contemporary warfare, and the very same companies involved in building logistics cities hold significant contracts with the U.S. military. The chapter thus moves to explore the privatization of military logistics, the complex circuits across military and civilian practice, and debates about military urbanism.

In addition to the imperial politics of logistics cities, this chapter explores the striking visual representations of these new forms in maps and plans that closely resemble computer motherboards. These sterile, engineered environments are without chaos, disorder, or detritus, let alone signs of life. Drawing on the work of Henri Lefebvre (1991) on the role of representation in the production of space, Foucault ([1997] 2003) on circulation and the city, and critical legal writing on old and new colonial forms, this chapter investigates the paradox of containment and flow and locates the urban centrally in the violent global social factory. It asks, what does it mean for the city to be made in the image of efficient cargo flow? What does it mean for the urban to be designed and governed in the service of efficient economic exchange? What does this mean for questions of citizenship and the city?

From Military Base to Logistics City

On December 31, 2010, The U.S. military hosted a ceremony "returning" the 740-acre Camp Bucca to "the Iraqi people." As part of the ceremony, the base's American flag was lowered and the Iraqi flag was raised, the army's 1st Infantry Division deputy commanding general fed cake to young male Iraqi children, and men in suits and uniforms all grinned widely for the cameras that rolled.[1] Camp Bucca, the deputy commanding general explained, would become Basra Logistics City, and a "gift" from the Americans would include $100 million in infrastructure on the site (including warehouses, roads, advanced water treatment and sewer systems, electricity, a recreational facility, a helicopter landing pad, and a thousand "modern and well-maintained housing units"). In addition to this infrastructure, Camp Bucca also boasts a fifteen-foot berm and dozens of guard towers. The same perimeter that contained Iraqis and subjected them to violent abuse is, according to CNN (2012), "nearly impossible to breach making it a relatively safe place for workers." Marking the deeply entangled geographies of rough trade, CNN explains how "entrepreneurs aim to make this former military jail into a key element of southern Iraq's quest to become a business hub along the new Silk Road."

Despite the highly masculine, geopolitical performance of the site-transfer ceremony with its focus on nations and sovereignty, the "return" of the land and the lowering of the U.S. flag were not entirely sincere. Basra Logistics City will be operated by the New York–based company Northern Gulf Partners, which holds a forty-year lease on the site. Northern Gulf and their investors will be exempted from all corporate taxes and fees for ten to fifteen years as they establish one of the largest centers for corporate petroleum logistics on earth. They are entitled to employ an entirely foreign work force, and they hold the right to repatriate all investment and profit. The American "gift" furthermore pales in comparison to the investment of the Basra Investment Commission, whose contribution is expected to exceed $2.6 billion. Bartle Bull, a founding member of Northern Gulf who was recently awarded for the excellence of his "Iraqi political analysis" by U.S. General Petraeus, explained, "This is an extremely important project for Iraq and for companies seeking to do business here. Basra Logistics City offers a secure, convenient, and hassle-free way for companies to set up and get to work in the booming Iraq market" (quoted in Jaffer 2013, xxix). CNN (2012) suggests that Basra "could soon become a weighpoint on the new Silk Road," a "link for commerce between Asia and Europe."

Camp Bucca was at one point the largest U.S. detention camp in Iraq and held twenty-two thousand detainees despite an official capacity built for eighteen thousand. Camp Bucca is deeply entangled in the controversies over U.S. detainee abuse that filled the airwaves in the early years of occupation. Bucca not only was home to some of the most serious and early accounts of detainee abuse but was also the home base of U.S. military personnel who would later become renowned for their role in the shocking acts at Abu Ghraib. Indeed, it was after early reports of detainee abuse at Bucca in 2003 that the commander of the camp—Lt. Col. Jerry L. Phillabaum—was promoted to manage Abu Ghraib ("US Jail Guards" 2008; Hirschfeld Davis and Sullivan 2004; Pryer 2009; Tilghman 2008).

Clark Air Force Base in the Philippines is another contemporary example of a U.S. military base transformed into a corporate logistics facility. Clark AFB operated from 1903 to 1991 and was once the largest overseas U.S. military facility in the world. Home to 30,000 personnel and comprising 156,204 acres, the base was a stronghold of the combined Filipino and American forces during the end of World War II. Until 1975, Clark provided the logistical support to the U.S. forces during the Vietnam War. Following the departure of American forces in 1991, the base became the site of Diosdado Macapagal International Airport and the Clark Freeport Zone. The site has since been transformed into the Global Gateway Logistics City (GGLC). The project was initiated in 2008, but "formal construction did not formally start until 2010 because all derelict structures, trees and *informal setters* had to be removed from the site" (Valencia 2012; emphasis mine). Completion of the project is expected to take another decade (Muñoz 2012; Valencia 2012).

FIGURE 30. Camp Bucca, 2011. Source: Photograph by Andrea Bruce/NOOR.

The GGLC website states that, like Camp Bucca, Clark offers "many state-of-the-art amenities, including controlled access with a comprehensive physical security system, a sound infrastructure capable of supporting the most sophisticated communication networks with inexpensive and stable power, along with good water and sewage treatment by virtue of the former U.S. Air Force base infrastructure." The Philippine government has contributed more than $3 billion in investment to build the GGLC. The project was conceived and is led by Peregrine Development International, an offshoot of the notorious private military contractor KBR, which is itself a former subsidiary of Haliburton. Dennis Wright, the president and CEO of Peregrine, served in an executive capacity with KBR and also has a background in the U.S. Navy as a logistician. A similar mixed pedigree of experience in public and private military work is common across the Peregrine executive team, with most having spent time as U.S. military logisticians followed by a period at KBR. On the company's web page, Peregrine proudly reports the completion of such projects as the prison facilities as Guantanamo Bay and the Camp Cropper detention facility in Baghdad. In addition to these more traditional private military projects, Wright's biography proudly notes that he "brought Seaworld and Busch Gardens to Dubai," pointing to the common planning and development techniques, and perhaps even "organization space" (Easterling 1999), at work in this unusual array of corporate and military megaprojects.

Dubai and the Birth of the Logistics City

While logistics cities proliferate around the world, it is enlightening to consider the prototype that inspires the form. The very first logistics city was an invention of Dubai and as such establishes some precise precedents for the urban and global politics of labor, citizenship, and security at play in their deployment. Itself a very recent phenomenon, Dubai Logistics City (DLC) was opened in 2007 as part of Dubai World Central—the largest master-planned settlement on earth and the United Arab Emirates' "most strategically important infrastructure development." Dubai World Central encompasses a wide range of specialized zones and uses, but its Logistics City is perhaps the most unusual and intriguing element of the plan. United Arab Emirate officials claim on the DP World website that DLC is "the world's first truly integrated logistics platform with all transport modes, logistics and value added services, including light manufacturing and assembly, in a single customs bonded and Free Zone environment." The plan unites the Port of Jebel Ali, the world's largest human-made harbor and the largest port in the Middle East, with the new Dubai World Central International Airport, planned to have the world's greatest capacity upon completion. Logistics City entices firms to become tenants with offers of fifty-year no-tax guarantees, no caps on capital inflows or outflows, and no labor restrictions. It is part of an aggressive effort to diversify the Emerati economy beyond oil into alternative growth industries (Fernandes and Rodrigues 2009).[2] Supply chain experts claim that Dubai's move toward "such a radical solution" in the construction of Dubai Logistics City, as opposed to the expansion of the current combined airport and cargo-processing zone, is a feature of the political context. Supply chain analysts (Mangan, Lalwani, and Butcher 2008, 310) explain, "A principal advantage for developments in Dubai compared with European countries is that the sheikhs are in the position to focus on a long-term investment horizon. This influenced their decision-making process since they do not have to focus on short-term success (e.g. to guarantee a re-election) but can instead focus on the long term and decide which solution is most beneficial for Dubai in the long run."

The emergence of the logistics city is significant. It marks a fundamental transition in the global space economy wherein the design and management of supply chains has become so critical to just-in-time production and distribution that there is now an urban form named in its honor. In the logistics city, urban space is conceived for the singular purpose of securing the management and movement of globally bound *stuff*. Dubai's boosters promote the city precisely in these terms, signaling its centrality in a changing global geopolitical economy. Writing in Dubai's high-profile self-promotional magazine *Vision*, Parag Khanna (2011) exclaims, "Dubai is the 21st-century Venice, a 'free zone' that efficiently re-exports the world's goods, confidently sitting at the crossroads of Europe, Africa, and Asia. We now call the deepening trade routes between the Gulf and Far East the 'New Maritime Silk Road.'" Recycling a simple and celebratory version of ideas that have circulated in urban scholarship for decades (Beaverstock et al. 2000; Brenner and Keil 2005; Friedman 2000; Sassen 1991), Khanna asserts that the rise of Dubai is a feature of epochal change wherein globalization is intimately coupled with the rising power of cities. He writes, "The emerging geopolitical and economic consensus is that the 21st century will no longer be dominated by nations such as America, Brazil and China, but, instead, by so-called global cities such as Dubai." Khanna writes in a mode where promotion and description are difficult to differentiate—a style with a long pedigree in urban boosterism (Logan and Molotch 1987) and certainly a familiar tone in the particular brand of boosterism deployed in the discursive production of "distributive cities" (Negrey, Osgood, and Goetzke 2011). He argues that Dubai's power is not seriously challenged by the global recession: "No matter who is up or down, Dubai wins." He offers as an example the capacity for a trading nation to "reroute" trade—in other words, manipulate globally uneven local and regional economies in the face of crisis. "When traffic between New York and Dubai dried up due to the 2008 financial crisis," he explains, "Emirates Airline rerouted its Airbus A380 planes to Toronto, whose banking system survived in better shape." While Dubai cannot stand outside of the global political economies it circulates, it is Dubai's role as a modern-day entrepôt that defines the city's prominence and the particular fate of its prosperity.

Dubai Logistics City is already setting standards that are reverberating along transnational supply chains. It sets momentous precedents for the production of urban space and the politics of infrastructure protection, reaching far beyond Dubai and the Gulf region. Dubai Logistics City prides itself for offering the "latest technology solutions," not only for transport and customer service, but for "security" as well (Steins 2006; see also Mangan, Lalwani, and Butcher 2008). Indeed, concern for the security of DLC is significant. The term is rarely defined, yet *security* is invoked as a self-evident priority in urban development and infrastructure projects around the world. But it is the security of *supply chains* rather than the people who live and work in the city that is at the focal point of a logistics lens. Order and efficiency guide the design of built form and govern the distribution of uses and users in space, as Figure 31 conveys.

While logistics is ostensibly about efficient movement and undisrupted flow, the plans for Dubai Logistics City reveal that flow is achieved through a proliferation of new borders and spatial ordering and control. Some forms are clearly visible in the landscape, while others are hidden from immediate view. On the one hand, the entire vision for the city resembles a computer motherboard. DLC is ordered electronically through biometric access cards, security gating, surveillance cameras, and other technologies. The most significant form of spatial containment is likely the "Labour Village." Officials promote the "village" as the "provision of integrated blue collar housing with full range of facilities." But despite the clean design and lavish landscaping, artists' renderings still conjure an air of prison architecture. Described by local media as a "luxury labour camp" (ArabianBusiness.com 2007), Labour Village will eventually occupy fourteen million square feet of land and hold 87,500 beds.[3] The provision of this "luxury" for foreign workers is part of a broader labor regime;

FIGURE 31. Dubai Logistics City, 2007. Source: Photograph by Brian McMorrow.

strikes and trade unions remain illegal in the UAE, and participation in either can result in permanent expulsion from the country. This is one stark indication of the extreme conditions operative in Dubai; the vast majority of workers are on temporary work permits without any formal citizenship. While Europe and the United States rely heavily on noncitizen labor, no place on earth matches the UAE in this regard. Noncitizens make up 99 percent of the private work force (two-thirds of which are South Asian), and while there are more than 4.5 million residents, there are only 800,000 Emirati citizens (Al Tamimi n.d.; Kapiszewski 2006; UAE Ministry of Labour 2001).

A paradox with transnational salience lies at the core of Dubai Logistics City. Ensuring flow and preventing disruption to commodity circulation seems to require containment. On the one hand, the building of a logistics city is an important event in the production of urban space and infrastructure dedicated entirely to supporting networked flows across global supply chains, but on the other hand, the very premise of protecting those flows from disruption entails new forms of political geographic enclosure. For a city dedicated to logistics, the interruption of flows becomes system vulnerability, and forces that interfere with flow are managed as security threats. According to the logic of supply chain security, threat can just as easily come from a labor action as a natural disaster or a terrorist act (see chapter 2).

DLC may be exceptional in the way it couples trade liberalization and authoritarian politics, but it is precisely this exceptional form that has made DLC particularly influential in the United States, the world's most powerful and active proponent of global supply chain security. Accumulation through dispossession of formal and substantive citizenship rights, managed through the production of securitized logistic space, is the ominous model that U.S. port cities are borrowing from Dubai. The UAE may seem a world away from the United States, and plans for Dubai Logistics City likely appear a far cry from the organization of space anywhere in the United States, including its ports. However, Dubai's geographic resolution to the problem of containing disruption and facilitating flow is now a model for port and infrastructure security in U.S. cities (Fattah and Lipton 2006; Flynn 2006; Jacobs and Hall 2007). Chapter 3 details some of the controversy that erupted when Dubai Ports World tried to assume operation of a string of ports in the United States. The controversy involved large-scale opposition to the plan by elected officials and the public over "Arab operation" of U.S. shipping terminals. The opposition soldered a potent mix of outright anti-Arab racism with a more progressive critique of Dubai's labor, environment, and human rights practices still inflected with nationalism. While the executive branch approved the sale despite bipartisan congressional opposition, the controversy nevertheless prompted Dubai Ports World (DP World) to sell its interests (Friedman 2006; Gibson 2006; Kirchgaessner 2006; "Peter King" 2006; Overby 2006; "Dubai Company" 2009). With its Orientalist depiction of shady Arabs sneaking around U.S. ports, the *New York Times* cartoon (Figure 32) from February 2006 by an animator who is heavily critical of the Bush administration captures well the racist tone of popular debate.

The failure of this deal was not the end of the relationship; while the proposal for direct ownership was abandoned, political forms still migrate. Dubai has long been touted as a model of success that the United States and the rest of the world should follow. In 2005, former president Bill Clinton said, "Dubai is a role model of what could be achieved despite the other negative developments in the region. Look at Dubai, which has achieved enormous economic growth in such a short period of time" (quoted in Bhoyrul 2005). George W. Bush echoed this sentiment on a presidential visit to the UAE. In January 2008, he exclaimed, "I'm most impressed with what I've seen here. The entrepreneurial spirit is strong, and equally importantly, the desire to make sure all aspects of society have hope and encouragement" ("Bush Regaled" 2008). In a 2009 speech, President Obama praised Dubai's "astonishing progress"

Bush Administration Cuts Deal with Dubai Government to Manage US Ports

FIGURE 32. Dubai ports security. Source: Cartoon by Jeff Danziger, 2006.

(Alrawi 2009). Dubai is specifically touted as a model for U.S. port security. To "American officials, the sprawling port along the Persian Gulf
here, where steel shipping containers are stacked row after row as far as
the eye can see, is a model for the post-9/11 world," Hassan Fattah and
Eric Lipton (2006) assert. "Fences enclose the port's perimeter, which is
patrolled by guards. Gamma-ray scanners peek inside containers to make
sure they carry the clothing, aluminum, timber and other goods listed
on shipping records. Radiation detectors search for any hidden nuclear
material." Leading maritime security experts and logistics trade publica-
tions reiterate the ironies of the failed DP World deal in the United States:
despite populist concern, Dubai is a global leader in port security (Flynn
2006; Jacobs and Hall 2007).

So what is specific to the plan for Dubai Logistics City that makes it of
more than fleeting significance beyond this particular site in the Persian
Gulf? There is nothing novel about the joint project of containing disruption and facilitating flow. As Christine Boyer (1986, 9) has argued, since
the emergence of the American metropolis in the post–Civil War era, two
problems defined its government: "How to discipline and regulate the
urban masses in order to eradicate the dangers of social unrest, physical
degeneration, and congested contagion, which all cities seemed to breed,
and how to control and arrange the spatial growth of these gigantic places

so that they would support industrial production and the development of a civilization of cities." Indeed, Boyer suggests this problematization of city space and the "quest for disciplinary control" forged a "new relationship between the urban public and social science knowledge, as well as the architectural adornment of urban space and the rational treatment of spatial development." In the process, this struggle for the city gave rise to the field of urban planning. Boyer argues that disciplinary order "begins with a fear of darkened places of the city," spaces that should be "open to light and ventilated by fresh air." Discipline "proceeds from the distribution of individuals in space" (ibid.).

If the general problem of reconciling sociospatial order with efficiency and productivity through urban space has a long history, it takes on a more specific form when cast through the geographies of logistics and the politics of security. As chapter 2 explored in some detail, post-9/11 securitization efforts have entailed a dramatic rethinking of the meaning and practice of security in response to the specific challenges of securing both movement and borders, and Dubai has been centrally implicated in the U.S. designs of these globalizing forms. A good example of this is the United States' Container Security Initiative (CSI). It posts U.S. customs officials in foreign ports to inspect U.S.-bound cargo and aims to "extend [the US] zone of security outward so that American borders are the last line of defense, not the first" (DHS 2009). Dubai was the first "Middle Eastern entity" to join the CSI in 2005, and as a result, U.S. Border Patrol works especially close with Dubai Customs to screen containers destined for the United States. Likewise, the Transportation Workers Identity Credential—a central pillar of U.S. supply chain security—can be understood as part of the effort to drag the cramped conditions of work in a place like Dubai into the radically different context of the global north's advanced liberal maritime space (Boske 2006). The refusal of workers' rights in the interests of trade flows is crucial to the Dubai model, and the Transportation Workers Identification Credential (TWIC) program can be understood as an attempt to institutionalize similar logics. As chapter 3 explains, labor actions in U.S. ports have recently been cast as security threats. The most dramatic instance came in 2002 when George W. Bush enacted the Taft-Hartley Act in the largest U.S. ports of Los Angeles/Long Beach. Protest at the increasing numbers of workplace injuries by the International Longshore and Warehouse Union (ILWU) and a subsequent lockout by employers led the U.S. vice president to declare ILWU actions a threat to national security, threatening fines, criminal charges, and even military deployment (OWCW 2002). TWIC aims to preempt such disruption.

TWIC creates special "security zones" around ports where normal civil and labor law is suspended. Access to "secure areas" is controlled by biometrics and security clearances, organized through extensive new fencing, security gating, cameras, and other surveillance technologies (Emsellem et al. 2009; McEllrath 2011). Secure areas are governed differently; political, social, and economic rights that are in force across the country are suspended within these exceptional zones in the name of national security.

It is not only specific policies and technologies that work to replicate the relations within the Logistics City that are migrating from Dubai to the United States; the urban *form* also travels. The phenomenon is striking not just U.S. military bases overseas but domestic ones, too. In the core states of the global north, this exceptional space sometimes emerges in a somewhat more circumscribed form as logistics parks or zones. In Oakland, California, intense controversy greeted the conversion of a military base into a logistics center. From 1941 to 1999, the Oakland Army Base (OAB), immediately adjacent to the city's port, served as a critical transfer point of goods and equipment for U.S. military deployments (Cockrell 2010). In 2012, what was once the world's largest military port complex was set to become "a world-class trade and logistics center," which will "strengthen the port's position as the leading export gateway on the United States West Coast" (Port of Oakland 2012). The project is led by ProLogis—the world's largest owner, manager, and developer of distribution facilities. A firm that holds six hundred million square feet of distribution space across North America, Asia, and Europe (Port of Oakland 2011), ProLogis was one of the first corporations to build a facility in Dubai Logistics City. The DLC site was also the company's first distribution center in the Middle East. In the summer of 2012, plans for "Oakland Global"—the military base-cum-logistics facility's new identity—were solidified when ProLogis and partner California Capital & Investment Group were promised $242 million from the state, $54 million from the city, and close to $300 million in federal grants (Artz 2012; Burnson 2012).

Oakland Global may well be one of the largest logistics facilities in the works in North America, and it illustrates the complex forms of public–private partnership that construct these spaces. Yet, 900 miles to the north, another logistics megaproject offers a glimpse at a different kind of state–corporate partnership, one that brings the settler-colonial politics of the logistics city to the fore. Three years before the Camp Bucca / Basra Logistics City ceremony in Iraq and more than 11,000 kilometers to the west, similarly suited figures performed another land transfer ceremony designed to mark the signing of the Tsawwassen Agreement and the transfer of lands and sovereignty from the Canadian state to the Tsawwassen First Nation (TFN). Chuck Strahl, the conservative minister for Indian affairs who opened the event, called the agreement a "historical milestone . . . a tremendous achievement . . . a truly historic event" (AADNC 2007). A few months after this ceremony took place, another one was staged: this time the groundbreaking for the Tsawwassen Gateway Logistics Park.

Marketed as Canada's first successful "modern urban land treaty," and touted by the government for its landmark status in the story of a postcolonial nation, the Tsawwassen Agreement has also been subject to devastating critique by Tsawwassen band members who see it as nothing more than a contemporary colonial land grab. The Tsawwassen Agreement came into effect in 2009, but the First Nation has been fighting for sovereignty over its traditional lands for decades. The lands in question are situated in the rapidly urbanizing lower mainland of Vancouver, immediately adjacent to Delta Port—the single most important facility in the Vancouver Port Authority's portfolio. The agreement transfers a relatively small amount of land from the provincial and federal governments to the Tsawwassen First Nation: approximately 700 acres in total, but that includes 400 acres of existing reservation lands. The actual new lands in question are thus only 334 acres (Gordon 2010), along with a miniscule cash transfer of $33.6 million. A key part of the agreement stipulates that the lands will "normalize"; they will be removed from the special status occupied by reserves within the Canadian legal system. The TFN will begin to pay taxes on the land after eight years, provoking serious concerns about a permanent individualized displacement of Tsawwassen band members through market mechanisms and gentrification.

Against Port Expansion (APE), a group that is fighting the project and process, highlights the fact that there "was no environmental assessment as required by Order-In-Council 908, the B.C. Environmental Assessment Act and the Canadian Environmental Assessment Act. No fiduciary responsibility was exercised towards other First Nations who have claims to this territory." Indeed, the agreement transfers almost 3,000 acres of land from environmental protection as part of the designated Roberts Bank Wildlife Management Area to the federal government to be managed by the Vancouver Port Authority. One Tsawwassen band member, Bertha Williams (2007), an outspoken critic of the agreement, took the matter to the United Nations Special Rapporteur in attempt to expose the violence at work under the government's gloss. The treaty "means that we will lose our inherent Title and rights and become assimilated into the mainstream legal system and our lands will fall under the jurisdiction and administration of the provincial and federal government," Williams wrote. "As much as the Indian Act system was an instrument of segregation and economic marginalization of our people, at least the Indian Reserve lands were inalienable and could not be alienated by non-natives." Indeed, if the meager terms of the agreement were not alarming in themselves, a key clause in the agreement certainly gives pause. Titled "Release of past claims" (Province of British Columbia 2013), section 16 of the agreement asserts the following: "Tsawwassen First Nation releases Canada, British Columbia and all other Persons from all claims, demands, actions or proceedings, of whatever kind, whether known or unknown, that Tsawwassen First Nation ever had, now has or may have in the future, relating to or arising from any act or omission before the Effective Date that may have affected, interfered with or infringed any aboriginal right, including aboriginal title, in Canada of Tsawwassen First Nation."

Williams has also described the process behind the actual referendum on the treaty as rigged, wherein the government extended support to a faction seeking power within the community in exchange for support of the highly questionable terms of the plan. The official leadership of the TFN and the government have sidelined opposition to the agreement, and yet opposition is never fully contained; it seeps out in unexpected places. In response to a special feature on the agreement in *Canadian Geographic*, critical reader responses poured in. One local reader suggests that the agreement had little to do with indigenous sovereignty and everything to do with logistics space:

> The TFN treaty was done without proper consideration of the Semi-ahmoo First Nation treaty, the protection of our Agricultural Land Reserve, or the Environment. This is not about giving TFN its due . . . it's about expanding DeltaPort at the expense of our farmland, the Fraser River estuary, and our air quality in an area that shouldn't have been considered for a port in the first place. Tsawwassen First Nations accepted individual cash payouts from the government for signing the treaty and now we will all have to live with the blight of container sprawl on some of the best farmland and most important wildlife habitat in the world. (MacNeil 2008)

These claims about the colonial nature of the process and terms of the agreement stand in strong contrast to the official line of the Tsawwassen chief: "We are looking forward to seeing the Logistics Centre play a significant role in the transportation and supply chains" (Infrastructure Canada 2010). The struggle for the lower mainland lands, and for the story that narrates them, continues.

Logistics Cities and City Logistics

What is this thing called the logistics city? And how are urbanists accounting for its rise? There is no critical scholarship that investigates these questions. The closest thing to scholarly discourse on the topic is an applied debate in the field of business management that is actively engaged in building a distinct project known as "City Logistics." A whole field of applied research has emerged since the late 1990s, which now includes regular conferences, textbooks, and an institute dedicated to city logistics or the "City Logistics Concept." In 1999, Japanese scholar and consultant Eiichi Taniguchi formed the Institute for City Logistics in Kyoto. Taniguchi also convened the City Logistics conference—an event that is now annual—and he edits a series of conference proceedings as well as the first textbooks on the topic. According to the Institute for City Logistics, "City Logistics is the process for totally optimizing the logistics and transport activities by private companies in urban areas while considering the traffic environment, the traffic congestion and energy consumption" (Tanaguchi et al. 1999, cited in Ehmke 2012). City logistics is a response to a series of major geographic shifts, including rapid global urbanization; DHL specifically cites that 70 percent of the global population will be urban by 2050 and suggests that city logistics will ensure a prosperous urban future (DHL n.d.; Taniguchi 2012). Gentrification is also explicitly flagged by city logisticians as having created particular challenges of distribution and delivery. In many cities around the world, this entailed the return of large retailers to the inner city in the wake of postwar suburbanization, although often in new big-box form (Parlette and Cowen 2011; Wrigley and Lowe 2002), which prompts the retrofitting of infrastructure and space to make core areas auto oriented. In addition, the rise of Internet shopping places newfound distributional challenges on retailers and logistics companies in terms of the volume of delivery and complexity of distribution. If these are the forces that set the scene for the project of city logistics, then the acute problem that fuels its growth is precise: cities are ridden with forces that disrupt efficient flows. Cities have immediate problems of disruption; they are congested, making both moving and stopping difficult. For city logisticians, the political nature of cities makes them difficult to manage, and indeed, Teodor Gabriel Crainic (2006) highlights that they are rife with "labor issues" and "community issues." Finally, cities are challenging for logistics because of risks classically associated with urban space. Crainic writes, "Cities are polluted; cities are not safe." Drawing on Jean-Paul Rodrigue and Laetitia Dablanc (2013), Crainic and Benoît Montreuil (2012) offer a definition of the city that is likely one of the least inspiring in the long tradition of urban thought but that captures the managerial antipolitics of the field beautifully. These leading city logistics researchers assert that "a city can be considered as a bottleneck where transportation resources are scarce relative to the potential demand and are thus highly valuable." Echoing the basic insights of the revolution in logistics, they explain that the fundamental idea of city logistics is for logisticians to "stop considering each shipment/company/vehicle individually" but "rather as components of an integrated logistics system." City logistics is fundamentally about coordinating and consolidating shippers, carriers, and deliveries with a focus on optimizing the logistics *system*.

A field largely dedicated to computer modeling of systems, the "City Logistics Concept" is gaining momentum. Large-scale private–public partnership initiatives are under way that seek to transform how space and circulation are coupled. In 2012, Germany-based logistics company DHL initiated a major research project in partnership with the city of Chengdu, China. DHL's "City Logistics concept approach" is anchored by the "implementation of urban freight centers that significantly decrease freight traffic, increase the quality of air, improve efficiency, reliability, service quality and offer a better control of the logistic processes by a higher visibility of the supply chain" (Hartman 2012). DHL's partnership with Chengdu seeks to be "a model for other megacities in China" but also follows on the heels of the corporation's partnership with Dubai, where in 2010 they launched a major city logistics pilot project—the first of its kind outside of Germany ("Dubai FDI, DHL" 2011).

Logistics cities can be distinguished from *city logistics* in a number of ways. The latter acts on already constituted urban spaces, aiming to transform dense and congested cities into more controlled and efficient spaces of circulation, whereas the former entails the wholesale production of entirely new urban formations for that same purpose. City logistics is a piecemeal practice that acts on already established urban fabric, reconstituting it and territorializing a logistics form. On the other hand, logistics cities are master-planned spaces, standardized and purpose-built. Thus, while these two forms have similar aims in terms of the functionality of urban space, as interventions and as urban forms they are quite distinct. Yet the truly striking difference in these projects is the seemingly civilian nature of city logistics in contrast to the exceptional and often explicit military and colonial context of logistics cities. The logistics city is more than a free trade zone, combining the discipline of the military base with the exceptionality of the camp. If the export-processing zone is an exceptional zone of hyperexploitation and spatial discipline focusing on production, the logistics city is all this and more, dedicated to servicing the system of stuff in motion. Logistics cities and city logistics are two faces of the urbanization of global trade and battle space; they are the two prominent forms of urban revolution in logistics.

While scholarly debate has yet to address either city logistics or the logistics city, there is research emerging in economic and transport geography that highlights the rise of specialized urban forms within global networks that are specifically dedicated to distribution. Rodrigue, Comtois, and Slack (2009) have approached the study of logistics in this way and offer Figure 33 to account for the "material function" of cities within a transnational system. They explain how some cities have developed "a pronounced tertiary function implying that consumption accounts for the dominant share of the total goods being handled, with the functions of production and distribution (supplying local needs) assuming a more marginal role." These "consumptive cities" are supported by what they term "distributive" and "productive" cities, ironically reinscribing a distinction between distribution and production that the revolution in logistics challenges (see chapter 3). Nevertheless the distinction between forms of production as marked by manufacturing (as one form of production) and distribution (as another) is significant. Scholarship on "global" or "world" cities that first emerged in the 1980s has long made this claim (Beaverstock et al. 2000; Brenner and Keil 2005; Friedman 2000; Sassen 1991). Particular activities that were historically distributed on a much

FIGURE 33. Global city types. Source: Rodrigue, Comtois, and Slack 2009, 181.

more local scale in zones within cities are increasingly concentrated into specific global hubs that come to service transnational urban systems. Scholars like Neil Brenner and Roger Keil (2005) and R. G. Smith (2005) among many others have argued that there is not one kind of global city but a number of types. Yet within this broader global cities literature, there has been little focus on the specificities of the "distributive city" (Negrey, Osgood, and Goetzke 2011) or on the broader transformations associated with the rise of logistics. As Negrey, Osgood, and Goetzke (2011, 812) explain, a concern for the distributive city "shifts the analysis away from the commonplace focus on finance and producer services to a different industry and global function, namely distribution . . . a different representation of a world city hierarchy and network emerges." Accounting for the distributive city is important not only because of the particular functions these places hold in global supply chains but also because of the particular class structure, social ordering, and political struggles that constitute these cities. Negrey, Osgood, and Goetzke (2011, 828) explain that the occupational structure of distributive cities is "unlike that of major world cities," in that it does not suggest a "dual city" (Mollenkopf and Castells 1991) form. Rather, they suggest that the "social structure as a distributive world city remains similar to that of some 50 years ago," in that it has a "small percentage of professional, managerial and technical occupations and a high proportion of working class occupations." The particular contours of class and social ordering are profoundly important for making sense of the diversity of struggles that characterize the standardization of global supply chains in the context of acutely uneven development (Parlette and Cowen 2011; Smith 1984; Tsing 2009).

Logistics has not simply reshaped cities that specialize in the circulation of stuff, however. The revolution in logistics underpins the dramatic transformation of the global space economy since the 1960s in such a way that production, distribution, and consumption are not only located in different places but organized in profoundly changed ways through networks of so-called global cities. The form these spheres assume is sometimes blurred and elsewhere disaggregated; they would be unrecognizable to an analyst, worker, consumer, or manager of an earlier era. With the rise of the "big box"—the retail form that dominates the field in terms of growth—competitive edge comes precisely from the blurring of distribution and consumption. The novelty of the big-box store is in its transformation of the warehouse into the showroom. On the other hand, production itself has been systematized, broken into component parts, and distributed into complex geographical arrangements. The factory is superseded by the supply chain; the factory is now "stretched" across a highly uneven economic and political geography (as explored in chapter 3; Bonacich 2005; Fishman 2006; Hernandez 2003; Spector 2005), exploiting and producing difference (Tsing 2009) around the world.

Circulation and the City

There is newfound interest in the ways that circulation is urbanized, not simply in the shape that transport takes in the city, but in how mobility constitutes particular forms of urban space and urban life (Hall 2007; Hesse 2008; Hesse and Rodrigue 2006; Negrey, Osgood, and Goetzke 2011). An applied approach to these questions has emerged in the fields of transport and economic geography since the late 1990s. This work looks specifically to logistics as a force creating profound challenges for the city and the contemporary city as a reality creating profound challenges for logistics. Markus Hesse (2008) hints at the powerful transformations that the rise of logistics has entailed for cities, though he does not mark the revolution in logistics as a turning point. Without naming this historical event as such, he does however highlight the effects of the revolution in terms of the shift in the power of logistics from a residual to a defining feature of the organization of space. He highlights the ways in which logistics "increasingly follows a distinct logic, likely to influence related parts of manufacturing or retail, rather than being determined by the place and the time of production or distribution" (2). Hesse and Rodrigue (2004, 171) suggest the scale of change implied in a focus on logistics when they write that "new modes of production are concomitant with new modes of distribution, which brings forward the realm of logistics; the science of physical distribution." For them, this is not simply a change in the location of these activities but in the more profound questions (which nonetheless imply the former) of how these activities take place. Centrally important in the rise of the logistical city is the remaking of urban spatial form. Indeed, the city has been systematized and networked, and "the spatial fix-point of the organization of everyday life is no longer the city centre, but are the individually shaped networks of activities which may stretch over the entire urban region and beyond" (Hesse 2008, 18). Scholars working on the contemporary geographies of logistics have traced the increasingly global networks and metrics that define contemporary cities, insisting that urban status and form must be understood in terms of a city's position and role in transnational logistical networks (Sheppard 2002, 324; Hesse 2010, 88).

Yet it is striking that the vast majority of recent attention to logistics in applied and scholarly urban work is characterized by an exclusive focus on the civilian. Authors might make mention of the historical role of logistics as a military art, but beyond that they usually presume an entirely civilian context and practice. This civilian story circulates despite the fact that logistics' military history was transformed rather than terminated over the last century (see chapter 1). The birth of business logistics was never a purely civilian affair, and to interpret it as such misses its meaning. The revolution in logistics should not be interpreted as a "civilianization" of the field. If the art of logistics came to drive geopolitical military strategy and tactics in the early twentieth century, today market models of economic space have increasingly come to drive the science of logistics across the blurring bounds of military and civilian domains (Allen 1997; Levinson 2006; Miller Davis 1974; Reifer 2004; Spencer 1967).

With the privatization of warfare of the last three decades, there has furthermore been a rapid march of corporate logisticians and firms onto the battlefield, most of whom were born out of training and institutional networks in "public" military logistics, as we saw with Peregrine and the GGLC. Indeed, an inventory of the current entanglement of corporate and military logistics would see not only military forces clearing the way for private logistics companies in logistics cities but the latter actively supporting the former, too. Logistics is one of the most heavily privatized areas of contemporary warfare. This is nowhere more the case than in U.S. military bases in Iraq and Afghanistan, where private companies are contracted to do much of the feeding and housing of troops. The notorious KBR has held the largest contracts with the U.S. military in Iraq for feeding and housing soldiers under the program that initiated the privatization of war in the United States, the Logistics Civil Augmentation Program (Holan 2010; SIGIR 2010; U.S. Department of the Army 2012). Brown Root Services (now KBR) was the first company awarded a contract under the program when it was initiated in 1985. There is furthermore a rapid circulation of personnel between public and private organizations in this area. Logisticians in the armed forces often end up in the private sector, but some military logisticians move precisely to facilitate the shifting of contracts. For instance, Supreme Foodservice, a logistics company that holds contracts for food provision with the U.S. military in Afghanistan, hired the former director of the Defense Logistics Agency (the unit that handles logistics for all the services) just prior to having a large contract renewed without competitive bid (Hegseth 2013; Wouters 2008).

This corporate–military cooperation is not so much concealed as unspoken and certainly unproblematized in the technical and antipolitical discourses of business management (Cahlink 2003; Carrico 2006; Georgi, Darkow, and Kotzab 2010; Maccagnan 2004; Skipper et al. 2008). There is no better example of this logic than in DHL's framing of its own work in warfare. The web page for DHL's "Warfighter Support" explains, "Being a market leader is all about combining agility and power to provide a complete service for our customers. Anywhere you need your shipment to be, we have the capability to get it there." DHL, also a leader in the city logistics movement, thus frames warfare work as a matter of providing good customer service, exculpating itself from the messiness of politics and violence. The image and motto that appears on their web page marketing these services performs this stance of being essential to defense work while being outside of politics. "Our mission is supporting theirs," the bold red type on DHL's gold background insists. The word "supporting" is emphasized, and the text is sharply separated from the image of the soldier above, providing a spatial metaphor for the work of DHL in literally underpinning the soldier. Indeed, as DHL asserts, the firm was "not only a pioneer in international shipping, DHL Express was the first express carrier to service all US Department of Defense theaters worldwide." DHL further explains that they "constantly monitor world events to spot crisis situations that may impact your shipment because DHL has the staff and equipment to manage those that occur. Worry free shipping to any region of the world; that's our foreign policy." This playful deployment of "foreign policy" again highlights the distanced, technical, and antipolitical role that DHL assumes in relation to its war work, even as they invoke a sacred domain of modern statecraft.

No doubt, there is a growing body of work that explores the rise of a "new military urbanism" (Graham 2010), the powerful architectures of urban warfare (Weizman 2006), the violent contours of "urbicide" (Coward 2008; Graham 2003; Gregory and Pred 2007; Kipfer and Goonewardena 2007; Ramadan 2009; Shaw 2004), and broadly, the everyday life of urban geopolitics (Graham 2004; Graham and Shaw 2008). The best of this work addresses the entanglement of this military urbanism with the politics and geographies of global trade. For example, Stephen Graham (2010, 77) asserts that "globally the new military urbanism is being mobilized for the securing of the strung-out commodity chains, logistics networks, and corporate enclaves that constitute the neoliberal geo-economic architectures of our planet." There is widespread recognition of the broad entanglements of markets and militaries, yet the specific domain of logistics is typically only mentioned in passing rather than treated as a key vector for these shifting boundaries. Logistics doesn't even earn an entry in the indexes of any of the key books in these debates. This is in part a feature of a persistent assumption that infuses much contemporary scholarship: that this entanglement is defined by the work of militaries and warfare in protecting trade, rather than an interrogation of the shared forms of calculation and common logics that underpin military and civilian urban operations. There is a tendency to reproduce the modern binary of military/civilian and public/private violence, even as it is being questioned or contested.

There are however some exceptions that approach the city less in terms of civilian space of commerce becoming militarized and more as a deeply contested space that is shaped by historically specific relations of coercion (both military and civilian) that are particularly concerned with the politics of circulation. This is evident in historical work where scholars have taken a longer lens on these questions and examined the city in relation to questions of mobility and flow in such a way that does not presume a distinction between urban political economies and urban geopolitics. The city has long been a key architecture of circulation, as it has also variously been a major obstacle to circulation. This is not simply to assert that transportation of various kinds has been definitive in terms of the rise of particular urban forms—be it canals, rail, ports, or more recently airports. It is well established that the initial build out of cities, as well as their future growth or decline, is often contingent on particular forms of connectivity that have lasting effects. The rise of Chicago as a key hub in massive rail networks was crucial for its historical development, and it remains essential to national, continental, and global flows today (see Hesse 2008, 15; Hesse and Rodrigue 2004, 173). Economic geographers are less likely to emphasize that this rise of Chicago through the expansion of rail networks was key in the genocidal movement westward of European settlers in North America. And yet, the vibrant and growing body of scholarship on the colonial city inevitably emphasizes this point. The city has long been a machine (Isin 2002, 2004) of social order and economic exchange; the space of circulation assumes both.

It is in scholarship on nineteenth-century Paris that some of the best insights about the urban geopolitical economies of circulation come into focus. Baron Von Haussmann's dramatic intervention in the physical form of the city was vital to the French Empire and the birth of modernity more broadly. Indeed, David Harvey (2003, 102) insists that the remaking of the "interior" space of Paris was coupled with the integration of French national space. He suggests that the transformation of what he calls "external space relations" put "intense pressure on the thrust to rationalize the interior space of Paris itself" and asserts that this is precisely what has made Haussmann's exploits into "great legends of modernist urban planning." Matthew Gandy (1999, 27) also emphasizes the urgency of the transformation of the physical structure of Paris in the 1850s as key to the changing role of the city within the newly integrated national economy. Most striking is the massive national expansion of rail infrastructure that took shape in France between the 1850s and 1890s. During this time, the network expanded from "a few strands of rail here and there in 1850," as Harvey (2003, 105) explains, "to an intricate web of some 17,400 kilometers in 1870" (see Figure 34, drawn from his discussion). Harvey notes that the volume of trade expanded at twice the rate of industrial output after it shifted to rail, with the effect of opening up "Parisian industry and commerce to interregional and international competition." This

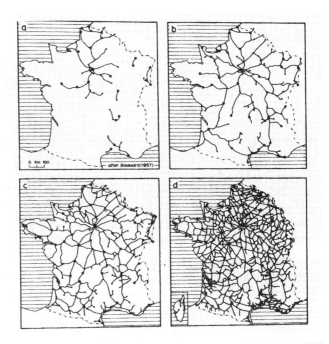

FIGURE 34. The expansion of the rail network in France, 1850–90. (a) 1850, (b) 1860, (c) 1870, (d) 1890. Source: Harvey 2003, republished with permission of Taylor and Francis Group LLC; permission conveyed through Copyright Clearance Center Inc.

infrastructural integration was critical in the making of national territory, identity, and economy, and yet, as a powerful and ambitious empire,
France was central in building not only a national economy but also the
global economy of the nineteenth century. France financed megaprojects like the Suez Canal, which remains at the center of global corporate
and military logistics today and marks the vast scale of the transport and
communications system laid out between 1850 and 1870 "that was to
be the foundation of a new world market and a new international division of labor" (Harvey 2003, 104). Haussmann was given extraordinary
powers directly from Napoleon in 1853, and he boldly exercised that
authority in a massive campaign of creative destruction. He introduced
the notion of a general plan to replace piecemeal planning in an effort to
rationalize and rescale planning to the city as a whole. He created new
institutional forms—hierarchical territorial administration that aimed to
govern the city in its entirety. Harvey explains how "urban space was
seen and treated as a totality in which different quarters of the city and
different functions were brought into relation to each other to form a
working whole," and others concur that a defining feature of modern
planning Haussmann introduced was its comprehensive and "total"
approach (Papayanis 2004, 247). Crucial to this new way of seeing and
governing the city was the map. Indeed, immediately upon his appoint-
ment, Haussmann undertook a detailed survey and triangulation of the
city and produced the first accurate cadastral and topographical map
of Paris (Gandy 1999; Harvey 2003, 107). He did so by first establish-
ing a department of the "Plan de Paris," which installed wooden towers
throughout the city that reached taller than the surrounding buildings and
allowed for surveyors to triangulate their points. The map produced from
this process was large and detailed; Haussmann kept a copy at the scale
of 1:5,000, which measured 9 by 15 feet, on a rolling stand in his office,
and smaller versions were distributed to city departments and the public
(see British Library Map Exhibition n.d.). Haussmann's specific interventions in Paris are well known: he plowed broad boulevards through the
dense and crowded streets of the city, destroying whole sectors of the
urban fabric and displacing thousands, with the goal of social control and
infrastructural modernization. His boulevards deliberately fractured the
networks and spaces of working-class organizing and aimed to preempt
future uprisings.

For Eyal Weizman (2006), Haussmann remains a crucial figure, but
one who needs to be understood more specifically in relation to the "boomerang" effect of colonial violence (Cesaire [1950] 1972; Foucault [1997]

2003) and the circulations of violent strategies of rule from colony to metropole. Weizman draws our attention to the fact that Haussmann implemented plans for Paris that had been developed elsewhere; it was colonial battlespace in Algeria that provided the template for violent reforms in Paris. Marshal Thomas Bugeaud, leader of the French forces in Algeria in 1840, found himself in a losing battle despite having a massive force of one hundred thousand to the Algerians' ten thousand. Weizman explains that he "managed to regain control over Algiers's dense Kasbahs only after destroying entire neighborhoods, in reprisals for guerrilla attacks, and breaking the resistance by cutting routes through the neighborhoods where insurgents were hiding. In the process Bugeaud reshaped the city, making it more manoeuvrable for the military. This was among the first instances in which demolition was used as a means of military urban planning." Upon his return from the violent campaigns in Algiers, Bugeaud authored a manual, *La Guerre des Rues et des Maison,* which Weizman calls "the first manual for the preparation and conduct of urban warfare." An avid reader of Bugeaud, Haussmann's reforms applied many of his lessons, as they aimed to open up the narrow and congested streets of the city to the deployment of state security forces. This engagement with Paris as a logistical space challenges a geopolitical vision that would naturalize national territoriality and instead insists on an imperial cartography where power travels vast distances but as part of particular geographies of rule. Shattering simple spatial assumptions also disrupts the presumed distinction between markets and militaries.

The Logistics City and the Logistical City

While the specific rise of the logistics city is recent, the violence of imperial trade is clearly not new to the city, and vice versa. Urban space has long been profoundly implicated in the imperial politics of circulation and remains so today, as both Haussmann's Paris of the nineteenth century and Dubai's Logistics City of the twenty-first suggest. In each place and time, the ordering of urban space and the remaking of the city through spectacular megaprojects are a vital part of a supranational geopolitical economy of moving people and things. Both relied on the authoritarian power to remake the city by stealth, and both interventions introduced visions for urban space that set important precedents for the production of space elsewhere. As we have seen, maps and plans were also important to each intervention. Haussmann's violent remaking of Parisian urban form could only proceed once a detailed map of the city had been constructed. The map became vital to envisioning the city and planning its transformation but also to executing control over people and places. Haussmann's map was thus not simply a way of representing the city but a technology for its management and reconstruction. Likewise, the mapping and planning of the contemporary logistics city—be it in Dubai or Basra—play this kind of active role in the making of space.

Plans play a powerful role in the making of urban space; they render new political forms, concretizing something virtual and helping to constitute it as actual. While these forms of spatial representation can never produce the order and certainty to which they aspire, they are nevertheless powerful tools for acting on and ordering life. For Lefebvre (1991), the work of elite actors in crafting models and representations of space—"conceived space"—is vital to the production of lived space. In a well-worn passage, he asserts, "Representations of space are certainly abstract," but they also "play a part in social and political practice" (41). Perhaps most important for Lefebvre, "Representations of space are shot through with a knowledge (*savoir*)—i.e. a mixture of understanding and ideology." Margo Huxley (2006) also emphasizes the importance of plans when she argues that we should not dismiss them as "expressions of naive or mistaken spatial or environmental determinisms," as they play "an important part in shaping practices of regulation and management of the urban." Stuart Elden (2001, 145–50; see also Huxley 2007, 194) further argues that plans and diagrams "serve as models, tests and ongoing aims against which programmes of government are evaluated and adjusted, with the continuous (but seldom attained) aspiration that reality can be made to conform to the truth of these schemes."

Planning urban space thus has its parallel in the mapping of the labor process discussed in chapter 3; in each case, mapping mobility, be it through the form of the city or the movement of commodities and workers' bodies, is fundamental to managing circulation. Management, especially supply chain management, requires the map. But if the technology of mapping was as important for Haussmann as it is for the DLC, is there anything specific to be gleaned in the plans for logistics cities? Plans for urban space are crucial in assembling governing visions and practices, and from time to time, a plan emerges that captures something particularly revealing of shifting political rationalities. Foucault (2007, 61) declares that he wants to examine "spaces of security" as vital to the constitution of changing political forms, and he immediately asserts, "Obviously, I will look at the case of towns." For Foucault, master plans for urban space are fragments that allow us to examine changing forms of political rule, from sovereignty to discipline to security. Looking to a series of historical plans for urban space, Foucault asserts that sovereignty literally "capitalizes a territory, raising the major problem of the seat of government, whereas discipline structures a space and addresses the essential problem of a hierarchical and functional distribution of elements, and security will try to plan a milieu in terms of events or series of events or possible elements of series that will have to be regulated within a multivalent and transformable framework." As Elden (2007, 564) asserts, "The spatial distribution for sovereignty, discipline, and security is equally important but differently organized." Melinda Cooper (2008) suggests that Foucault's account of the rise of urbanism is promising because it focuses "on circulation rather than the localization of power, but also because it suggests a genealogy of the event and its relationship to infrastructure." Indeed, across these different space-times of government, "the problem of the town was essentially one of circulation." This problem of circulation is central to the whole enterprise of logistics, and the fact that it is conceptualized not as an element of urban form but as an urban form unto itself is indicative of the building of Dubai Logistics City as a significant event. DLC is a reflection of the rise of logistics over the past few decades from a residual to a leading concern of business strategy and a part of institutionalizing logistics at the core of globalized production, trade, and security.

If the power of circulation in the making of urban space has such a long history, the rise of the logistics city also marks crucial transitions. In other words, the *logistics city* exposes dramatic shifts in the *logistical city*. Martin Coward (2009) has offered some particularly thoughtful reflections on the specific ways in which contemporary warfare targets the city in contrast to the long history of military targeting of infrastructure, which was at times also urban. His insights are prescient for making sense of the specificity of contemporary urbanism vis-à-vis global violence. "Historically, the targeting of urban infrastructures might be seen as independent of the relation between those infrastructures and urbanity itself," he writes (409). Yet he argues that contemporary urban war "represents a distinctive attempt to disrupt urbanity through the destruction of that substrate which is central to contemporary cities: critical infrastructure." Coward argues that critical infrastructure is not simply *located in* the contemporary city but *constitutive of* contemporary urbanity. He writes that conceptualizing "contemporary urbanization as a network (which is defined by relationality and connectivity) revolves around a representation of the technical systems of critical infrastructure as a distinctive feature of contemporary existence" (409). He argues that urbanism today must be understood as "metropolitanization," which "comprises the emergence of multicentred assemblages predicated on interconnective technical systems." The relationship between the attack on infrastructure and the city are defining features of contemporary violence rather than merely contingent, as they have been in the past.

"Occupied" Cities

Both the *logistics city* as a specific project of select corporations and states and the *logistical city* as a broader urban moment in "supply chain capitalism" (cf. Tsing 2009) highlight the increasing global integration of urban space into managed networks of goods circulation underpinning both trade and warfare. As service centers to the world's container traffic, they are also built in its image; the standardization of space, movement, and infrastructure is the guiding design logic. But this urban form is not only material; it is also—through this materiality—centrally political. Efficient movement, an economy of space and time, becomes antipolitics. The replacement of objectives with efficiency is the tyranny of techne.

Standardization and authoritarian forms of management mark these cities; however, diverse forms of resistance and refusal also define the form. Logistics cities and logistical cities manage flows, but they also provoke disruption. In Dubai—the first logistics city—built form tells a political tale. One of these stories is spoken through the design of the "labor village." This form tells us that the reproduction of relations of production is precarious and potentially volatile. The labor village is an offer to workers of better living facilities to stem the rising tide of worker organizing, but it also establishes surveillance and isolation as a clear strategy of rule. CEO of Dubai Logistics City Michael Proffitt politely highlights this managerial thrust in the labor village, explaining that "with the community being managed and maintained directly by Dubai Logistics City, we can assure standards can be adhered to throughout" ("DLC to Build New Labor Village" 2006). The physical architecture of the DLC labor village betrays a social architecture of control in the face of struggle.

In Tsawwassen, the "lay of the land" also provides hints of the complex politics and contestations that surround the establishment of the logistics center. As the critics of the Tsawwassen Agreement that underpins the logistics center suggest, far from a peaceable postcolonial chapter in the story of Turtle Island, the Tsawwassen Logistics Centre is instead a significant new chapter in the long story of dispossession. A small group of Tsawwassen band members continue to fight the theft of land, scale jumping (Smith 1984) from this small and marginalized community to the south of Vancouver to the United Nations in order to make their claims audible. Band member Bertha Williams and others have written letters, appeared in media, spoken widely at public meetings, and participated in key events and organizations working toward indigenous sovereignty, like the annual Indigenous Sovereignty Week organized by Defenders of the Land. Williams's (2007) forceful challenge to the official story of her people's lands outlines how the treaty process aims for the "extinguishment of our Aboriginal Title and Rights and their modification into very limited treaty rights," where "within the first few years of the treaty a lot of the lands will be bought by non-natives, because the lands will now be on the open market." Williams suggests that this particular form of dispossession entails the state "gifting" land to the band in a manner that ensures that market mechanisms will be the force of displacement. The predicted loss of lands will thus appear as a failure of band members to maintain ownership despite the fact that the state engineered the conditions for dispossession through the agreement.

If one of the most powerful and globalizing forms of social protest to emerge in recent years was the "Occupy" movement, we might also say that it was in Oakland more than New York where the movement best demonstrated its capacity for analysis and action, and here the question of the port and global logistics was central. Oakland's Occupy movement builds on long traditions of radical organizing around a variety of issues, most notably antiracist and labor organizing. Referring to the Oakland port as a "Wall Street on the Water" in 2011, organizers drew connections between the dramatic decline of the city and the booming prosperity of the port. With the city facing economic crisis, the port was bankrolling revenues of $27 billion per year while operating rent free on public lands (Bady 2011). The city's financial crisis (acute enough to provoke the closure of public schools) was in part a result of Goldman Sachs's predatory lending in financing Oakland's debts (McBride 2012). Occupiers drew many lines of connection between finance capital and commodity circulation, one of the most direct connections being Goldman Sachs's majority ownership of global shipping company SSA Marine. On November 2, 2011, in a breathtaking move that drew global media attention, a few thousand protesters managed to bring one of the largest ports in North America to a complete halt. Once again in December 2011, but this time with a chorus of other West Coast port cities in tow, Occupy Oakland occupied the port.

In each of these events, through radically different means, protesters contest a particular form of logistics city or logistical city. These and other episodes of resistance and refusal are often invisible to a broader public; they are often made invisible by corporate media. Landscape can furthermore conceal as much as reveal; the lay of the land often becomes the *lie* of the land, as Don Mitchell (1996) reminds us. But the fact that many acts of contestation to the global logistics city remain localized, disconnected from each other, and without the capacity to remake the city in their own image diagnoses only a moment, not a condition. The obstacles to coalition are gargantuan, not only in practical terms of distance, language, and capacity, but even more so in terms of the fraught and fragile politics of solidarity across race, class, status, sexuality, gender, and location. Yet in this new logistical imperialism, the occupation of the city remains a question of not only which "citizens" (human, commodity, or corporate) occupy but whether indeed acts of urban citizenship can produce a city *after occupation*.

Rough Trade?

Sex, Death, and the
Queer Nature of Circulation

Figure 35 captures one moment in the extraordinary migration of the pronghorn antelope. Taking the longest trek of any land mammal in the United States, their migration follows the western mountain range. Increasingly treacherous as a result of human development and enclosure, their fraught migration has led the population of pronghorn to plummet to only 158 animals. This scene of seasonal circulation is captured in a major recent National Geographic production titled *Great Migrations*. The series explains that the precarious life of the pronghorn rests on the protection of their mobility. In fact, this is the recurring theme of the program across the hundreds of species and seven continents it surveys—that life itself relies on circulation, captured boldly in the show's motto: "Move or Die." National Geographic calls *Great Migrations* "its most ambitious programming initiative to date," with the effort to collect footage "the most arduous undertaking in the 122-year history of the National Geographic Society" (National Geographic 2010). The show premiered in 2010 in 330 million homes, 166 countries, and 34 languages. A hefty three-hundred-page coffee-table book with color photos and extended text serves as the official companion to the global television event. The text is a sensational mixture of science and fiction, quite literally; the descriptions of mating and migrating are mixed with the words of explorers and poets from the high period of European imperialism. The series offers a thrilling four-part romp through a ruthless, often violent, deeply racialized, social Darwinist world defined by necropolitics and reproductive heteronormativity. The individual episodes, like the book chapters, carry the titles "Born to Move," "Need to Breed," "Race to Survive," and "Feast or Famine." Like most nature shows of this genre,

FIGURE 35. Pronghorn antelope migration, 2009. Source: Photograph by Drew Rush/National Geographic Creative.

Great Migrations often hovers on the edge of gruesome: one species grabbing another with outstretched teeth or claws and ripping open flesh or one species hunting then eating the young of another. Yet distinct from similar scenes in the established archive of nature shows is the framing of this violence as a *problem of disruption*. As the online social gaming companion to the National Geographic series (*MOVE!*) suggests, "With potential risks looming at every turn—from unforgiving terrain to ferocious predators—the decision to keep moving or stop to graze could be one of life or death."

Great Migrations's narrative of the survivalist imperative to circulation is a story of not only animal migration but also trade flows. It is not just the species of the natural world that must keep circulating; capital, too, must move or die, and thus commodities must keep in motion. The connection drawn between animal migrations and trade flows is direct. In fact, the United Parcel Service (UPS) provided the major corporate sponsorship for the series as part of their dramatic recent rebranding initiative (Miller 2012). Rich Goldfarb, the vice president of media sales for National Geographic, explains how the partnership with UPS worked specifically "to create an association between animal migratory behavior and the logistics that allow UPS to unfailingly ship millions of packages around the globe" (Crupi 2010b). He continues, highlighting how the

UPS "emphasis on logistics proved to be a great contextual fit with what *Great Migrations* is all about. It was sort of a marriage made in heaven." In the UPS partnership with National Geographic, logistics becomes the bloody ripping flesh of one species eating another in order to move and survive. This "nonhuman" story of logistics is animated by procreative sex and gruesome death. "Move or Die" is the story of *logistics at war*.

But the sponsorship of *Great Migrations* is only one side of the massive UPS campaign. A second thread tells a very different tale, anchored in images of happy singing workers and consumers united in their love for efficient goods movement. In the civilian story of logistics, UPS promises its audience the ordering of chaos and the satisfaction of deep consumer desire. The UPS marketing campaign brings logistics out of the background and into center stage. It aims centrally at expanding corporate sales and normalizing global sourcing and supply but also at cultivating affect for logistics' logics. The art and science of logistics is presented not only as efficient but also as *lovable*.

Like the field of logistics more broadly, the UPS "We ♥ Logistics" campaign is impossible to ignore because of its massive scale. Logistics is big. According to industry estimates, it involves $8 trillion in global economic activity and nearly $1.3 trillion of trade just within the United States (Miller 2012). The ad campaign is also marked by its scale; it emerged out of a $200 million contract that UPS signed with New York–based firm Ogilvy & Mather in 2009 involving "tightly integrated media of every kind; television, print, online, outdoor, radio, special events, targeted sponsorships, and social media" (Ogilvy 2012). This coordination of flows across multiple platforms and media mirrors the actual intermodal assemblage of contemporary global supply chain management. Advertising Director Betsy Wilson describes "We ♥ Logistics" as "more than an advertising campaign, it's really a global communications platform" (quoted in Dickens 2010).

Both the corporate identity of logistics and the specific image of this technoscientific assemblage presented in the campaign are worth scrutinizing. Beyond the scale and complexity of global logistics, the campaign also renders its defining political logics: the rationalization of space—the reduction of complexity into a singular system of order and the simultaneous privatization, standardization, and commodification of matter. Yet in "splitting the screen" of circulation between the corporate world of commodity flows and the natural territory of animal migration, the UPS campaign inserts a profoundly social Darwinist politics of species survivalism deep into the "♥" of the human life of logistics. Rather than segregate these scenes and their respective affective logics, the dual UPS campaign underscores their profound entanglement. This is no simple story of a warring Hobbesian nature overwhelming a civilized/civilian logistics. As I have insisted throughout this book, the revolution in logistics is not a story of the militarization of trade but of a much more complicated coproduction of corporate and military calculation and space. In fact, the logic of "Move or Die" is already interspecies; it animates recent (decidedly human) efforts to secure the circulation of trade and the growing entanglement of military and civilian logistics.

This concluding chapter interrogates these campaigns—their political logics and political geographies—engaging debates about more-than-human worlds and the complicated role they play in producing very human futures. Taken together, the "We ♥ Logistics" and "Move or Die" threads of the campaign offer important insight into the biopolitical, necropolitical, and antipolitical renderings of logistics space. I argue that the stakes in this crossing of the human and nonhuman worlds are profound; it marks the reorganization of the everyday and the exceptional in the social and spatial ordering of war and peace. The politics of "Move or Die" inhabit the forms of futurity produced by logistics space. The logistics love that is also anchored in the survivalist politics of "Move or Die" animates an emerging new normal of sex, death, and empire and new cartographies of the political. Connecting back to themes raised in the introductory chapter and encountered throughout the book, this concluding chapter explores visions of violence and desire in the social and spatial assembly of logistics space while highlighting queer paths toward alternative futures—even alternative economies—of rough trade.

We ♥ Logistics

"We ♥ Logistics" was launched in 2010 by a television ad that aired in myriad countries and dozens of languages. A $30 billion enterprise that handled more than eighteen million shipments per day in 2011, UPS launched this massive campaign as part of their efforts to compete globally, especially with DHL and FedEx. The commercial spot defines the broader campaign in terms of style and imagery: happy workers and consumers and high technology integrate seamlessly around a complex transnational logistical network. The screen is constantly in motion, guided by a thick golden arrow that sprouts from the text of the UPS logo and travels the world, leading a smooth cargo flow. Distinct locales are traversed: New York City, Venice, Paris, as well as some generic logistics landscapes—distribution centers, highways, and ports of unknown address. Images of unspecified Chinese urban spaces flash across the screen. UPS workers sing and UPS customers smile. Parcels move, barcodes are scanned, vehicles of all kinds connect—planes, trains, and automobiles, but also bicycles, cargo ships, and even Venetian gondolas. Scenes of factory production lines are seamlessly interspersed with those of supply lines, marking a central lesson from the revolution in logistics: that production is merely one element in a broader system of circulation.

The most striking aspect of the ad is undoubtedly the soundtrack; the tune of Dean Martin's "That's Amore" starts immediately after the opening shot of a young, white, able-bodied male donning signaling gear on a tarmac, proudly announcing, "Logistics makes the world work better." The UPS version of the 1940s classic offers a different set of lyrics; in place of Dean Martin we are given the distinctively young and feminine voice of singer Nadia Ackerman. The singing voice narrates the globetrotting thirty-second spot, and the ad ends with a girlish vision of a young white woman excitedly embracing her UPS delivery man as he hands her a package, at once attributing the singing voice to the event of consumer affect and assigning it to the domain of feminine consumption.

For all the newness presented in UPS's brief glance at global logistics, old gendered tropes of feminine consumption persist, while the labor that makes logistics space circulate is largely male, highly segmented, and

FIGURE 36. UPS advertisement: "We ♥ Logistics." Source: Copyright 2013 United Parcel Service of America Inc. All rights reserved.

deeply racialized. Yet from the vantage point of the industry, even producers have become consumers of outsourced third-party logistics providers,
thus the complex feminization of logistics in the ad is not restricted to
consumption in any simple sense. As chapter 1 explores in some detail,
the logistics revolution has seen the rise of distributors over manufacturers (Aoyama and Ratick 2007; Bonacich 2005), blurring the line between
production and circulation.

FIGURE 37A–B. Screenshots from a UPS television commercial. Source: Copyright
2013 United Parcel Service of America Inc. All rights reserved.

The ad's song lyrics highlight these and other trends and are worth quoting in their entirety:

> When it's planes in the sky for a chain of supply
> That's logistics
> When the pipes for the line come precisely on time
> That's logistics
> A continuous link that is always in sync
> That's logistics
> Carbon footprint's reduced, bottom line gets a boost
> That's logistics
> With new ways to compete there will be cheers on Wall Street
> That's logistics
> When technology knows right where everything goes
> That's logistics
> Bells will ring, ring-a-ding
> Ring-a-ding, ring-a-ding
> That's logistics
> There will be no more stress 'cause you called UPS
> That's logistics

With its reference to transportation infrastructures, just-in-time production techniques, systematic synchronicity and efficiency, and "green" cost savings, the segment provides a sketch of the corporate *fantasy* of logistics. The campaign emphasizes two central lessons. First, it aims to define logistics for a broad public audience. As UPS explains in their winning submission to the Effie advertising awards, "A survey of customers had revealed that even the people that do logistics for a living all defined it differently. So we defined it for them." The corporation did not pull any punches; their sweeping definition highlights the vitality of logistics: "*Logistics is the force that enables the modern economy*" (Ogilvy & Mather 2012). Logistics makes markets live, and UPS is the corporation that ♥s that biopolitical force.

The corporate branding of logistics—at once the redefinition of UPS and the logistics that it loves—is the second lesson of the commercial. The branding is clearly rendered in the preceding print advertisement: the ordering of chaos in the upper end of the panel occurs in tandem with the emergence of the UPS brand along the bottom of the frame. These two acts—defining the contours of logistics and the corporation—are presented as one, and this is a deliberate effect of the campaign design. In their video submission to the Effie awards, UPS explains how the campaign's success was in simultaneously redefining logistics and redefining its corporate image: "Let's say you're respected, you're admired, you're liked. But you stand for something that most people think is boring. Old. That is—shipping." After quoting Jim Casey, the founder of UPS, in his claim that "anyone can deliver a package," the video defines the discursive challenge: "You're UPS. And what you do is actually very sophisticated. It requires billions of dollars of investment in technology. Huge amounts of innovation and creativity. Is so incredibly complex that it makes your brain hurt. How do you make it simple? Simple enough that people will get it. But powerful enough that it will change the way people think about you. The answer? It's not shipping. It's logistics." Further marking the contours of this attachment, logistics is presented as not simply a vital management science but also *a good*. The video asserts the artistic and scientific dimensions of logistics, again emphasizing its globality. "Everybody loves something. We love logistics. We love its precision, its epic scale, its ability to make life better for billions of people. Each day, our customers count on us to choreograph a ballet of infinite complexity played across skies, oceans and borders. And we do. What's not to love?" Like the actual assemblage of logistics as a management science and a complex set of physical and informational infrastructures, the advertisement renders the simultaneous decentralization and centralization under way in the industry. If "industrial discipline" or the scientific management of production entailed "the breaking down of a given factory practice into micro-movements, and the streamlining of these movements for greater efficiency and centralized management control" (De Landa 2005, 120), it also was a process of reducing the complexity of acts and motions of individual workers while increasing the complexity of the total production system by rescaling coordination and control to the production line. The fantasy of choreography and the creative craftwork of ballet alluded to thus underdescribes the vast networks of surveillance and control that define the industry. Logistics has shed its history as an art to become a highly standardized and mechanized management science organized by electronic and digital surveillance and heavy securitization. And as Anja Kanngieser (2013, 598) writes, the "calibration of technologies" in the sector monitors not only the flow of goods in supply chains but "the workers and machines that move them." Kanngieser argues that the tracking and tracing of laboring bodies in the logistics industry through radio frequency identification, the extended monitoring networks of GPS telematics, and the implementation of voice picking in warehouses involve the "technological extension of governance onto the registers of bodily movement and expression." The tracking of movement of the laboring body is hardly a new development. As chapter 3 illustrates, managing the laboring body—and making the laboring body's movements visible to management—have been at the core of industrial discipline at least since the birth of scientific management. Nevertheless, there has been a massive expansion of efforts to track the laboring body and profound developments in the nature of tracking technologies that implicate not only the intimacy of surveillance but so too the mechanics of power in which they are embedded (cf. Foucault 1977). Kanngieser (2013, 596) is particularly interested in the emergence of tools like Google's "Map Coordinate," which allows employers to track mobile employees in real time. These and other technologies of "electronic governance," she suggests, act "to redefine and normalise behavior, displac[ing] traditional disciplinary control" (see also Catá Backer 2008). Kanngieser elaborates on the effects of these "bio-techno-disciplinary techniques," specifically emphasizing how they are refining the spatial and temporal existence of bodies, what Foucault referred to as the "temporal elaboration of the act," through a "positive economy" of time that seeks the "intensification and maximisation of efficiencies."

Perhaps most interesting is the way in which the advert presents core elements of the dramatic recasting of economic geography and spatial calculation of the revolution in logistics. "It wasn't long ago that the most important rule of business was 'location is everything.' If you had location in your favor, you were more or less protected against competitors of every shape and size. Things are different now. Business is global in a way we could only imagine ten years ago. Markets are everywhere and new ones open constantly. Suppliers shift, supply chains adapt. And location has been supplanted by a new force in business: logistics." It is far too simple (and not entirely coherent) to suggest that location has been supplanted by logistics. Yet while *geography* has hardly lost its importance in an era of global logistics, it is has indeed changed. Logistics relies heavily on complex calibrations of multiple locations, but the advertisement is on target insofar as trade is less defined by location in the simple or singular sense of the production facility and more by coordination across networks and systems (see chapter 1). It is in this sense—in its bold declaration of the arrival of supply chain capitalism (Tsing 2009) and its distinct spatialities—that the UPS campaign offers more than just a sales pitch. The campaign captures dramatic shifts that have taken place with the rise of a civilian science of logistics and invests them with an affective intensity. UPS is not only interested in the "peaceful" politics of logistics love, however. In highly coded terms, the corporation is also profoundly attuned to the logistics of war.

Move or Die

The *Great Migrations* thread of UPS's advertising campaign looks very different from its musical commercial. In this part of the campaign, the human joy of efficient cargo circulation is replaced with the life or death nonhuman struggle for species survival through migration. Violence does not appear as a problem in itself but only insofar as it disrupts the immediate physical circulation of a species *or* the generational cycling of the species and so its future mobility. The show narrates how interspecies violence, while natural in itself, nevertheless disrupts the fundamental imperative to keep *life in motion*, thus recursively fueling further migrations. The violence of disruption is both a threat to circulation and a force prompting circulation. There is thus no avoiding violence; disruption must be anticipated such that survival figures as a matter of *resilience*.

Deliberate or not, the title gestures at a different "Great Migration"—the movement of African Americans from the rural south to the northeastern industrial cities in the early to mid-twentieth century—and so at the history of internal colonialism. And while *Great Migrations* does not portend to tell a directly human tale, as we will see, it nevertheless narrates the politics of race, reproduction, and empire.

Great Migrations not only brings the natural world of nonhuman life to a large human audience; the transmedia event was in fact launched in the urban center of the American Empire. New York City was temporarily transformed into a space of circulation of a whole different kind, with the aim of juxtaposing and so contrasting nonhuman and capital mobilities and also perhaps naturalizing both. National Geographic executives comment not only on the immense scale of the *Great Migrations* launch but also on its deliberate disruption of—and entanglement in—the everyday circulation of New York City (Mustain 2010): "On an unseasonably warm October evening in Manhattan, thousands of creatures were on the move. Marching westward, they moved with purpose down 41st street, drawn by the rose-gold light of a disappearing sun—or perhaps just the Port Authority, a couple blocks away, and the promise of home. As the daily human migration proceeded outside the Times Center, inside the building life-size blow-up zebras were carefully placed, glassware was unpacked, and National Geographic Channel staff prepared for an event to highlight migrations of a more dramatic sort than most New Yorkers typically experience." This event unfolded just twelve miles southwest of the Bronx Zoo—an everyday space of nonhuman animal adventure within New York City founded by the powerful social Darwinist Madison Grant, who famously argued, "The laws of nature require the obliteration of the unfit," as he advocated "sterilization for the criminal, diseased, insane . . . and for those he termed 'worthless race types,' by which he meant Jews, blacks and indigenous peoples" (McWhorter 2010, 83). As the executives' comments suggest, the launch, as part of the broader *Great Migrations* event, aimed in part to contrast human and nonhuman migrations, thus marking their difference. *Great Migrations* had pedagogical intent, as David Hamlin, the senior producer of the series, suggests: "One of the big messages of this project is that migrations aren't just these epic global movements, they're incredibly difficult, torturous journeys that animals wage every year" (Mustain 2010). He continues to explain the story of the show: "It's about the need to feed and the need to breed" and "nature's power and the inexorable drive of life." Biologist Rory P. Wilson, the chief scientific advisor on the project, further highlights this biology lesson, pointing to one of the show's key taglines: "Move as millions, survive as one."

Yet if these comments imply that the aim or effect of the series is to hold a firm distinction between human and nonhuman circulatory worlds, the UPS sponsorship shatters this illusion. UPS executives, excited about the "marriage" and featured in the same article as the National Geographic executives quoted earlier, stated, "There's a nice alignment between the stories National Geographic Channel is telling in the Great Migration series and the particulars behind moving goods around the world every day . . . We take seriously how we associate our brand and this is a quality effort." It is not simply the brand association of logistics at stake here but the very vision of what defines the field. While UPS defined the meaning of logistics in its "We ♥ Logistics" campaign as "the force that enables the modern economy," the firm offers a different definition of logistics as part of the *Great Migrations* sponsorship. Here UPS expounds, "*Logistics is nature's way of surviving.*" Natural selection, it would seem, is a matter of logistics. These lessons are repeated over and over again in the *Great Migrations* programming; nonhuman animals survive by keeping in motion, and species survive when groups of animals remain in motion and reproduce themselves for future migrations—mammals, reptiles, birds, and even single cell organisms. *Life itself must move or die.*

The Birds and the Bees

Taking a closer look at the UPS campaign reveals how nature's survival through logistics relies on the naturalization of reproductive heterosexuality and a violent competition for species survival—a necropolitical racial

FIGURE 38A. "Great Migrations: Move as Millions, Survive as One."
Source: National Geographic/Anup Shah.

FIGURE 38B. "Great Migrations: Move as Millions, Survive as One." Source: National Geographic/Anup Shah.

<small>FIGURE 39.</small> Screenshot from UPS/National Geographic television commercial.

project, all organized by the logistics logic of "Move or Die." A string of UPS television ads aired with the National Geographic series, borrowing extravagant footage directly from the main show. In one segment that ran immediately prior to a commercial break, herds of bright red crabs desperately claw their way across treacherous obstacles to maritime breeding grounds only to reappear in the first advertising segment for UPS, deliberately confusing ad and program. The motion is seamless, such that the viewer is not immediately aware that they have entered the commercial break. There are only a very few subtle visual markers that indicate that the show has paused and the ad has begun. As the animals move, translucent vectors emerge out of their bodies and movements to digitized sounds, transforming the migratory species into high-tech nonhuman cyborgs. Whether National Geographic meant the vectors to be *revealed* (soaring out of and so native to the migratory bodies) or *engineered* (added by the logistics lens) is unclear, but this ambiguity is productive. In the voiceover, too, a definite parallel between human and nonhuman migration is proposed, but the nature of the relationship remains ambiguous:

> Every fall, the red crabs of Christmas Island undertake a Great Migration made possible by great logistics. They have limited time to ensure the survival of their species. Departures are synchronized, contingency planning overcomes obstacles, and just in time, they deliver their eggs. In their world just like ours, on time arrivals depend on logistics.
>
> *UPS is a proud sponsor of Great Migrations on the National Geographic Channel.*

The other ads in the series feature different species (albatross, ants, jelly-fish) and lessons but echo the same message:

> The black-browed albatross log enough miles to circle the globe one hundred and forty times over. Their Great Migration depends on great logistics. Despite months at sea, they can locate their mate among thousands, and a new generation takes flight to travel the globe. In their world just like ours, global operations depend on logistics.
>
> *UPS is a proud sponsor of Great Migrations on the National Geographic Channel.*

> Every night, army ants in the Costa Rican rainforest mobilize in a Great Migration made possible by great logistics. Loaded with their precious cargo, the fleet sets out. Communicating through chemical signals and touch, their cooperation propels them to their journey's end, sustaining a whole new generation. In their world just like ours, successful supply chains depend on logistics.
>
> *UPS is a proud sponsor of Great Migrations on the National Geographic Channel.*

Narrated by a confident masculine voice, the ads repeat the same refrain at the close of each segment: "In their world just like ours . . ." Nonhuman migrations, we are told repeatedly, have a likeness to the human world of logistics, and this likeness has particular contours. The management of *time* (on-time arrivals), *space* (global operations), and their *calibration* through material circulations (supply chains) are common to the animal and logistical worlds. Even more precisely, we learn that the mobility of objects and organisms is vital for survival. But if physical mobility is required for survival, so too is generational mobility; reproductive sex secures future circulation. "The need to breed is the very backbone of existence," the show asserts (Kostyal 2010, 78). Most poignant in scenes of the great white albatross, a species that is applauded for mating for life, procreative sex and monogamous coupledom dedicated to privatized parenting are framed as fundamental for the species to "move as millions" and "survive as one." The circulation of nonhuman bodies—and the endurance of these migrations across time and space globally and generationally—naturalizes the circulation of stuff.

Border Crossing

For as long as we have had nature shows, the genre has been animated by imperial pedagogies of species survivalism and reproductive hetero-normativity. However, *Great Migrations* doesn't simply recirculate these long-established lessons; there are some much more precise and urgent deployments that explain its extended appearance here. What makes *Great Migrations* worth this special scrutiny is the specific rendering of the mobile nature of logistics space and supply chain capitalism. The *Great Migrations* story is not simply one of resilient relations between species on the move but a story about the geography of their journeys, most acutely demonstrated through a focus on border crossings. Not only must species and the logistics system move or die; according to UPS, their migrations must transgress human crafted enclosure. Supply chain security explicitly takes up the national border as a threat to the security of logistics systems by virtue of its capacity to impede flow (see chapter 2); so too, *Great Migrations* presents the border as a threat to the integrity of species' migrations. The audience learns this lesson in the crucial scene this chapter opened with—one of a small handful that includes any sign of human life. Here, the herd of pronghorn antelope encounters a farmer's fence as they undertake their annual migration. The farmer's fence, the show explains, allows the farmer to maintain livestock and thus serves a critical economic function. Yet *Great Migrations* also exposes its violence. The camera follows the herd jumping through the fence and dwells on the animals as they are snagged in the barbed wire. Flesh tears, fur rips, and legs are snared as the antelope try desperately to get through the treacherous obstacle in their path. A lineup of pronghorn wait their turn to make the crossing, as in Figure 40, much like the backup of trucks at inland border crossings in the wake of border securitization. The *Great Migrations* book also reflects explicitly on this problem, outlining how "for the long haul migrants—the white sharks and sea turtles, the arctic terns and pronghorn—the borders of nations and reserves hold no meaning" (Kostyal 2010, 290). In the series, as in the world of logistics, this caption is not quite right. The border may "hold no meaning" insofar as it does not define the routes along which species and stuff respectively circulate. Yet the ripping of nonhuman flesh along the fence in *Great Migrations*, and the millions of dollars in costs for border delays in cargo flow, certainly register. The National Geographic series and the project of supply chain security in fact both work to mediate the problem of the border for their respective circulation systems. This is the effect of the series: it aims to convince the viewer that national borders must be transformed so that they do not impede desirable flows. In this sense, *Great Migrations* aims to institutionalize the conditions that it already purports to represent.

In fact, *Great Migrations* simultaneously justifies the national border (the natural needs of the farmer) and rationalizes its transgression (the

FIGURE 40. Pronghorn antelope, 2009. Source: Photograph by Joe Riis.

natural needs of the antelope), pointing directly at the central challenge of the emergent paradigm of global supply chain security. Neither *Great Migrations* nor supply chain security intend to do away with borders or make any claim in favor of their dismantling, yet both are very explicit about the need to *border differently*. Chapter 3 explored how a decade of experimentation has given rise to network or systems models of security that reconstitute borders and govern them differently, prioritizing flow through new forms of containment. For the emergent paradigm of supply chain security, as for the narrative of nonhuman migrations presented in *Great Migrations*, borders are both justified and transgressed. Staging this critical scene of the series in the old frontier of empire (the American West) along with the launch of the series in the urban center of empire (New York City) perhaps additionally codes the contemporary realities of human migration and so the global south in the global north. In contrast to the classic narrative of white scientist in dark Africa, here we are given a story of *living with* border crossings—a story that can also code the political economy of precarious migrant labor and the deeply racialized labor migrations that constitute key sectors of the contemporary logistical economy like warehouse work and port trucking.

More broadly, the emphasis in the series on species crossing each other's territories suggests a notion of relational space without romance.

Overlapping migratory routes—for "migrants whose migration never ends" (Kostyal 2010, 25)—means constant danger and the need for constant preparedness. Unlike the geopolitical imaginaries of the modern state, species war is not waged in blocks of national territory but perpetually through small wars across network space (Graham and Shaw 2008; Gregory and Pred 2007). This is the perpetual danger for the wildebeest of the lion attacks that "explode out of the night, racing towards the most vulnerable targets" (Kostyal 2010, 34). According to repeat claims in *Great Migrations* (Kostyal 2010, 38), "danger lurks" for this and countless other profiled species, "but the wildebeests have one strategic advantage. They—including their young—were built to stay on the move." Such irregular warfare and counterinsurgency become the paradigmatic form of battle animated by the politics of species resiliency in the nonhuman world like in the worlds of contemporary warfare and supply chain security (Anderson 2011; Cassidy 2008; Duffield 2008; Kilcullen 2010, 2012; Petraeus 2006). The border that was once supposed to stabilize the Hobbesian distinction between anarchy and order (the acceptable contours of exceptional politics) are no longer framed in national terms but defined by species; national war becomes transnational race to survive through resilient circulation.

Organized violence has certainly not lost its geographies, but they assume a different spatial and ontological form. Warfare and supply chains both have taken up network or supply-line cartographies that postdate and predate the modern warfare of national territoriality. The two threads of the UPS campaign—"We ♥ Logistics" and "Move or Die"—offer a Jekyll and Hyde lens on the contemporary logics and practice of logistics; both perspectives are crucial, yet so is the imagined distinction between them. As the corporate executives indicate, "Move or Die" is a story about logistics as much as it is a story about nonhuman animal migrations, but telling a story about the latter allows for specific kinds of learning about the former. The story of a violent race for survival is more easily set in the nonhuman world of "nature," even as its deployment there becomes a metric for the very human worlds where it would be difficult to disseminate directly. "Move or Die" would be a scandalous way for UPS to describe their business practices in the corporate world, even as it serves as bedfellow for the love of logistics. Yet in the very human world of supply chain security, "Move or Die" is indeed mobilized. As this book illustrates, martial law and military force are unleashed on land and on sea against pirates, indigenous organizers, and workers that threaten the smooth circulation of stuff.

War and Resilient Organisms

Great Migrations offers not simply a pedagogy for survival and reproductive heterosexuality in the animal kingdom but a lesson about the violent nature of trade. Rough trade takes on a biological imperative, and biology is infused with economic logics, with the laws of nature at once constitutive of and constituted by logistics. Causality is not attributed to one domain or the other; rather, logistics and species survival are animated by common logics, as the tag line *"in their world just like ours"* suggests. Today, the politics of trade, nature, and war are profoundly entangled through the problem of resilience. In corporate and government practice, trade is understood as a key domain of life wherein resilience marks the fitness of the system. As earlier chapters of this book have explored, the circulation of stuff through global logistics networks now figures as a matter of national security and a key vital system (see chapter 2). Because it is oriented toward threats that may be impossible to predict, supply chain security mobilizes preemption techniques to mitigate vulnerability (see Cooper 2006; Amoore and De Goede 2008) and preparedness measures to build resilience and recover circulation in the wake of disruption (see Collier and Lakoff 2007; Pettit, Fiskel, and Croxton 2010). "Resilience" has become the dominant paradigm for conceptualizing the security of logistics systems, and it emerges from the natural sciences (Christopher and Peck 2004; Gerven 2012; Sheffi 2006, 2007; Waters 2007). Most notably, Israeli American scholar Yossi Sheffi's book *The Resilient Enterprise: Overcoming Vulnerability for Competitive Advantage* has taken business management schools and the corporate world by storm. The book emerged out of a three-year research effort at MIT funded by the U.K. government and a long list of transnational corporations including Monsanto, Lucent, Intel, and Texas Instruments. The book (and the project that motivated it) aim to help companies recover from "high-impact disruptions" and was prompted by the 2001 attacks on the World Trade Center and Pentagon. Sheffi (2007, ix) notes in the preface that the "notion is borrowed from materials sciences," where "resilience represents the ability of a material to recover its original shape following deformation." As Jeremy Walker and Melinda Cooper (2011, 144) have outlined, the term *resilience*—itself an ecological concept—has been profoundly successful in "colonizing multiple arenas of governance due to its intuitive ideological fit with a neoliberal philosophy of complex adaptive systems" (see also Davoudi and Porter 2012).

Mark Duffield (2011, 761) argues that the discourse of resilience blurs war, nature, and economy precisely because it casts both social and natural worlds as threatened vital systems. Ecology and economy figure as dynamic though vulnerable organic systems, essential to human (and planetary) life, that therefore need to be secured. He explores how ecologist C. S. Holling's work in the 1960s and 1970s "reflected in nature how contemporary society mobilizes for war" and argues that "ecology naturalized war." Duffield outlines a break "with modernist conceptions of social protection that are based upon knowing and protecting against the future through statistically derived forms of insurance . . . resilience positively embraces uncertainty and the ultimate unknowability of the future." Highlighting the imperial circulation of the concept, he continues, "An organism, an individual, an eco-system, a social institution, an engineered infrastructure, even a city—in fact, anything that is networked, evolving or 'life-like' in some way—is now said to be resilient in so far as it able to absorb shocks and uncertainty, or reconfigure itself in relation to such shocks while still retaining its essential functionality." While resilience has become a mobile metaphysics blurring economy, ecology, and war, this is not the first time that theories of the natural world have migrated to and from these other domains. The notion that capital must circulate in order to accumulate—that the very survival of capitalism is contingent on circulation—is a foundational premise of Marx's critique of political economy, examined in more detail in chapter 3. Marx suggests in conversation with Engels that Darwin's vision of species competition was borrowed from the social relations of production that constituted early industrial capitalism (Ball 1979, 473). In yet another interesting twist, modern geopolitics, most notably Friedrich Ratzel's nineteenth century theories of the geopolitical state as competitive "organism," borrowed directly from Darwin's theories of species competition (Cowen and Smith 2009). Thus modern theories of warring nation-states were modeled on evolutionary theories of species competition, which were themselves modeled on historically and geographically contingent capitalist social relations.

And yet perhaps most immediately significant here is the entanglement of nature, war, and trade that made the post–World War II revolution in logistics and the rise of supply chain capitalism possible. Historically, a systems theory that emerged largely out of biology and the natural sciences contributed in important ways to the broad discursive shift in which the 1960s revolution in logistics was an important effect and actor (see chapter 1). Since the mid-twentieth century revolution in logistics, systems thinking has become ubiquitous, most importantly through the rise of the concept of ecosystems fueled by environmental movements (Duffield 2011; Dyckhoff, Lackes, and Reese 2004), such that today the systems approach in logistics and supply chain management is unquestioned, seemingly natural. While organic theories of systems were critically important to the revolution in logistics, so too were military models of physical circulation practiced during World War II and military conceptions of systems derived from the closed economies of defense procurement in the work of agencies like RAND, which gave us early systems analysis. Thus concern for the resilience of global logistics systems is a powerful contemporary installment in a long history of the tangled ontopolitics of war, trade, and the bios.

In this engagement with the natures/cultures of war and trade, it is worth reiterating Foucault's insights on the profound connections between sexuality and warfare in his early writing on biopolitics in volume 1 of the *History of Sexuality.* Foucault (1978, 137) famously writes, "It is as managers of life and survival, of bodies and the race, that so many regimes have been able to wage so many wars, causing so many men to be killed." In waging war and regulating sexuality, "at stake is the biological existence of a population." These are some of the stakes when he suggests that modern Western sexuality took shape at the interstices of a biology of population and a medicine of sex (Sandilands and Erickson 2010, 7) and that the biopolitics that emerged in the classical age was defined by "the administration of bodies and the calculated management of life." Indeed, *Great Migrations* connects the politics of life and death directly through optimism about the *fertility* of war. In contrast to the devastation "you expect to find" in the aftermath of war—in this case, in southern Sudan—National Geographic instead outlines its creativity: "You don't expect to rediscover one of the greatest migratory spectacles on Earth. But there it is, some 1.3 million white eared kob, tiang and mongalla gazelle, filing across a landscape where just a few years before, war ravaged, seeming to suck the life out of the boundless savannas. Yet the urge to create life was strong and more relentless, winning out in the end against war and destruction" (Kostyal 2010, 120). It is not just logistical war but the securitization of mobility more broadly that is under way in both logistical and animal kingdoms. Convergence in the politics of nonhuman animal migration and human commodity circulations are more clearly visible if we look beyond the *narratives* at work in the transmedia campaign and instead consider the *practices and technologies* used to "capture" the migrations of each. Here we see that human and nonhuman worlds are not only alike in terms of the allusions of marketers and the narratives guiding imaginaries of each—in fact, the same technologies of surveillance are deployed across the human/nonhuman divide. We see this in particularly stark ways in relation to the tracking of bodily movement, discussed earlier in the world of logistics labor management. Directly mirroring the use of surveillance technologies in logistics management, *Great Migrations* also relies on new technologies to remotely track animal movements, using a device that is nicknamed the "daily diary" and that "provides astounding data on animals' movements and their environments" (Mustain 2010). The technology, initially developed to track penguins in South Africa, has been expanded for use with others species by the National Geographic show. "It's a self-contained, maniacal scribe," explained the researcher who developed the technologies. "Once it's attached to an animal, whether fish, beast or fowl, the device records a mass of data—everything from the animal's minute movements through space and time to the temperature of its environment and light levels." Outlining the ecstasy of surveillance that seems to characterize natural and management sciences alike, *Great Migrations* Chief Scientific Advisor Wilson exclaims, "In other words you can be there—really be there—with the animal when you couldn't be otherwise." It is notable that the use of tracking technologies in logistics labor and nonhuman animal migrations are expected to have human consequences. Camera operator Bob Poole suggests that after viewing the series, which makes elaborate use of tracking technologies, "when you lie down to go to sleep at night, you'll realize the whole world is moving. And when you wake up and you see a flock of birds flying by, or a school of fish, you won't just think, 'Oh isn't that pretty!' You'll be wondering, 'Where did they come from? And where are they going?'" (Mustain 2010). Picking up on these comments, Wilson suggests, "That's really critical . . . The fact that they're all doing it together is part of the thing that keeps the species alive." In other words, the tracking technologies allow for a particular image and understanding of the necessity of mobility as a matter of survival that the show directly links to economic circulation (Mustain 2010).

We Have Never Been Human

How do the political geographies and affective economies of "Move or Die" work alongside those of "just-in-time"? In the UPS campaign, we are told that the *love of order and efficiency* defines logistics in the human world. This is a biopolitical logistics that enables the economy and so prosperity, vitality, and life itself. Yet when traced through nonhuman worlds, logistics figures as a necropolitical game of survival; the ethos transforms into *move or be killed*. On the one hand, the national border is explicitly and deliberately problematized and traversed by both animal and cargo circulations. On the other hand, a new kind of bordering is under way, but this is a species border rather than an immediately territorial one.

Visions of nature's migrations are deeply entangled in the building of logistical futures and spaces. The "human campaign" lays out important logistical lessons, but it also requires the nonhuman supplement. As Sarah Franklin et al. (2000, 9) suggest, heavy traffic or "borrowings" between global nature and culture is leading to their increasing isomorphism, even as their distinctiveness remains crucial. Indeed, as Donna Haraway (1989, 139) elaborates so eloquently in the context of Cold War representations of nonhuman bodies, "The media and advertising industries of nuclear culture produce in the bodies of animals—paradigmatic natives and aliens—the reassuring images appropriate to this state of pure war." Visions of nature can make stark claims on the social while avoiding directly discussing it, and "Move or Die" is an *unspeakably* important ethos of logistics space. By talking nature in addition to singing culture, National Geographic and UPS at once invest logistics with a biological imperative and infuse the nonhuman world with market logics. They herald a future of "Move or Die" where circulation is not simply a social good but a necessity for life, where disruption is a matter of *when* not *if,* where the powerful rule by virtue of their natural capacity for force, where borders can be both justified and transgressed, and where distinctions between military and civilian authority have no salience and so can be sidestepped.

Great Migrations is one recent installment in a broader genre of nature stories that narrate human social and intimate life by nonhuman means. More than two decades ago, Donna Haraway (1992) described the significant contribution of National Geographic in narrating human racial and imperial politics through the intimate tropes of family, trust, and love. Her analysis of what was (before *Great Migrations*) National Geographic's most popular production—Jane Goodall's adventures with the chimpanzees of Tanzania—highlights the global political context of this white woman's "communion" with the primates. Most important, Haraway emphasized the work of this interspecies intimacy in framing the postwar era of African decolonization on aggressively colonial terms. The meeting of the white woman's and nonhuman animal's hands in a key scene both renders and obliterates the presence of African subjects, positioning the white scientist (not accidentally feminine) as the authority that "speaks for nature." In the same piece, Haraway (1992, 296) eloquently argued, "Efforts to travel into 'nature' become tourist excursions that remind the voyager of the price of such displacements—one pays to see fun-house reflections of oneself." As heir to the throne of National Geographic's most watched program, *Great Migrations* explicitly calls on the legacy of "Miss Goodall and the Wild Chimpanzees" in the first pages of the book. *Great Migrations* positions itself in direct relation to this 1965 program—"one of the Geographic's first television programs" (Kostyal 2010)—as the advanced technology installment in the march of progress of geographic knowledge. National Geographic outlines how, in ways the founding members of the society could "only fathom . . . migration is the key to the intricacy of life on Earth" (Kostyal 2010, 19).

Feminist scholars in particular have further developed this critical engagement with the "culture" of "nature," looking at the ways in which narratives of the nonhuman shape human sociality (cf. Lancaster et al. 2000; Mitman 1999), with some key contributions specifically taking up the work of the National Geographic Society (Haraway 1997; Lutz and Collins 1993; Rothenberg 2007). Much of this work emphasizes the profoundly racialized, gendered, classed, and heteronormative ways in which discourses of nature and the natural operate, approaching nature as a "shifting classificatory process" (Franklin et al. 2000, 1) with powerful effects rather than a distinct sphere or logic. More recently, a literature has emerged specifically concerned with the sexual politics of nature and the natural politics of sexuality. Building on the insights of scholars like Haraway but with a particular concern for sexual normativity, the field of "queer ecologies" investigates how ideas, spaces, and practices of "nature" compel particular sexual and social formations, valorizing some acts and identities while castigating others. This work is centrally concerned with the ways that sexual normativities are constituted by allusion to nature—be it environmental or nonhuman animal. This work is also interested in how the "naturalness" of particular sexual and environmental formations is questioned and how alternatives are introduced. Catriona Sandilands (Sandilands and Erickson 2010, 4) argues, "Ideas and practices of nature, including both bodies and landscapes, are located in particular productions of sexuality, and sex is, both historically and in the present, located in particular formations of nature." Nature is powerfully, discursively tethered to sexuality in ways that exceed particular forms, but this intimacy is not "natural" in itself; their marriage is historically and geographically specific, in addition to being profoundly fraught.

Much of this story centers on Darwin's evolutionary theory and its legacies. Sandilands argues that "although Darwin would likely cringe at some of the uses to which evolutionary thought has been put, with the popularization of his work came an increasing naturalization of sexual politics." Normal sex and sexuality were interpreted as biologically reproductive, with the naturalness of heterosexuality confirmed by functional reproductive capacity. The take-up of Darwin's work and evolutionary thinking more broadly institutionalized not only reproductive heteronormativity but also scientific racism. *Social* Darwinism of Herbert Spencer's variety gave us the dictum "survival of the fittest," directly influencing late-nineteenth-century thinking on race and social evolution, and helped usher in eugenics and the politics of "racial improvement" at the turn of the century (Moore, Pandian, and Kosek 2003, 21). The supposedly biological basis for this political logic led directly to a reproductive response—most notably, the sterilization of bodies who would "pollute" the human race. The take-up of Darwin's thinking in the United States was simultaneously a project of sexual and social order where "debates over Social Darwinism often hinged on the natural order of things and the social hierarchies of race, class, and sex seen to reflect a universal design" (22). As Ladelle McWhorter (2010, 75) reminds us, the concept of "species," which acquired initial scientific meaning in the late eighteenth century, was only "stabilized again in the wake of Charles Darwin's work" and "often brought great harm to both racial and sexual minorities over the past two hundred years." Homosexual and transgendered people were often managed as "menacing degenerates," and in the context of "Race Hygiene" and "Race Betterment" movements, they were subjected to sustained social and medical violence (76). "Queer people—like dark-skinned (savage) people, disabled (defective) people, chronically ill (weak, feeble) people, and so on—were degenerates who might contaminate the bodies and bloodlines of the evolutionary avant-garde and thus derail *Homo sapiens* biological advance." These people, McWhorter asserts, "were held to be, literally, *biological enemies of the human species*, pollutants and pathogens, whose very presence posed a physical and possibly moral threat not only to individuals but to the species as a whole" (emphasis mine). The tradition of social Darwinism and the specific field of sociobiology make a prominent and perhaps predictable appearance in *Great Migrations*. Biologist E. O. Wilson's characterizations of species' sexual practices grace the chapter of the National Geographic tome titled "Need to Breed"—for instance, describing male army ants in dramatically functional terms that turn a life form into merely a tool for biological reproduction: "flying sperm dispensers" (Kostyal 2010, 114).

Can the naturalness of supply chain capitalism as a feature of the supposed naturalness of reproductive heterosexuality or species war be not only called into question but exposed for the violence it executes every day on alternative bodies, ways, and forms? If this "natural" vision of sex and death is deployed to *naturalize* the violence of supply chain capitalism, how might different engagements with nature's reproduction help cultivate alternative futurities, including alternative forms of economic organization? Can we engage logistics on different terms, through desire for a different *rough trade*? Can logistics space be disrupted by efforts to "queer capitalism"?

Queering Logistics?

What might a queer engagement with logistics space look like? Energetic interdisciplinary debates have recently focused on the uses of queer theory beyond the explicit surfacings of sex and sexuality. In "After Sex: Writing after Queer Theory," Janet Halley and Andrew Parker (2007) outline how leading figures in queer theory including Butler, Warner, Klein, and Sedgwick began to address a range of questions seemingly beyond the purview of sexuality, including matters of faith, geopolitics, and settler colonialism. This prompts them to ask, "Does the very distinction between the sexual and the nonsexual matter to queer thinking and, if so, when, where, and how? Can work be regarded as queer if it's not explicitly 'about' sexuality?" Elizabeth Povinelli (2007, 576) argues that the promise of sexuality, queer, and gender studies lies in "the degree to which, in disturbing identities and identifications, in pushing against legibility they illuminate how these relations and identities are held in a larger social matrix itself separating people and placing them on different trajectories of life and death," rather than in the "appropriateness of social relations, identifications, and identities on the basis of their proximity to a disciplinary name." Likewise, Peter Limbrick (2012, 104) suggests that scholarly readings of queerness typically "attend to a literal presence of non-normative figurings of gender or sexuality or sex in the text, especially those embodied by a self-identified queer subject." Drawing on the work of Amy Villarejo (2005), Limbrick suggests that such readings can "narrowly delimit or overlook the ways in which queer theory has the potential to unsettle our understandings of normative nationalisms, racialisations, temporalities, and their sexualised and gendered logics." Limbrick is committed to the potential for queer theory to "uncouple the pathologies of symptom from the potential for queer agency," well beyond the immediate domain of

CONCLUSION   223

sexuality. The promise of a queer engagement is thus in its potential for transforming relations of rule through the desire and occupation of those relations differently.

This is not a move away from sexuality but a deepened engagement with the ways that sexual desire and its government are profoundly entangled in contemporary bio-, necro-, and geopolitics. The language of biopolitics is often the language of eugenics, race, population, death, life, health, risk, and today "resilience." Yet as Foucault elaborates, biopolitics is profoundly about the history of sexuality, even as it may never utter these words. While there may be a newfound expansiveness to queer objects of study—for instance, terrorists (Puar 2005), animals (Chen 2012), and ecologies (Sandilands and Erickson 2010)—the issue of sex in strange places is hardly a new queer question. Elizabeth Freeman (2007) playfully asks, "Wasn't my being queer, in the first instance about finding sex where it was not supposed to be, failing to find it where it was, finding that sex was not, after all, what I thought it was?" Indeed, a conception of desire as simultaneously intimate and infrastructural is a hallmark of queer theory, which as Antke Engel (2010) argues, "proposes to understand desire as not solely a category of subjectivity, of sexual practices or intimate relations, but as productive in and of the social—which includes macropolitical processes and institutions." Across its diverse iterations, queer theory holds desire as simultaneously intimate and infrastructural, crossing public/private divides and collapsing spatial scale.

The writing that might seem most immediately relevant to a queer engagement with logistics is the early and groundbreaking work of J. K. Gibson-Graham, who famously mobilizes queer theory to challenge discourses that totalize and universalize capitalism, even those within radical political economy. Gibson-Graham (1996, 139) asserts a project of "rethinking capitalist morphology" in order to "liberate economic development from the hegemonic grasp of capitalist identity" and points to queer theory as a key resource. She is concerned with the ways in which gendered and sexual metaphors inscribe capitalist relations and the potential for imaging economy otherwise. "A queer perspective," in this reading, "can help to unsettle consonances and coherences of the narrative of global commodification" (144). And while this work has been enormously generative in provoking fresh debates and projects, there are also limits to such an approach. As Engel (2010) argues in an appreciative but critical engagement with this work, "queer theory is presented as a politics of language and a technique of rereading rather than of taking part in the process of 'resubjectivation,' the mobilization and transformation of desires, the cultivation of capacities, and the making of new identifications." Indeed, this "new economic language" (Engel 2010) that Gibson-Graham proposes engages "queer" as primarily a project of thinking differently rather than a question of materiality and affect. Sexuality is more than metaphor. As the projects of these queer theorists suggest, it is calibrated to, installed within, and productive of infrastructures of political and economic life. It is neither a stepping outside of power nor a figuring of sexuality as liberatory, as Gibson-Graham seems to suggest. As Duggan (2003), Puar (2007), Oswin (2008), Lamble (2013), and others articulate, homonormativity, homonationalism, and "queer necropolitics" are centrally implicated in the production of globalization, the carceral state, and empire. It is not just normative sexuality but many of its alternatives that are woven into relations of rule. This means that a queer engagement adequate to the challenge of a simultaneously martial and organic discourse of resilient systems must refuse the romance of queering and approach sexuality as immanent to empire. If capitalism, war, and normative sexuality are increasingly governed by the bio/necropolitics of species, systems, circulation, and sex, then cultivating alternatives to logistics space demands not only imagining economy differently but building different economies of (human) natures.

Recent feminist work in the "new materialities" is animated by an engagement with the queer and more than human, which is not bound by constructivism. Elizabeth Grosz's (2011) work on natural and sexual selection is particularly helpful in resisting resilience and cultivating alternative feminist futurities. She has called on Darwin's work to think about the becoming and transformation of things differently. This is a surprising move in many regards, not least because of the deeply fraught legacies of his evolutionary thinking, particularly in so far as they gave shape to the social Darwinism discussed earlier. But Grosz suggests that the politics of survivalism, racist species competition, and an all-encompassing evolutionary functionalism should not be attributed to Darwin's thought, per se, but rather to a limited reading of his work that has nevertheless become an established interpretation. Specifically she argues that the collapse of sexual and natural selection in his work has done tremendous political damage and that disaggregating them is a necessary and productive political act. She thus finds surprising resonance between the recasting of evolutionary thought and insights from queer theory that engage science and materiality differently and are prescient in the project of moving beyond "Move or Die."

Grosz writes (2011, 118), "Darwin understood, far better than his contemporaries and successors, the irreducibility of sexual selection to strategies of survival." For Grosz, natural selection is mimetic—reproducing biologically with explicitly functionalist ambitions. However, sexual selection is different: it has no obvious, immediate, or practical function. Sexual selection is excessive, and this is precisely what gives it value and makes it *creative* practice. She continues, "Darwin's conception of sexual selection is irreducible to natural selection, and thus is relatively independent of the principles of fitness or survival that regulate natural selection." Darwin's account of sexual selection must be understood, according to Grosz (119), "as a principle different from and at times opposed to natural selection, a view entirely contrary to the tradition of social Darwinism, which sees them as ultimately two versions of the same principle." This in turn allows for "a new and quite different understanding of sexual selection than that which dominates sociobiology," she argues, "one more resonant with a feminism of sexual difference, a feminism beyond the constraints of identity." The conflation of natural and sexual selection forecloses the possibility of creative transformation, addressing difference as deviance rather than embracing its potential for introducing the new. Sexual selection "insists on a dimension of taste, on a recognition of beauty, and on the assertion of preferences based on the perception of appeal that complicate the relentless operations of natural selection." The *promise* of sexual selection is not simply in the way it insists on the autonomy of sexuality from reproduction, though this is crucial. For Grosz (2011, 141), sexuality "intensifies the everyday by making it spectacular, exciting, intense, stimulating, not a preparation for something else but an experience for its own sake, for the sake of what it does to the body of the subject." Most profoundly, sexual selection insists on the autonomy of creativity and desire from the systems that aim to foreclose political transformation in the interests of their own reproduction—eco, economic, and beyond. Precisely because sexual desire has been captured so powerfully by the politics of survivalism, its capacity to transform relations of rule as it engages them holds such promise. Sexual selection (Grosz 2011, 118), its "energetic excess," is "the condition for the production of biological and cultural extravagance, the uncontainable production of intensification, not for the sake of the skills of survival but simply because of its force of bodily intensification, its capacity to arouse pleasure or 'desire,' its capacity to generate sensation." Playing directly with Clausewitz's maxim regarding war as a continuation of politics by other means—a claim that has been interpreted as crucial to the modern making of national and territorial war and to conceptualizing war as an exceptional event always outside supposedly peaceful national borders (Arendt 1970; Foucault 1977, 1997; Hardt and Negri 2000, 2004)—Grosz (2011, 76) playfully asserts, "Art is not the antithesis of politics, but politics continued by other means." In inverting Clausewitz's maxim and positing politics as a continuation of war by other means, Foucault ([1997] 2003, 16) resists the purging of social war within national space and the violence of the supposedly peaceful politics of the national state. Instead he insists that power is organized by a "relationship of force that was established through war at a given historical moment" and that modern politics "sanctions and reproduces" the violence operative in war. If Foucault aims to recover the historic violence of our present, then Grosz insists that the recovery of sexual selection is a claim on the place of artistic practice in organizing future politics.

Desiring a Different "Rough Trade"

In a bold and insightful paper written twenty years ago, feminist scholar Anne McClintock (1993) engages with the queer power of BDSM play (bondage, discipline, dominance, submission, sadism, masochism). Counter to interpretations of BDSM that interpret its performances, roles, and costumes as literal renderings of fixed inequalities and desire for actual violence and inequality, McClintock highlights its transgressive potential. She writes, "S/M manipulates the signs of power in order to refuse their legitimacy as nature." That the term *rough trade* is already in play in myriad ways in popular culture and sexual slang itself suggests a kind of queer engagement with the organization of power and its signs. A refusal of the nature of things by taking them up differently and with desire is precisely the power of BDSM play and culture. According to McClintock (1993, 91), BDSM "performs social power as both contingent and constitutive, as sanctioned neither by fate nor by God, but by social convention and invention, and thus as open to historical change." While BDSM "seems to parade a servile obedience to conventions of power," McClintock argues "on the contrary" that "with its exaggerated emphasis on costume and scene," it instead "performs social power as *scripted,* and hence as permanently subject to change" (89; emphasis in the original). Thus BDSM, as a "theatre of conversion . . . reverses and transmutes the social meanings it borrows." The promise of refiguring sexual selection and so too desire, unhinging it from the imperatives of efficient war anchored in permanent accumulation, is profound in a time of logistics space. BDSM may thus offer a kind of queer method for constructing countercartographies of logistics space. In engaging the logistics maps and plans as the scripting of geopolitical economic power, I highlight their constitutive struggles and violence and insist that this too is subject to change.

Writing about a very different time and mobilizing a different theoretical architecture, Peter Linebaugh and Marcus Rediker (2001, 6) describe the unlikely ways in which the geographies of early Atlantic imperialism also provided a skeleton for the emergence of a surprising flesh of connections across vast spatial networks. Precisely because the organized violence of empire threw spatially dispersed social orders into heterogeneous relations of rule—exploitation, slavery, incarceration, dislocation, diaspora, and so forth—it also brought peoples into relation differently. Without guarantee or even intentionality, these relations could at times produce creative solidarities. "Sailors, pilots, felons, lovers, translators, musicians, mobile workers of all kinds made new and unexpected connections," they write, "which variously appeared to be accidental, contingent, transient, even miraculous." Connections forged through the violent infrastructures of relations of rule may become the connective tissues of alternative futurities if they are occupied differently.

Writing without romance in 2013, it is impossible to avoid the movements and actions that have emerged in recent years around the world that respond to or target logistics space. Some of these—the Arab Spring, the Occupy movement, so-called Somali pirates, a global wave of logistics labor actions, and indigenous protest of new rounds of dispossession— are discussed in chapters 3, 4, and 5. While they make a wide variety of claims that cannot be reduced to simple questions about supply chains, this book has explored how the assemblage of logistics space entails the elaborate recasting of not just political economy but also international law, urban space, and the relationship of all these to warfare. Much like the many-headed hydra, the seemingly disparate lives of these movements are connected through the infrastructures of logistics space. Alongside profound differences in strategy, tactics, and logistics of struggle, and the very real distance (socially and spatially) between these collectivities, there has also at times been exchange between members and overlap in organizers, events, and ideas that point to the potential for a different occupation and organization of logistics space.

In this sense, we might follow Jasbir Puar (2005, 126) in "encouraging subjects of study to appear in all their queernesses, rather than primarily to queer the subjects of study." The image in Figure 41, which circulated on social media through the networks of the Idle No More movement in North America, may be an oblique symbol of that potential. The North American indigenous warrior in the Guy Fawkes mask does not scream "*logistics*," but this may well be the perfectly queer figure of rough trade. It is this kind of image of the "Indian" (less the mask) that haunts narratives of the

FIGURE 41. Image of indigenous warrior wearing Guy Fawkes mask that circulated in social media during Idle No More uprising.

American western frontier. Like the pirates that troubled maritime commerce at the high point of European imperialism, the Indians that attacked stagecoaches on their colonial journeys westward came to define the era. Thus the Indian in full battle dress is a potent symbol of the histories of the colonial supply line in both its explicitly military and everyday colonial guise. But the added element of the Guy Fawkes mask makes this image acute in whole new ways. The mask—a symbol that became associated with the Occupy movement—suggests a powerful irony, for the indigenous warrior can really only be understood to "occupy" *again*. As Stuart Elden (2013) argues, by virtue of its emergence as a trademarked Hollywood symbol, the mask also highlights "the use of the tools of capitalism against capitalism that is one of the most striking elements of the protests." This image and the movements out of which it emerged are tethered to logistics space more tightly then a cursory glance might suggest—in the particular targets of their actions (circulatory systems like rail corridors, ports, and logistics cities) and through the "queer" play of recycling "conventions of power" (McClintock 1993). The very possibility of this image speaks to this profound circulation of opposition and alternatives. Perhaps most notably, the image captures the profound potential for ironic alliance across diverse networks that mark the logistics space of rough trade.

That the same infrastructures of oppression may be creatively reused toward their transformation is a hallmark of activism in an era of global circulation. The capacity for the tools of oppression to potentially reframe the master's house may be most readily evident in the complex life of the Internet, which is well known to be a network of both control and resistance. The Internet is not only a crucial technology of logistic space and its massive flows of information, real-time inventories, and GPS surveillance tools; the Internet provides a fascinating metaphor for the "physical Internet" of logistics systems. Indeed, the World Bank (Arvis et al. 2007, 3) asserts that the degree of a country's connectivity to "physical Internet" is "fast becoming a key determinant of a country's competitiveness." The *Economist* (2006) also deploys the term, claiming that the "physical Internet" of global logistics systems brings "access to vast new markets" and contrasts this to the growing exclusion of those who have only weak connection. The use of the virtual space of the Internet as a metaphor for the actual material space of supply chains is fascinating and ironic. It presumes a discernable distinction between the physical and informational infrastructures and flows of logistics on the one hand and Internet on the other and thus that there could be some prior and fixed spatiality to the Internet, autonomous from the spatiality of the "physical Internet." But if the Internet connects people and movements even as it subjugates them, so too does the "physical Internet," paradoxically in ways that are often *more* material and *less* visible. Logistical networks of circulation connect consumers and producers as they also challenge that distinction. Supply chains connect people across vast distances and provide the networked "grounds" for a commons. This is the potential of logistics space done differently.

The move to include protection of global trade as a pillar of national security, as so many states now do, stems from the central role that trade plays in reproducing a corporate-managed and transnationally networked way of life. Yet a slippage occurs where protection of the economy as a route to protection of life is replaced with the protection of the economy as protection of life itself. Writing in 1966, Aaron Wildavsky offers a compelling critique of the "encroachment of economics on politics" that he sees in cost-benefit analysis, systems analysis, and project budgeting. He suggests that the economizer "claims no special interest in or expertise concerning the decision apparatus outside of the market place" yet "pursues efficiency to the heart of the political system." Wildavsky sees a danger in the replacement of objectives with efficiency and the relativization of means and ends. But the rise of "techné," the conflation of ends with means, of strategy with logistics, is precisely the achievement of business logistics. Exactly forty years later, Wendy Brown (2006, 693) suggests that "neoliberal rationality is not merely the result of leakage from the economic to other spheres but rather of the explicit imposition of a particular form of market rationality on these spheres." The move to

FIGURE 42. "Occupy Logistics," Toronto, Canada, 2011. Source: Photograph by the author.

govern supply as a problem of security is a further attempt to remove it from the realm of political contestation—*to make economy policy.*

Disruption is thus a profoundly political tactic—for instance, of workers protesting graphic deaths on the docks associated with demands for higher productivity in California's ports or of Somali pirates contesting the European dumping of toxic wastes in the Gulf of Aden. These disparate groups and many others are governed as threats to the security of supply, concealing complex social worlds animated by the violence of efficient global trade. There are thus heavy stakes in the technical, even technocratic debates over the protection of logistics from systemic failure.

Logistics clearly has a long history as a military art and business science, and both market and military forces have been critical in transforming the field. And yet, these actors do not exhaust the terrain. Recently logistics has become important to the management of many forms of complex systems and operations to a wider range of actors—most notably emergency response, humanitarian aid, organized labor, and even protest movements. Logistics management is so frequently mobilized for humanitarian aid that there are now a number of institutes, textbooks, and since 2011 even a professional journal devoted entirely to the subject. The labor movement has initiated its own logistics think tank in California in collaboration with scholars in order to rethink the *socially just supply chain.* And in activist worlds such as those protesting G8 and G20 meetings, as well as more recently the Occupy movement, logistics have become a crucial resource.

Logistics is more than haunted by its military, imperial, and more recent corporate past. In training programs, professional circuits, institutional expertise, and its primary sites of deployment, corporate and military men and methods dominate. Logistics also drives neoliberal forms of bio-, necro-, and antipolitical calculation where cost-benefit analysis and assumptions of market efficiency are embedded into its basic techniques. Nevertheless, emerging in other sites is a claim on logistics as a technique for organizing around the "how" problems of material life where both ends and means matter.

ACKNOWLEDGMENTS

This book is a fragment of many years of learning and of many people's teaching. Like any fragment, it is constituted by rough edges, soft spots, and strange absences. Generous engagement from many inspiring people points to complexity beyond what I render here and makes it tempting to hold the text close and refuse its release. Tim Mitchell's words, shared with me when I was a postdoc anxiously reviewing the proofs of my first book, are always helpful. He encouraged me to consider the text simply (and spatially) as a collection of bread crumbs that mark a trail. I therefore offer this book hoping that it maps useful paths for colleagues and comrades.

But I had so much help! In an incredibly violent world, I have been fortunate to land in beautifully nurturing environments. First, I must thank Tom Dufresne, longtime president of the International Longshore and Warehouse Union (ILWU) Canada area. Not only did he teach me invaluable lessons about the materiality and hypermobility of contemporary capitalism; he also came to trust me and call me sister. Tom and the ILWU introduced me to courageous people in ports around the world who shared so much with me. Thank you especially to brothers and sisters Rob Ashton, Mandy Chan, Linda Maxwell, Glen Edwards, Jyalmen Sidhho, Steve Nasby, Chris Verbeek, Tim Farrell, Tim Footman, Peter Lahay, Rino Voci, Luisa Gratz, Peter Peyton, Peter Olney, Terry Engler, Cynthia Brooke, Paul Uppal, and Dean Summers.

If longshore workers taught me about their world and how it is changing global landscapes and livelihoods, intransigent scholars pushed me to think carefully and expansively about the implications and effects of these transformations. My earliest research in this area—on transport labor and security—began while I was a postdoctoral fellow at York

University working with Leah Vosko. I thank her and her crew for their nonstop challenge, support, and interest. I am also deeply grateful to Tim Mitchell and the incredible seminar "Rethinking the Social" at NYU's International Center for Advanced Study, where the ideas of this book were born. A year of conversation with this group—especially Miriam Ticktin, Jane Anderson, Julia Elyachar, Alondra Nelson, Peggy Sommers, Ella Shohat, Maimuna Huq, Tom Bender, Andy Lakoff, Sherene Seikaly, Chris Otter, Diana Yoon, and others—was truly magical and gave me an experience of generous and challenging collectivity that I aspire to cultivate wherever I go.

There have been so many who changed how and what I know, but most important for this project I thank Mimi Sheller. Inspiring in work and beyond, Mimi patiently read the manuscript at different stages and was even more patient with my attempts to respond to her insightful and provocative comments. I had helpful conversations with Bobby Noble while working through questions of piracy and rough trade, and I thank him for sharing his brilliance. Enormous thanks to the amazing Caren Kaplan, Inderpal Grewal, and Minoo Moallem for inviting me into the Faculty Seminar on Culture and Militarism at Berkeley, and to the phenomenal group of UC scholars who have kept the conversations going since, especially Jennifer Terry, Peter Limbrick, and Toby Beauchamps. Thank you to John Morrisey, Anna Stanley, and Ulf Strohmayer at the National University of Ireland, where I presented parts of this work two years running. At NUI I had the pleasure to meet and learn from Mick Dillon and then Marc Duffield, who engaged my work with extraordinary care and generosity. I am indebted to Steve Graham, Marc Salter, Vron Ware, Janine Brodie, François Debrix, Derek Gregory, Gavin Smith, Stephen Collier, Mariana Valverde, Stuart Elden, Natalie Oswin, Mary Thomas, Nik Heynen, Melissa Wright, Louise Amoore, Jennifer Ridgley, Michelle Buckley, Peter Gratton, Tyler Wall, Matt Coleman, Joel Wainwright, Scott Prudham, Anna Zalik, Jin Haritaworn, David McNally, Leo Panitch, Sharzad Mojab, Lauren Berlant, Rita Murad, David Grondin, Sarah Koopman, Craig Gilmore, Larry Kowalchuk, David Miller, Heidi Nast, Max Rameau, Elizabeth Knafo, Zoltán Glück, Geoff Mann, Debanuj DasGupta, Laurel Mei, Elizabeth Sibilia, Lauren Pearson, Eliza Darling, Julian Brash, Héctor Agredano Rivera, Mazan Labban, Jessica Miller, Malav Kanuga, Steve Tufts, Mary-Joe Nadeau, Cynthia Wright, John Eyles, Richard Harris, Suzanne Mills, Juanita Sundberg, Amy Kaplan, Emma Sommers, Ron Stuber, Ross Johnstone, Amy Siciliano, Tania Li, Genevieve LeBaron, Natasha Myers, and always, Engin Isin.

I am grateful to lots of locals in and around Toronto. Vanessa Parlette provided generous bibliographic and editing assistance in the last stretches of the process. David Seitz, David Roberts, and Jordan Hale provided invaluable research assistance. I feel fortunate to have such a remarkable community at the University of Toronto. Thanks to Emily Gilbert, Judy Han, Brett Story, Katie Mazer, Alexis Mitchell, Martin Danyluk, Debra Pogorelsky, Nemoy Lewis, Lia Frederiksen, Kanishka Goonewardena, Tammy George, Shaista Patel, Matt Farish, Rajyashree Reddy, Sheila Htoo, Carla Klassen, Sue Ruddick, J. P. Catungal, Jeff Tanaka, Lauren Ash, Jessica Wilczak, Maya Eichler, Connor Pion, Shiri Pasternak, Sonia Grant, Nadia Hedar, Scott Prudham, Rachel Silvey, Lisa Freeman, Dina Georgis, Jennifer Chun, Ahmed Allahwala, Martine August, Charles Levkoe, Lauren Ash, Katharine Rankin, Michelle Murphy, Rhys Machold, Sue Bunce, Alissa Trotz, and Sherene Razack. I thank my collaborators from the National Film Board of Canada—Kat Cizek, Paramita Nath, Maria-Saroja Poonambolam, Heather Frise, Cass Gardiner, Gerry Flahive, and Emily Paradis from the University of Toronto—who have been inspiring beyond words and patient with my fractured focus.

The Social Science and Humanities Research Council of Canada supported this work in two significant ways: first through a postdoctoral fellowship and then through a Standard Research Grant.

It is impossible to know how to acknowledge the presence of Neil Smith in this work or his absence in my life. Indeed, I finished this book at a time of profound loss, yet astonishing support surrounded me. I am most deeply grateful to David Harvey. While I was in the depths of grief, he opened his heart, helped me forgive myself, and then told me to finish this book. Ruthie Gilmore is always inspiring politically and intellectually, but her solidarity over the past sixteen months was intimate and artful. I am eternally grateful to her. I miss Randy Kapashesit. He was an inspiring teacher who helped me understand the persistence of imperialism despite its changing forms. I feel fortunate to know his life partner, Donna Ashamock, and to learn from her strength as we each navigate new worlds. Don Mitchell has moved from someone I deeply admire to someone who made laughter possible. Cindi Katz is simply amazing. Thank you always to Leah, Leslie, Jeremy, Noah, Miles, Robert, Audrey Cowen, Judy Low, Troy Ketela, Robynne McKinley, and Jacques Paris. Uzma Shakir and Jane Farrow inspire me to be ruthless with hypocrisy, courageous politically, and to love hard. My gratitude to Carey Gray is tectonic.

1. The Revolution in Logistics

1. In 1985, the National Council of Physical Distribution Management (NCPDM) became the Council of Logistics Management (CLM), which has 11,500 members (an increase of 248 percent since 1985).

2. From National Borders to Global Seams

1. Lisa Gow, Executive Director, Pacific Gateway Branch, Ministry of Transportation and Infrastructure, Government of British Columbia, interview with author, Vancouver, June 10, 2009.

2. John Rehn, Gest régional, Opérations de la sûreté des transports (Marine), Sûreté et préparatifs d'urgence, Transports Canada, interview with author, Toronto, July 7, 2009. See also Transport Canada 2011.

3. Mike Henderson, Regional Director, General Pacific Region, Transport Canada, interview with author, Vancouver, June 10, 2009.

4. Raymond Schaible, Vice President, Operational Logistics Division, Logistics Management Institute, interview with author, April 16, 2010.

5. Ports that are currently operational within the CSI include those of Buenos Aires, Argentina; Freeport, The Bahamas; Antwerp and Zeebrugge, Belgium; Santos, Brazil; Montreal, Vancouver, and Halifax, Canada; Hong Kong, Shenzen, and Shanghai, China; Cartagena, Colombia; Caucedo, Dominican Republic; Alexandria, Egypt; Le Havre and Marseille, France; Bremerhaven and Hamburg, Germany; Piraeus, Greece; Puerto Cortes, Honduras; Ashdod and Haifa, Israel; La Spezia, Genoa, Naples, Gioia Tauro, and Livorno, Italy; Kingston, Jamaica; Yokohama, Tokyo, Nagoya, and Kobe, Japan; Port Klang and Tanjung Pelepas, Malaysia; Rotterdam, The Netherlands; Port Salalah, Oman; Port Qasim, Pakistan; Balboa, Colon, and Manzanillo, Panama; Lisbon, Portugal; Singapore; Durban,

South Africa; Busan (Pusan), South Korea; Algeciras, Barcelona, and Valencia, Spain; Colombo, Sri Lanka; Gothenburg, Sweden; Kaohsiung and Chi-Lung, Taiwan; Laem Chabang, Thailand; Dubai, United Arab Emirates; Felixstowe, Liverpool, Thamesport, Tilbury, and Southampton, United Kingdom.

6. John Rehn, 2009.

3. The Labor of Logistics

1. U.S. Customs and Border Protection agents frequently refer to Canadian ports as the "foyer" to the United States.

2. For a news archive of the struggle, see "Longshore and Shipping News," http://www.longshoreshippingnews.com/tag/egt-development.

4. The Geo-Economics of Piracy

1. For a list of the resolutions, see "United Nations Documents on Piracy," http://www.un.org/Depts/los/piracy/piracy_documents.htm.

2. A "binder" is a temporary contract that provides proof of insurance before a permanent policy is issued.

3. Signatories of the Djibouti Code include Comoros, Djibouti, Egypt, Ethiopia, France, Jordan, Kenya, Madagascar, Maldives, Oman, Saudi Arabia, Seychelles, Somalia, South Africa, Sudan, the United Republic of Tanzania, and Yemen.

4. Captain Steve Poulin, Chief of the Coast Guard's Maritime and International Law Division, interview with author, Washington, D.C., May 19, 2011.

5. Logistics Cities

1. At the time of this writing, footage was available on YouTube: "Camp Bucca Transfer to Government of Iraq," https://www.youtube.com/watch?v=y4zNSp GYc-8.

2. Already making up more than 10 percent of the nonoil revenue in the UAE, and with global revenue accounting for $3.4 trillion in 2006 and projected growth at 4.5 percent annually for the next five years, logistics offers a promising risk: UAE Interact 2007.

3. "Beds" best describes the extent of the facilities, as they are designed according to a bare minimum provision of space. New regulations developed in response to the workers' protests to inhumane living conditions (DeParle 2007) provide that there should be no more than eight residents to a room and toilet, and each person should have a minimum of three square meters of floor space.

AADNC (Aboriginal Affairs and Northern Development Canada). 2007. "Welcoming Ceremony at the Royal BC Museum—Tsawwassen Treaty." http://www .aadnc-aandc.gc.ca/aiarch/mr/spch/2007/bcm-eng.asp.

Abeyratne, Ruwantissa. 2010. "Managing the Twenty-First Century Piracy Threat: The Somali Example." In *Supply Chain Security: International Practices and Innovations in Moving Goods Safely and Efficiently,* edited by Andrew R. Thomas, 121–34. Santa Barbara, Calif.: Praeger.

ADB (Asian Development Bank). 2008. "Lao People's Democratic Republic and Socialist Republic of Viet Nam: Greater Mekong Subregion: East–West Corridor Project: Evaluation Report." Operations Evaluation Department. http:// www.adb.org/sites/default/files/29271-LAO-PPE.pdf.

———. 2009. *Infrastructure for a Seamless Asia.* Tokyo: Asian Development Bank Institute.

———. 2010. *Institutions for Asian Connectivity.* Working paper #220. http:// www.adbi.org/files/2010.06.25.wp220.institutions.asian.connectivity.pdf.

———. 2012. "Assessment of Public–Private Partnerships in Viet Nam: Constraints and Opportunities." http://www.adb.org/publications/assessment-public-private -partnerships-viet-nam-constraints-and-opportunities.

Against Port Expansion (APE). n.d. "The Issues." http://www.againstportexpansion .org/issues.html.

Agnew, John. 1999. "Mapping Political Power beyond State Boundaries: Territory, Identity, and Movement in World Politics." *Millennium* 28, no. 3: 499–521.

———. 2005. *Hegemony: The New Shape of Global Power.* Philadelphia: Temple University Press.

———. 2010. "Making the Strange Familiar: Geographical Analogy in Global Geopolitics." *Geographical Review* 99, no. 3: 426–43.

Agnew, John, and M. Coleman. 2007. "The Problem with Empire." In *Space, Knowledge, and Power: Foucault and Geography,* edited by Jeremy W. Crampton and Stuart Elden, 317–40. Hampshire, UK: Aldershot.

"Agreement between the United States of America and the Socialist Republic of Vietnam on Trade Relations." 2000. http://www.bilaterals.org/IMG/pdf/US-VN_FTA.pdf.

Ali, Muna, and Zahra Murad. 2009. "Unravelling Narratives of Piracy: Discourses of Somali Pirates." *Darkmatter: In the Ruins of Imperial Culture.* December 20. http://www.darkmatter101.org/site/2009/12/20/unravelling-narratives-of-piracy-discourses-of-somali-pirates.

Allen, W. Bruce. 1997. "The Logistics Revolution and Transportation." *Annals of the American Academy of Political and Social Science* 553:106–16.

Al Mashni, R. 2011. "Kufan Group and Northern Gulf Partners Launch Transformative Logistics and Business Investment in Iraq." *AMEinfo: The Ultimate Middle East Business Resource.* January 4. http://www.ameinfo.com/252895.html.

Alrawi, Mustafa. 2009. "Education Key to Progress." *Emirates 24/7.* June 5. http://www.emirates247.com/eb247/economy/uae-economy/education-key-to-progress-2009-06-05-1.33379.

Al Tamimi. n.d. "Labour Law in the UAE." http://www.aluminium.gl/sites/default/files/12_PDF/arbejdskraft/UAE%20-%20Appendix%201%20Labour%20Law%20in%20the%20UAE.pdf.

Amin, Ash. 1994. "Post-Fordism: Models, Fantasies, and Phantoms of Transition." In *Post-Fordism: A Reader,* edited by Ash Amin, 1–40. Oxford, UK: Blackwell.

Amin, Ash, and Nigel Thrift, eds. 2004. *The Blackwell Cultural Economy Reader.* Oxford, UK: Blackwell.

Amoore, Louise, and Marieke De Goede. 2008. *Risk and the War on Terror.* New York: Routledge.

Amsterdam, Robert. 2009. "Fret over Freight—Why Piracy Happens." *Corporate Foreign Policy.* April 20. http://corporateforeignpolicy.com/africa/fret-over-freight-why-piracy-happens.

Anderson, Ben. 2011. "Population and Affective Perception: Biopolitics and Anticipatory Action in UU Counterinsurgency Doctrine." *Antipode* 43, no. 2: 205–36.

Antràs, Pol, Luis Garicano, and Esteban Rossi-Hansberg. 2005. *Offshoring in a Knowledge Economy.* No. w11094. Cambridge, Mass.: National Bureau of Economic Research.

Aoyama, Yuko, and Samuel J. Ratick. 2007. "Trust, Transactions, and Information Technologies in the US Logistics Industry." *Economic Geography* 83, no. 2: 159–80.

APF (Asia Pacific Foundation of Canada). 2008. "The Asia-Pacific Gateway and Corridor: Gaining a Competitive Edge by Doing Security Differently." *Canada-Asia Commentary* 51. http://www.asiapacific.ca/sites/default/files/archived_pdf/commentary/cac51.pdf.

APGST (Asia Pacific Gateway Skills Table). 2009. *Security in the Asia Pacific Gateway: Human Resources Issues and Strategies*. Vancouver: Context Research Limited and Izen Consulting.

ArabianBusiness.com. 2007. "Dubai Opens First 'Luxury' Labour Camp." http://www.arabianbusiness.com/index.php?option=com_content&view=article&id=8473.

Arce, Dwyer. 2010. "Seychelles Court Convicts Somali Pirates." *Jurist*. July 26. http://jurist.org/paperchase/2010/07/seychelles-court-convicts-somali-pirates.php.

Arendt, Hannah. 1970. *On Violence*. New York: Harcourt.

Arthur, Maurice P. 1962. "Federal Transport Regulatory Policy." *American Economic Review* 52, no. 2: 416–25.

Artz, Matthew. 2012. "Council Approves $1 Billion Oakland Army Base Deal." *Mercury News*. June 20. http://www.mercurynews.com/breaking-news/ci_20892750/oakland-army-base-vote-scheduled-tuesday-night.

Arvis, Jean-François, Monica Alina Mustra, John Panzer, Lauri Ojala, and Tapio Naula. 2007. *Connecting to Compete: Trade Logistics in the Global Economy; The Logistics Performance Index and Its Indicators*. Washington, D.C.: World Bank.

Arvis, Jean-François, Monica Alina Mustra, Lauri Ojala, Ben Shepherd, and Daniel Saslavsky. 2010. *Connecting to Compete: Trade Logistics in the Global Economy; The Logistics Performance Index and Its Indicators*. Washington, D.C.: World Bank.

———. 2012. *Connecting to Compete: Trade Logistics in the Global Economy; The Logistics Performance Index and Its Indicators*. Washington, D.C.: World Bank.

Asad, Talal. 2007. *On Suicide Bombing*. New York: Columbia University Press.

Asia Pacific Gateway and Corridor Initiative. 2009. *National Policy Framework for Strategic Gateways and Trade Corridors*. Government of Canada. http://www.canadasgateways.gc.ca/nationalpolicy.html.

Associated Press. 2012. "Seychelles to Transfer Pirates to Somalia." *FOX News*. March 5. http://www.foxnews.com/world/2012/03/05/seychelles-to-transfer-pirates-to-somalia.

Badiou, Alain. 2002. "Philosophical Considerations of Some Recent Facts." *Theory and Event* 6, no. 2. https://muse.jhu.edu/login?auth=0&type=summary&url=/journals/theory_and_event/v006/6.2badiou.html.

Bady, Aaron. 2011. "Occupy Oakland's Port Shutdown Has Re-energised the Movement." *The Guardian*. December 13. http://www.guardian.co.uk/commentisfree/2011/dec/13/port-blockade-occupy-oakland.

Bahnisch, Mark. 2000. "Embodied Work, Divided Labour: Subjectivity and the Scientific Management of the Body in Frederick W. Taylor's 1907 'Lecture on Management.'" *Body and Society* 6, no. 51: 51–68.

Balibar, Étienne. 2002. *Politics and the Other Scene.* London: Verso.

Ball, Terence. 1979. "Marx and Darwin: A Reconsideration." *Political Theory* 7, no. 4: 469–83.

Ballantine, Duncan S. 1947. *US Naval Logistics in the Second World War.* Princeton, N.J.: Princeton University Press.

Ballou, Ronald H. 2006. "The Evolution and Future of Logistics and Supply Chain Management." *Produção* 16, no. 3: 375–86.

"Bangladesh Port Back to Work after Army Ends Strike." 2010. *Himalayan Times.* October 20. http://www.shippingreporter.com/shipping-news/bangladesh-port -back-to-work-after-army-ends-strike.

Barkawi, Tarak. 2011. "From War to Security: Security Studies, the Wider Agenda, and the Fate of the Study of War." *Millennium: Journal of International Studies*: 1–16.

Barker, Kezia. 2010. "Biosecure Citizenship: Politicising Symbiotic Associations and the Construction of Biological Threat." *Transactions of the Institute of British Geographers* 35:350–63.

Barnard, Bruce. 2011. "Global Container Traffic Hits All Time High." *Journal of Commerce Online.* April 5. http://www.joc.com/maritime/global-container -traffic-hits-all-time-high.

Barnes, Trevor J. 2002. "Performing Economic Geography: Two Men, Two Books, and a Cast of Thousands." *Environment and Planning A* 34:487–512.

———. 2004. "The Rise (and Decline) of American Regional Science: Lessons for the New Economic Geography?" *Journal of Economic Geography* 4:107–29.

Barton, Jonathan. 1999. "Flags of Convenience: Geoeconomics and Regulatory Minimization." *Royal Dutch Geographical Society* 90, no. 2: 142–55.

Beaverstock, Jonathan V., Richard G. Smith, and Peter J. Taylor. 2000. "World City Network: A New Metageography?" *Annals of the Association of American Geographers* 90, no. 1: 123–34.

Bell, Daniel. 1974. *The Coming of Post-Industrial Society: A Venture in Social Forecasting.* London: Heinemann.

Belzer, Michael H. 2000. *Sweatshops on Wheels: Winners and Losers in Trucking Deregulation.* Oxford, UK: Oxford University Press.

Benjamin, Walter. 1978. "Critique of Violence." In *Reflections: Essays, Aphorisms, Autobiographical Writing,* edited by Peter Demetz, 277–300. New York: Schocken.

Bennett, Jane. 2010. *Vibrant Matter: A Political Ecology of Things.* Durham, N.C.: Duke University Press.

Benton, Lauren. 2005. "Legal Spaces of Empire: Piracy and the Origins of Ocean Regionalism." *Comparative Studies in Society and History* 47:700.

———. 2010. *A Search for Sovereignty: Law and Geography in European Empires, 1400–1900.* Cambridge, UK: Cambridge University Press.

Bertalanffy, Ludwig von. 1951. "General System Theory: A New Approach to Unity of Science." *Human Biology* (December): 303–81.

———. 1973. *General System Theory: Foundations, Development, Applications.* Harmondsworth: Penguin.

Bigo, Didier. 2001. "To Reassure, and Protect, after September 11." Brooklyn, N.Y.: Social Science Research Council. http://www.ssrc.org/sept11/essays/bigo .htm.

Blackstone, William. (1755) 1922. *Commentaries on the Laws of England: In Four Books.* Philadelphia: Geo Bisel.

Blank, Stephen. 2006. "North American Trade Corridors: An Initial Exploration." Faculty Working Papers, Paper 50. http://digitalcommons.pace.edu/lubinfaculty _workingpapers/50.

Blank, Stephen, Stephanie R. Golob, and Guy Stanley. 2006. "Staying Alive: North American Competitiveness and the Challenge of Asia." Faculty Working Papers, Paper 55. http://digitalcommons.pace.edu/lubinafaculty_working papers/55.

BMP4. 2011. *Best Management Practices for Protection against Somalia Based Piracy.* Edinburgh: Witherby. https://homeport.uscg.mil/cgi-bin/st/portal/uscg _docs/MyCG/Editorial/20110817/BMP4%20August%202011.pdf?id=dfdc60 1ceae6cc261dbebddc96f8622256185988&user_id=0b2f018ca622dba1b57bc 578e969e0ec.

Bonacich, Edna. 2003. "Pulling the Plug: Labor and the Global Supply." *New Labor Forum* 12, no. 2: 41–48.

———. 2005. "Labor and the Global Logistics Revolution." In *Critical Globalization Studies,* edited by Richard P. Appelbaum and William I. Robinson, 359–68. New York: Routledge.

Bonacich, Edna, and Khaleelah Hardie. 2006. "Wal-Mart and the Logistics Revolution." In *Wal-Mart: The Face of Twenty-First-Century Capitalism,* edited by Nelson Lichtenstein, 163–87. New York: New Press.

Bonacich, Edna, and Jake B. Wilson. 2008. *Getting the Goods: Ports, Labour, and the Logistics Revolution.* New York: Cornell.

Bonner, Robert C. 2002. "Statement by U.S. Customs Commissioner Robert C. Bonner: Hearing on Security at U.S. Seaports." U.S. Senate Committee on Commerce, Science, and Transportation, Charleston, South Carolina, February 19. http://www.cbp.gov/xp/cgov/newsroom/speeches_statements/archives/2002/ feb192002.xml.

Boske, Leigh B. 2006. "Port and Supply-Chain Security Initiatives in the United States and Abroad." Prepared for the Congressional Research Service, Lyndon B. Johnson School of Public Affairs, University of Texas at Austin.

Bowersox, Donald J. 1968. "Emerging Patterns of Physical Distribution Organization." *Transportation and Distribution Management* (May): 55–56.

Boyer, M. Christine. 1986. *Dreaming the Rational City: The Myth of American City Planning.* Cambridge, Mass.: MIT Press.

Bhoyrul, Anil. 2005. "Clinton Leads Dubai Praise." *Arabian Business* (Dubai). December 4. http://www.itp.net/business/news/details.php?id=18919&category=arabianbusiness.

Bradford, Marianne, and Juan Florin. 2003. "Examining the Role of Innovation Diffusion Factors on the Implementation Success of Enterprise Resource Planning Systems." *International Journal of Accounting Information Systems* 4, no. 3: 205–25.

Branch, Alan E. 2008. *Global Supply Chain Management and International Logistics.* New York: Routledge.

Brand, Colin George. 2011. "A Model for the Formulation of Strategic Intent Based on a Comparison of Business and the Military." Research report presented to the Unisa School of Business Leadership, Pretoria, October 10.

Braudel, Fernand. (1979) 1998. *Civilization and Capitalism: 15th–18th Century, vol. 3.* Berkeley: University of California Press.

Braun, Bruce, and Sarah J. Whatmore, eds. 2010. *Political Matter: Technoscience, Democracy, and Public Life.* Minneapolis: University of Minnesota Press.

Braverman, Harry. 1974. *Labor and Monopoly Capital: The Degradation of Work in the Twentieth Century.* New York: Monthly Review Press.

Brenner, Neil, and Roger Keil. 2005. *The Global Cities Reader.* Oxford, UK: Routledge.

Brenner, Neil, and Nick Theodore. 2002. *Spaces of Neoliberalism: Urban Restructuring in North America and Western Europe.* London: Wiley-Blackwell.

Brewer, Stanley H., and James Rosenzweig. 1961. "Rhochrematics and Organizational Adjustments." *California Management Review* 3 (Spring): 52–71.

British Library Map Exhibition. n.d. "An Imperial Capital: Baron Haussmann's Transformation of Paris." MapForum.com. http://www.mapforum.com/15/blmap.htm.

Brooks, Mary R. 2001. "NAFTA and Transportation: A Canadian Scorecard." *Transportation Research Record* 1763:35–41.

Brown, Carol V., and Iris Vessey. 2003. "Managing the Next Wave of Enterprise Systems: Leveraging Lessons from ERP." *MIS Quarterly Executive* 2, no. 1: 45–57.

Brown, Wendy. 2006. "American Nightmare: Neoliberalism, Neoconservatism, and De-democratization." *Political Theory* 34:690–714.

Browning, Douglas. 2003. "Trade Facilitation Policy and New Security Initiatives." In *Sharing the Gains of Globalization in the New Security Environment: The Challenges to Trade Facilitation,* edited by the Economic Commission for Europe, 169–78. New York: United Nations.

Buck-Morss, Susan. 1995. "Envisioning Capital: Political Economy on Display." *Critical Inquiry* 21:434–67.

Bugeaud, Thomas. 2006. "The War of Streets and Houses." *Insecurity* 22. http://cabinetmagazine.org/issues/22/bugeaud.php.

Bumstead, Charles. 2010. "Barbary Coast Revisited: International Maritime Law and Modern Piracy." In *Supply Chain Security: International Practices and Innovations in Moving Goods Safely and Efficiently,* edited by Andrew R. Thomas, 144–58. Santa Barbara, Calif.: Praeger.

Burchell, Graham. 1996. "Liberal Government and Techniques of the Self." In *Foucault and Political Reason: Liberalism, Neoliberalism, and Rationalities of Government,* edited by Andrew Barry, Thomas Osborne, and Nikolas Rose, 19–36. London: University College London Press.

Burghardt, Andrew F. 1971. "A Hypothesis about Gateway Cities." *Annals of the Association of American Geographers* 61, no. 2: 269–85.

Burnson, Patrick. 2012. "Port of Oakland and ProLogis Move Forward on Oakland Army Base Development." Logistics Management. August 28. http://www.logisticsmgmt.com/article/port_of_oakland_an_prologiis_move_forward_on_oakland_army_base_development.

Busch, Lawrence. 2007. "Performing the Economy, Performing Science: From Neoclassical to Supply Chain Models in the Agrifood Sector." *Economy and Society* 3:437–66.

"Bush Regaled in United Arab Emirates." 2008. *CBS News.* January 14. http://www.cbsnews.com/news/bush-regaled-in-united-arab-emirates.

Buxton, Graham, and Let Lee. 1974. "A Profile of the UK Distribution Executive and His Organizational Responsibilities." *International Journal of Physical Distribution* 5, no. 5: 280–93.

Cafruny, Alan. 1987. *Ruling the Waves: The Political Economy of International Shipping.* Berkeley: University of California Press.

Cahlink, George. 2003. "Logistics Lessons." *Government Executive* 35, no. 13: 61–65.

Callon, Michael. 1998. *The Laws of the Markets.* Oxford, UK: Blackwell.

Canada Border Services Agency. n.d. "Partners in Protection." http://www.cbsa-asfc.gc.ca/security-securite/pip-pep/menu-eng.html.

Carmody, Pádraig. 2012. *The New Scramble for Africa.* Cambridge, UK: Polity.

Carrico, Jason A. 2006. "Mitigating the Need for a Logistic Pause." Army Command and General Staff Coll. Fort Leavenworth School of Advanced Military Studies. Accession Number: ADA450161.

Carter, Donald Martin. 2010. *Navigating the African Diaspora: The Anthropology of Invisibility.* Minneapolis: University of Minnesota Press.

Cassidy, Robert M. 2008. *Counterinsurgency and the Global War on Terror: Military Culture and Irregular War.* Westport, Conn.: Praeger.

Castells, Manuel, and Peter Hall. 1994. *Technopoles of the World: The Making of Twenty-First-Century Industrial Complexes.* London: Routledge.

Catá Backer, Larry. 2008. "Global Panopticism: States, Corporations, and the Governance Effects of Monitoring Regimes." *Indiana Journal of Global Legal Studies* 15, no. 1: 101–48.

CENTCOM (Central Command). 2008. "Maritime Security Patrol Area to be Established." http://www.cusnc.navy.mil/articles/2008/105.html.

Cesaire, Aimé. (1950) 1972. *Discourse on Colonialism.* Translated by Joan Pinkham. New York: Monthly Review.

Chalk, Peter. 2010. "Piracy off the Horn of Africa: Scope, Dimensions, Causes and Responses." *Brown Journal of World Affairs* 16, no. 11: 89–108.

Chan, Felix T. S. 2003. "Performance Measurement in a Supply Chain." *International Journal of Advanced Manufacturing Technology* 21:534–48.

Chen, Mel. 2012. *Animacies: Biopolitics, Racial Mattering, and Queer Affect.* Durham, N.C.: Duke University Press.

Chestermann, Simon, and Chia Lehnardt. 2007. *From Mercenaries to Market: The Rise of Private Military Companies.* Oxford, UK: Oxford University Press.

Chivers, C. J. 2012. "Seized Pirates in High-Seas Legal Limbo, with No Formula for Trials." *New York Times.* January 27. http://www.nytimes.com/2012/01/28/world/africa/seized-pirates-in-legal-limbo-with-no-formula-for-trials.html?ref=piracyatsea.

Christopher, Martin, and Helen Peck. 2004. "Building the Resilient Supply Chain." *International Journal of Logistics Management* 15, no. 2: 1–14.

Cicero, Marcus Tullius. (44 BC) 1887. *Cicero De Officis: Book III.* Boston: Little, Brown.

Clausewitz, Carl von. (1873) 2007. *On War.* Oxford, UK: Oxford University Press.

Clayton, Anthony. 1986. *The British Empire as a Superpower, 1919–1939.* Athens: University of Georgia Press.

CNN. 2012. "Basra Logistics City." March 1. Television Broadcast.

Cockrell, Cathy. 2010. "Oral History Weaves Story of the Oakland Army Base and Its Profound Region-Wide Impact." *UC Berkeley News Center.* October 4. http://newscenter.berkeley.edu/2010/10/04/oaklandarmybase.

Cole, Teju. 2012. "The White Savior Industrial Complex." *Atlantic.* March 12. http://www.theatlantic.com/international/archive/2012/03/the-white-savior-industrial-complex/254843.

Collier, Stephen J., and Andrew Lakoff. 2007. "On Vital Systems Security." *Anthropology of the Contemporary Research Collaboratory.* http://anthropos-lab.net/collaborations/vital-systems-security/vss-documents.

Combined Maritime Forces. n.d. "CTF-151: Counter-Piracy." http://combinedmaritimeforces.com/ctf-151-counter-piracy.

Converse, Paul. 1954. "The Other Half of Marketing." Presentation at the Twenty-Sixth Boston Conference on Distribution.

Coole, Diana, and Samantha Frost, eds. 2010. *New Materialisms: Ontology, Agency, and Politics.* Durham, N.C.: Duke University Press.

Cooper, Martha C., Douglas M. Lambert, and Janus D. Pagh. 1997. "Supply Chain Management: More than a New Name for Logistics." *International Journal of Logistics Management* 8, no. 1: 1–14.

Cooper, Melinda. 2006. "Preempting Emergence: The Biological Turn in the War on Terror." *Theory, Culture, and Society* 23, no. 4: 113–35.

———. 2008. "Infrastructure and Event—Urbanism and the Accidents of Finance." Presentation at the Center for Place, Culture, and Politics, City University of New York.

Cordingly, David. 1996. *Under the Black Flag: The Romance and the Reality of Life among the Pirates*. New York: Random House.

Cordon, Hector. 2012. "US Coast Guard to Escort Grain Ship against Dockworkers' Protest." World Socialist Website, International Committee of the Fourth International. January 12. http://www.wsws.org/articles/2012/jan2012/dock-j12.shtml.

Corvin, Aaron, and Marissa Harshman. 2011. "Longshore Workers Rally at Downtown Railroad Tracks." *Columbian*. September 7. http://www.longshoreshippingnews.com/2011/09/longshore-workers-rally-at-downtown-vancouver-railroad-tracks.

Coward, Martin. 2008. *Urbicide: The Politics of Urban Destruction*. Oxon, UK: Routledge.

———. 2009. "Network-Centric Violence Critical Infrastructure and the Urbanisation of Security." *Security Dialogue* 40, no. 4/5: 399–418.

Cowen, Deborah. 2005. "Welfare Warriors: Towards a Genealogy of the Soldier Citizen in Canada." *Antipode* 37, no. 4: 654–78.

———. 2007. "Struggling with 'Security': National Security and Labour in the Ports." *Just Labour: A Canadian Journal of Work and Society* 10:30–44.

———. 2008. *Military Workfare: The Soldier and Social Citizenship in Canada*. Toronto: University of Toronto Press.

———. 2009. "Containing Insecurity: US Port Cities and the 'War on Terror.'" In *Disrupted Cities: When Infrastructure Fails*, edited by S. Graham, 69–84. New York: Routledge.

———. 2010. "A Geography of Logistics: Market Authority and the Security of Supply Chains." *Annals of the Association of American Geographers* 100, no. 3: 1–21.

Cowen, Deborah, and Emily Gilbert, eds. 2008. *War, Citizenship, Territory*. New York: Routledge.

Cowen, Deborah, and Neil Smith. 2009. "After Geopolitics? From the Geopolitical Social to Geoeconomics." *Antipode* 41:22–48.

Cox, Robert W. 1993. "Production and Security." In *Building a New Global Order: Emerging Trends in International Security*, edited by David Dewitt, David Haglund, and John Kirton, 141–58. Toronto: Oxford University Press.

Coyle, John J., and Edward J. Bardi. 1976. *The Management of Business Logistics*. Boston: West.

Crainic, Teodor Gabriel. 2006. "City Logistics." NSERC Industrial Research Chair in Logistics Management. http://www.chairecrsnglogistique.uqam.ca/pdf/city logistics06.pdf.

Crainic, Teodor Gabriel, and Benoît Montreuil. 2012. "ITS for City Logistics and the Physical Internet." ITS Society of Canada, ACGM Quebec, June 10–13. http://www.itscanada.ca/files/Reports/4%20MPF%20CVO%20CityLogistics -PhInternet-ITS_Canada2012.pdf.

CRS (Congressional Research Service). 2002. "Homeland Security Office: Issues and Options." Foreign Affairs, Defense and Trade Division. http://www.fas .org/irp/crs/RL31421.pdf.

———. 2005. "Border and Transportation Security: The Complexity of the Challenge." Domestic Social Policy Division. http://www.fas.org/sgp/crs/homesec/ RL32839.pdf.

———. 2009. "Security and Prosperity Partnership of North America: An Overview and Selected Issues." http://www.fas.org/sgp/crs/row/RS22701.pdf.

Crumlin, Paddy. n.d. "Health and Safety." International Transport Federation. http://www.itfglobal.org/dockers/health.cfm.

Crupi, Anthony. 2010a. "Honda Tries 'Geo' Targeting." AdWeek. June 2. http:// www.adweek.com/news/advertising-branding/honda-tries-geo-targeting-102490.

———. 2010b. "Exclusive: Nat Geo Wraps Mega-Deal with UPS." AdWeek. October 18. http://www.adweek.com/news/television/exclusive-nat-geo-wraps -mega-deal-ups-116346.

Cutshell, Richard B. 1985. "Our Changing Times." Handling and Shipping Management (May): 7.

Dalby, Simon. 1999. "Against Globalization from Above: Critical Geopolitics and the World Order Models Project." Environment and Planning D: Society and Space 17, no. 2: 181–200.

Darwin, Charles. (1859) 1996. The Origin of the Species. Oxford, UK: Oxford University Press.

Davidson, Sharon M., and Amy B. Rummel. 2000. "Retail Changes and Walmart's Entry into Maine." International Journal of Retail and Distribution Management 28, no. 4/5: 162–69.

Davis, Grant M., and Stephen W. Brown. 1974. Logistics Management. Lexington, Mass.: D. C. Heath.

Davis, Grant M., and Joseph Rosenberg. 1974. "Physical Distribution Management: A Collage of 1973 Observations." Transportation Journal 13, no. 4: 50–56.

Davoudi, Simon, and Libby Porter. 2012. "Resilience: A Bridging Concept or a Dead End?" Planning Theory & Practice 13, no. 2: 299–307.

Dawson, John. 2000. "Retailing at Century End: Some Challenges for Management and Research." International Review of Retail, Distribution, and Consumer Research 10, no. 2: 119–48.

Dawson, John, Roy Larke, and Masao Mukoyama. 2006. *Strategic Issues in International Retailing.* New York: Routledge.

DefenceWeb. 2011. "Private Navy to Protect Convoys." November 10. http://www.defenceweb.co.za/index.php?option=com_content&view=article&id=20 969:private-navy-to-protect-convoys&catid=51:Sea&Itemid=106.

DeHayes, Daniel W., Jr., and Robert L. Taylor. 1974. "Moving Beyond the Physical Distribution Organization." *Transportation Journal* 13, no. 3 (Spring): 30.

De Landa, Manuel. 1991. *War in the Age of Intelligent Machines.* New York: Zone.

———. 2005. "Beyond the Problematic of Legitimacy: Military Influences on Civilian Society." *Boundary 2* 32, no. 1: 117–28.

Deleuze, Gilles. 1980. "Lecture on Spinoza." December 12. *Cours de Vincennes 1980–1981.* http://www.gold.ac.uk/media/deleuze_spinoza_affect.pdf.

Deleuze, Gilles, and Félix Guattari. 2009. "Capitalism: A Very Special Delerium." In *Felix Guattari Chaosophy: Texts and Interviews,* edited by Sylvè Lotringer, 35–52. Los Angeles: Semiotext(e).

Deloitte. 2011. *Logistics and Infrastructure: Exploring Opportunities.* http://www.deloitte.com/assets/Dcom-India/Local%20Assets/Documents/aLogistics%20and%20infrastructure%206%20Aug.pdf.

DeMello, Chanelcherie. 2011. "A New Dawn for Basra Logistics City." *Blackanthem Military News.* January 10. http://www.blackanthem.com/News/newdawn/A-new-dawn-for-Basra-Logistics-City23168.shtml.

Dempsey, Judy. 2012. "Taking on Somalia's Pirates on Land." *Strategic Europe.* April 12. http://carnegieeurope.eu/strategiceurope/?fa=show&id=47821.

DeParle, Jason. 2007. "Fearful of Restive Foreign Labor, Dubai Eyes Reforms." *New York Times.* August 6. http://www.nytimes.com/2007/08/06/world/middleeast/06dubai.html?_r=0.

DHL. n.d. "Solutions for Tomorrow's Megacities." http://dsi.dhl-innovation.com/en/aboutus/projects/focusprojects/city.

DHS (Department of Homeland Security). 2007. "Strategy to Enhance International Supply Chain Security." http://www.dhs.gov/xprevprot/publications/gc 1184857664313.shtm.

———. 2009. "Secure Borders, Safe Travel, Legal Trade: U.S. Customs and Border Protection Fiscal Year 2009–2014 Strategic Plan." http://www.cbp.gov/linkhandler/cgov/about/mission/strategic_plan_09_14.ctt/strategic_plan_09_14.pdf.

———. 2012. "National Strategy for Global Supply Chain Security." https://www.hsdl.org/?view&did=698202.

Dicken, Peter. 2003. *Global Shift: Reshaping the Global Economic Map in the 21st Century.* New York: Guilford.

Dickens, Mark. 2010. "UPS's New Ad Campaign Explains Why Everyone Should Love Logistics." *Upside: The UPS Blog.* September 13. http://blog.ups.com/2010/09/13/upss-new-ad-campaign-explains-why-everyone-should-love-logistics.

"DLC to Build New Labor Village." 2006. *Gulfnews.* April 2. http://m.gulfnews .com/dlc-to-build-new-labour-village-1.231300.

Downey, Gregory J. 2002. *Telegraph Messenger Boys: Labor, Technology, and Ge-ography, 1850–1950.* New York: Routledge.

DP World. n.d. "Hinterland." http://www.dpworld.ae/en/content.aspx?P=PB2ke %2fQITcirK8Movga67Q%3d%3d&mid=mLF114FrgMKSas7eQ7kGLw% 3d%3d.

Drucker, Peter F. 1962. "Big Business and the National Purpose." *Harvard Busi-ness Review.* March–April, 49–59.

———. 1969. "Physical Distribution: The Frontier of Modern Management." In *Readings in Physical Distribution Management,* edited by Donald J. Bower-sox, Bernard J. LaLonde, and Edward W. Smykay, 3–8. New York: Collier MacMillan.

———. 1973. *Management: Tasks, Responsibilities, Practices.* New York: Harper and Row.

"Dubai Company Gives Up on Ports Deal." 2009. *CBS News*/Associated Press. Feb-ruary 11. http://www.cbsnews.com/stories/2006/03/09/politics/main1385030 .shtml.

"Dubai FDI, DHL Launch Fully Automated DHL Service Point 24/7 in Dubai as Part of City Logistics Partnership." 2011. *PR Newswire.* http://www.prnews wire.co.uk/news-releases/dubai-fdi-dhl-launch-fully-automated-dhl-service -point-247-in-dubai-as-part-of-city-logistics-partnership-145328425.html.

Duclos, Leslie K., Robert J. Vokurka, and Rhonda R. Lummus. 2003. "A Con-ceptual Model of Supply Chain Flexibility." *Industrial Management and Data Systems* 103, no. 6: 446–56.

Duffield, Mark. 2007. *Development, Security, and Unending Warfare.* Cambridge, UK: Polity.

———. 2008. "Global Civil War: The Non-Insured, International Containment, and Post-Interventionary Society." *Journal of Refugee Studies* 21, no. 2: 145–65.

———. 2011. "Total War as Environmental Terror: Linking Liberalism, Resilience and the Bunker." *South Atlantic Quarterly* 110:770–79.

Duggan, Lisa. 2003. "The New Politics of Homonormativity: The Sexual Politics of Neoliberalism." In *Materializing Democracy: Toward a Revitalized Cultural Politics,* edited by Russ Castronovo and Dana D. Nelson, 175–93. Durham, N.C.: Duke University Press.

Dwyer, John B. 2006. "Facts after the Fact on the Dubai Ports Deal." *Ameri-can Thinker.* March 10. http://www.americanthinker.com/blog/2006/03/facts _after_the_fact_on_the_du.html.

Dyckhoff, Harald, Richard Lackes, and Joachim Reese. 2004. *Supply Chain Man-agement and Reverse Logistics.* Berlin: Springer.

Easterling, Keller. 1999. *Organization Space.* Cambridge, Mass.: MIT Press.

Economist. 2006. "The Physical Internet." June 15. http://www.economist.com/node/7032165.

Edelstein, Dan. 2009. *The Terror of Natural Right: Republicanism, the Cult of Nature, and the French Revolution.* Chicago: University of Chicago Press.

Elden, Stuart. 2001. *Mapping the Present: Heidegger, Foucault, and the Project of a Spatial History.* London: Continuum.

———. 2007. "Governmentality, Calculation, Territory." *Environment and Planning D: Society and Space* 25:562–80.

———. 2009. *Terror and Territory. The Spatial Extent of Sovereignty.* Minneapolis: University of Minnesota Press.

———. 2013. "V Is for Visibility." *Interstitial Journal* (March): 1–4.

Ehmke, J. F. 2012. *Integration of Information and Optimization Models for Routing in City Logistics.* International Series in Operations Research & Management Science 177. New York: Springer.

Emsellem, Maurice, Laura Moskowitz, Madeline Neighly, and Jessie Warner. 2009. "A Scorecard on the Post-9/11 Port Worker Background Checks: Model Worker Protections Provide a Lifeline for People of Color, While Major TSA Delays Leave Thousands Jobless during the Recession." National Employment Law Project, New York. http://nelp.3cdn.net/0714d0826f3ecf7a15_70m6i6fwb.pdf.

Engel, Antke. 2010. "Desire for/within Economic Transformation." *E-flux* #17. http://www.e-flux.com/journal/desire-forwithin-economic-transformation.

Engels, Donald W. 1980. *Alexander the Great and the Logistics of the Macedonian Army.* Berkeley: University of California Press.

Enke, Stephen. 1958. "An Economist Looks at Air Force Logistics." *Review of Economics and Statistics* 40, no. 3: 230–39.

Ethington, Philip J. 2007. "Placing the Past: 'Groundwork' for a Spatial Theory of History." *Rethinking History* 11, no. 4: 465–94.

"EU Forces in Anti-Piracy Raid on Somali Mainland." 2012. *Guardian.* May 12. http://www.guardian.co.uk/world/2012/may/15/eu-anti-piracy-raid-somalia.

Evans, Brad, and Michael Hardt. 2010. "Barbarians to Savages: Liberal War Inside and Out." *Theory and Event* 13, no. 3, http://dx.doi.org/10.1353/tae.2010.0013.

Everett, H. R., and Douglas W. Gage. 1999. "From Laboratory to Warehouse: Security Robots Meet the Real World." *International Journal of Robotics Research, Special Issue on Field and Service Robotics* 18, no. 7: 760–68.

Faiola, Anthony. 2010. "China Buys up 'Bargain-Basement' Greece and Extends Its Global Reach." *Guardian Weekly.* June 18, 9.

Fattah, Hassan M., and Eric Lipton. 2006. "Gaps in Security Stretch from Model Port in Dubai to U.S." *New York Times.* February 26. http://www.nytimes.com/2006/02/26/national/26port.html?_r=0.

Fernandes, Cedwyn, and Gwendolyn Rodrigues. 2009. "Dubai's Potential as an Integrated Logistics Hub." *Journal of Applied Business Research* 25, no. 3: 77–92.

Festa, Lynn. 2006. *Sentimental Figures of Empire in Eighteenth-Century Britain and France.* Baltimore: Johns Hopkins University Press.

Fisher, G. H. 1956. "Weapon System Cost Analysis." *Operations Research* 56, no. 4: 558–71.

Fishman, Charles. 2006. *The Walmart Effect.* New York: Penguin.

Flynn, Stephen E. 2002. "Constructing a Secure Trade Corridor." Paper presented at the Council on Foreign Relations, New York, March 11. http://www.cfr.org/defensehomeland-security/constructing-secure-trade-corridor/p5442.

———. 2003. "The False Conundrum: Continental Integration versus Homeland Security." In *Rebordering North America,* edited by Peter Andreas and Thomas J. Biersteker, 110–27. London: Routledge.

———. 2006. *The Edge of Disaster: Catastrophic Storms, Terror, and American Recklessness.* New York: Random House.

Foucault, Michel. 1977. *Discipline and Punish: The Birth of the Prison.* Translated by A. Sheridan. New York: Vintage.

———. 1978. *The History of Sexuality.* New York: Pantheon.

———. 1980. *Power/Knowledge: Selected Interviews and Other Writings, 1972–1977.* New York: Knopf.

———. (1997) 2003. *Society Must Be Defended: Lectures at the College de France.* New York: Picador.

———. 2007. *Security, Territory, Population: Lectures at the College de France.* New York: Palgrave Macmillan.

Franklin, Sarah, Celia Lury, and Jackie Stacey. 2000. *Global Nature, Global Culture.* London: Sage.

Freeman, Elizabeth. 2007. "Still After." *South Atlantic Quarterly* 106, no. 3 (Summer): 27–33.

Friedman, Milton. 2002. *Capitalism and Freedom.* Chicago: University of Chicago Press.

Friedman, Thomas L. 2000. *The Lexus and the Olive Tree: Understanding Globalization.* New York: Farrar, Straus, and Giroux.

———. 2006. "Port Controversy Could Widen Racial Chasm." *Deseret News.* February 25. http://www.deseretnews.com/article/635187293/Port-controversy-could-widen-racial-chasm.html.

Gandy, Matthew. 1999. "The Paris Sewers and the Rationalization of Urban Space." *Transactions of the Institute of British Geographers, New Series* 24, no. 1: 23–44.

Gavouneli, Maria. 2007. *Functional Jurisdiction in the Law of the Sea.* Leiden: Martinoff Nijhoff.

Geisler, Murray A. 1960. "Logistics Research and Management Science." *Management Science* 6, no. 4: 444–54.

Gentili, Alberico. 1589. *De Jure Belli Commentationes Tres.* London: Apud Iohannem Wolfium.

Georgi, Christoph, Inga-Lena Darkow, and Herbert Kotzab. 2010. "The Intellectual Foundation of the Journal of Business Logistics and Its Evolution between 1978 and 2007." *Journal of Business Logistics* 31, no. 2: 63–109.

Gerven, Arthur van. 2012. "Guest Commentary: Beyond Sustainability to Supply Chain Resilience." *Logistics Viewpoints.* October 9. http://logisticsviewpoints .com/2012/10/09/guest-commentary-beyond-sustainability-to-supply-chain -resilience.

Gettlemen, Jeffrey. 2012. "Toughening Its Stand, European Union Sends Forces to Strike Somali Pirate Base." *New York Times.* May 15. http://www.nytimes .com/2012/05/16/world/africa/european-forces-strike-pirate-base-in-somalia .html?_r=1&ref=piracyatsea.

GGLC (Global Gateway Logistics City). n.d. "Frequently Asked Questions." http://ggdc.ph/faq.html.

Gibbs, Jack P., and Harley L. Browning. 1966. "The Division of Labor, Technology, and the Organization of Production in Twelve Countries." *American Sociological Review* 31:81–92.

Gibson, John. 2006. "U.S. Ports Should Be Off Limits to Foreign Companies." *Fox News.* February 24. http://www.foxnews.com/story/0,2933,186029,00.html.

Gibson-Graham, J. K. 1996. *The End of Capitalism (as We Knew It): A Feminist Critique of Political Economy.* Oxford, UK: Blackwell.

Giddens, Anthony. 1985. *The Nation-State and Violence.* Berkeley: University of California Press.

Gillen, David, Graham Parsons, Barry Prentice, and Peter Wallis. 2007. "Pacific Crossroads: Canada's Gateways and Corridors." Paper prepared for Canada's Asia-Pacific Gateway and Corridor Initiative, Regina, Winnipeg, and Calgary, May 2007. Transport Canada.

Gindin, Sam, and Leo Panitch. 2012. *The Making of Global Capitalism.* New York: Verso.

Glassman, Jim. 2011. "The Geo-Political Economy of Global Production Networks." *Geography Compass* 5, no. 4: 154–64.

Globerman, Steven, and Paul Storer. 2009. "The Effects of 9/11 on Canadian-U.S. Trade: An Update through 2008." Brookings Institute. http://www.brookings .edu/papers/2009/0713_canada_globerman.aspx.

Goralski, Robert, and Russell W. Freeburg. 1987. *Oil and War.* New York: William Morrow.

Gordon, Avery F. 2008. *Ghostly Matters: Haunting and the Sociological Imagination.* Minneapolis: University of Minnesota Press.

Gordon, Katherine. 2010. "Landmark Land Settlement: No Reservations." *Canadian Geographic*. April. http://www.canadiangeographic.ca/magazine/apr08/indepth.

Goss, Thomas. 2006. "Who's in Charge? New Challenges in Homeland Defense and Homeland Security." *Homeland Security Affairs* 2:1–12. http://www.hsaj.org/pages/volume2/issue1/pdfs/2.1.2.pdf.

Grabski, Severin V., and Stewart A. Leech. 2007. "Complementary Controls and ERP Implementation Success." *International Journal of Accounting Information Systems* 8, no. 1: 17–39.

Graham, Ben. 2008. "The Roots of Business Process Mapping." *BPT Trends*. June. http://www.nqi.ca/en/knowledge-centre/articles/process-mapping-the-roots-and-weeds-of.

Graham, Stephen. 2003. "Lessons in Urbicide." *New Left Review* 19:63–77.

———. 2004. *Cities, War, and Terrorism: Towards an Urban Geopolitics*. Oxford, UK: Blackwell.

———. 2006. "Cities and the 'War on Terror.'" *International Journal of Urban and Regional Research* 30, no. 2: 255–76.

———. 2010. *Cities under Siege: The New Military Urbanism*. New York: Verso.

Graham, Stephen, and Martin Shaw, eds. 2008. *Cities, War, and Terrorism: Towards an Urban Geopolitics*. Malden, Mass.: Blackwell.

Gramsci, Antonio. 1985. *Selections from the Prison Notebooks*. New York: International.

Greenpeace. 2010. "The Toxic Ships: The Italian Hub, the Mediterranean Area, and Africa." http://www.greenpeace.org/italy/Global/italy/report/2010/inquinamento/Report-The-toxic-ship.pdf.

Gregory, Derek. 1994. *Geographical Imaginations*. London: John Wiley and Sons.

Gregory, Derek, and Allan Pred. 2007. *Violent Geographies: Fear, Terror, and Political Violence*. New York: Routledge.

Gregory, Todd. 2009. *Rough Trade*. Johnsonville, N.Y.: Bold Strokes.

Griggers, Camilla. 1997. *Becoming Woman*. Minneapolis: University of Minnesota Press.

Grosz, Elizabeth. 2005. *Time Travels: Feminism, Nature, Power*. Durham, N.C.: Duke University Press.

———. 2011. *Becoming Undone: Darwinian Reflections on Life, Politics, and Art*. Durham, N.C.: Duke University Press.

Guled, Abdi. 2012. "EU Navy, Helicopters Strike Pirate Supply Center." *Jakarta Post*. May 16. http://www.thejakartapost.com/news/2012/05/16/eu-navy-helicopters-strike-pirate-supply-center.html.

Gupta, Akhil, and James Ferguson. 1992. "Beyond Culture: Space, Identity, and the Politics of Difference." *Cultural Anthropology* 7, no. 1: 6–23.

Haghighian, Natascha Sadr, and Ashley Hunt. 2007. "Representations of the Erased." *16 Beaver Group*. http://www.16beavergroup.org/ashley/ahunt_3.pdf.

Hall, Peter V. 2007. "Seaports, Urban Sustainability, and Paradigm Shift." *Journal of Urban Technology* 14, no. 2: 87–101.

Halley, Janet, and Andrew Parker, eds. 2011. *After Sex? Writing Since Queer Theory.* Durham, N.C.: Duke University Press.

Hallinan, Conn. 2011. "The New Scramble for Africa." *Foreign Policy in Focus.* September 14. http://www.fpif.org/articles/the_new_scramble_for_africa.

Hamel, Gary, and Liisa Välikangas. 2003. "The Quest for Resilience." *Harvard Business Review.* September, 1–15.

Hammond, Debora. 2002. "Exploring the Genealogy of Systems Thinking." *Systems Research and Behavioural Science* 19, no. 5: 429–39.

Hands off Somalia. 2012. "EU Bombs Somalia—First Reports." May 15. http://handsoffsomalia.co.uk/2012/05/15/eu-bombs-somalia-first-reports.

Haraway, Donna. 1989. *Primate Visions: Gender, and Nature in the World of Modern Science.* New York: Routledge.

———. 1992. "The Promises of Monsters: A Regenerative Politics for Inappropriate/d Others." In *Cultural Studies*, edited by Lawrence Grossberg, Cary Nelson, and Paula A. Treichler, 295–337. New York: Routledge.

———. 1997. *Modest_Witness@Second_Millenium: Femaleman_Meets_Oncomouse.* New York: Routledge.

Hardt, Michael, and Antonio Negri. 2000. *Empire.* Cambridge, Mass.: Harvard University Press.

———. 2004. *Multitude: War and Democracy in the Age of Empire.* New York: Penguin.

Harland, C. M. 2005. "Supply Chain Management: Relationships, Chains, and Networks." *British Journal of Management* 7, no. 1: S63–S80.

Harley, J. Brian. 1988. "Maps, Knowledge, and Power." In *The Iconography of Landscape: Essays on the Symbolic Representation, Design, and Use of Past Environments*, edited by D. Cosgrove and S. Daniels, 277–312. Cambridge, UK: Cambridge University Press.

———. 1989. "Deconstructing the Map." *Cartographica* 26:1–20.

Harlow, Barbara, and Mia Carter. 2003. *Archives of Empire: Volume 1; From the East India Company to the Suez Canal.* Durham, N.C.: Duke University Press.

Harrod, Jeffrey, and Robert O'Brien, eds. 2002. *Global Unions? Theory and Strategies of Organized Labour in the Global Political Economy.* London: Routledge.

Hartman, Sabine. 2012. "DHL Marks the Start of a Unique Logistics Project in China." *Deutsche Post DHL.* July 24. http://www.dp-dhl.com/en/media_relations/press_releases/2012/dhl_marks_start_unique_city_logistics_project_china.html.

Harvey, David. 1973. *Social Justice and the City.* London: Edward Arnold.

———. 1989. *The Condition of Postmodernity: An Enquiry into the Origins of Cultural Change.* Cambridge, Mass.: Blackwell.

———. 2003. *Paris, Capital of Modernity.* New York: Routledge.

———. 2010. *A Companion to Marx' Capital*. London: Verso.

Haskett, J. L., R. Ivie, and N. Glaskowsky. 1964. *Business Logistics*. New York: Ronald.

Hassan, Mohamed. 2010. "Somalia: How Colonial Powers Drove a Country into Chaos (Interview)." *Investig'Action*. http://www.michelcollon.info/Somalia -How-Colonial-Powers-drove.html?lang=fr.

Haveman, Jon D., Ethan M. Jennings, Howard J. Shatz, and Greg C. Wright. 2007. "The Container Security Initiative and Ocean Container Threats." *Journal of Homeland Security and Emergency Management* 4, no. 1.

Haveman, Jon D., and Howard J. Shatz, eds. 2006. *Protecting the Nation's Seaports: Balancing Security and Cost*. San Francisco: Public Policy Institute of California.

Hawthorne, Daniel. 1948. *For Want of a Nail: The Influence of Logistics on War*. New York: Whittlesey House, McGraw-Hill.

Heaver, Trevor. 2007. "Tying It All Together: The Challenges of Integration in and through Gateways." Paper prepared for Canada's Asia-Pacific Gateway and Corridor Initiative, Vancouver, May 2–4. Transport Canada.

Hegseth, Pete. 2013. "GAO Report: Government Spending Is 'Unsustainable.'" Concerned Veterans for America. January 23. http://concernedveteransforamerica.org/2013/01/23/gao-report-government-spending-is-unsustainable.

Heinemann, Guy, and Donald Moss. 1969–70. "Federal Labor Law and the Foreign Flagged Vessel—An Inversion of the Doctrine of Preemptive Jurisdiction." *Journal of Maritime Law and Commerce* 1, no. 3: 415–42.

Heller-Roazen, Daniel. 2009. *The Enemy of All: Piracy and the Law of Nations*. New York: Zone.

Hernandez, Tony. 2003. "The Impact of Big Box Internationalization on a National Market: A Case Study of Home Depot Inc. in Canada." *International Review of Retail and Consumer Research* 13, no. 1: 77–98.

Heskett, James L. 1977. "Logistics—Essential to Strategy." *Harvard Business Review*. November–December, 85–96.

Hesse, Harmut, and Nicolaos L. Charalambous. 2004. "New Security Measures for the International Shipping Community." *WMU Journal of Maritime Affairs* 3, no. 2: 123–38.

Hesse, Markus. 2008. *The City as a Terminal: The Urban Context of Logistics and Freight Transport*. Hampshire, UK: Ashgate.

———. 2010. "Cities, Material Flows, and the Geography of Spatial Interaction: Urban Places in the System of Chains." *Global Networks* 10, no. 1: 75–91.

Hesse, Markus, and Jean-Paul Rodrigue. 2004. "The Transport Geography of Logistics and Freight Distribution." *Journal of Transport Geography* 12:171–84.

———. 2006. "Global Production Networks and the Role of Logistics and Transportation." *Growth and Change: A Journal of Urban and Regional Policy* 37, no. 4: 499–509.

Heyman, Jack. 2012. "A Class Struggle Critique: The ILWU Longshore Struggle in Longview and Beyond." *Counter Punch*. August 10–12 weekend edition. http://www.counterpunch.org/2012/08/10/the-ilwu-longshore-struggle-in-longview-and-beyond.

Higgins, Vaughan, and Wendy Larner, eds. 2010. *Calculating the Social: Standards and the Reconfiguration of Governing*. Basingstoke, UK: Palgrave Macmillan.

Hino, Hisato, Satoshi Hoshino, Tomoharu Fujisawa, Shigehisa Maruyama, and Jun Ota. 2009. "Improvement of Efficiency of Transportation in Harbor Physical Distribution Considering Inland Carriage." *Journal of Mechanical Systems for Transportation and Logistics* 2, no. 2: 145–56.

Hirschfeld Davis, Julie, and Laura Sullivan. 2004. "Abuse Incident Foreshadowed Abu Ghraib." *Baltimore Sun*. May 14. http://www.baltimoresun.com/news/bal-te.prisoner14may14,0,7589545.story.

Holan, Angie Drobnic. 2010. "Halliburton, KBR, and Iraq War Contracting: A History So Far." *Tampa Bay Times Polifact*. http://www.politifact.com/truth-o-meter/statements/2010/jun/09/arianna-huffington/halliburton-kbr-and-iraq-war-contracting-history-s.

Holzgrefe, J. L., and Robert Keohane. 2003. *Humanitarian Intervention: Ethical, Legal, and Political Dilemmas*. Cambridge, UK: Cambridge University Press.

Houlihan, John B. 1987. "International Supply Chain Management." *International Journal of Physical Distribution and Logistics Management* 17, no. 2: 51–66.

HSE (Health and Safety Executive). 2012. "Annual Statistics Report 2011/12." http://www.hse.gov.uk.

Huxley, Margo. 2006. "Spatial Rationalities: Order, Environment, Evolution, and Government." *Social and Cultural Geography* 7, no. 5: 771–87.

———. 2007. "Geographies of Governmentality." In *Space, Knowledge, and Power: Foucault and Geography*, edited by Jeremy W. Crampton and Stuart Elden, 185–204. Hampshire, UK: Ashgate.

IBRD (International Bank for Reconstruction and Development/World Bank). 2009. *Supply Chain Security Guide*. http://siteresources.worldbank.org/INTPRAL/Resources/SCS_Guide_Final.pdf.

ICS (International Chamber of Shipping). 2008. "Joint Statement: Response to Somali Pirates Inadequate Says International Shipping Industry." International Transport Federation. September 29. http://www.itfglobal.org/press-area/index.cfm/pressdetail/2624.

IGI (Idea Group Inc.). 2010. *Enterprise Information Systems: Concepts, Methodologies, Tools, and Applications*. 3 volumes. Google E-book.

IMB (International Maritime Bureau). 2009. "Report of the Secretary-General Pursuant to Security Council Resolution 1846." United Nations Security Council, March 16 (S/2009/146).

IMO (International Marine Organization). 2004. "ISPS Code and Maritime Security." http://www.imo.org/dynamic/mainframe.asp?topic_id=897.

———. 2009a. "Piracy and Armed Robbery against Ships in Waters off the Coast of Somalia." http://www.imo.org/OurWork/Security/SecDocs/Documents/Piracy/SN.1-Circ.281.pdf.

———. 2009b. "Protection of Vital Shipping Lanes: Sub-Regional Meeting to Conclude Agreements on Maritime Security, Piracy, and Armed Robbery against Ships for States from the Western Indian Ocean, Gulf of Aden, and Red Seas Areas." Note by the Secretary-General. http://www.imo.org/OurWork/Security/PIU/Documents/DCoC%20English.pdf.

———. 2012. "International Shipping Facts and Figures—Information Resources on Trade, Safety, Security Environment." Maritime Knowledge Centre. http://www.imo.org/KnowledgeCentre/ShipsAndShippingFactsAndFigures/The RoleandImportanceofInternationalShipping/Documents/International%20 Shipping%20-%20Facts%20and%20Figures.pdf.

Infrastructure Canada. 2010. "Groundbreaking for Tsawwassen First Nation Industrial Park." http://www.infrastructure.gc.ca/media/news-nouvelles/2010/20 100621tsawwassen-eng.html.

International Chamber of Commerce (ICC) and International Maritime Bureau (IMB). 2008. "Piracy and Armed Robbery against Ships. Report for the Period 1 January—30 September." http://www.icc-deutschland.de/fileadmin/icc/Meldungen/2013_Q2_IMB_Piracy_Report.pdf.

Intertanko. 2009. "Gulf of Aden Internationally Recommended Transit Corridor & Group Transit Explanation." http://www.intertanko.com/upload/IRTC%20 %20GT%20Explanation%20-%20March%202009%20%282%29.pdf.

InterVISTAS. 2007. Canada's Asia-Pacific Gateway & Corridor: A Strategic Context for Competitive Advantage. Prepared for Transport Canada.

Isenberg, David. 2012. "The Rise of Private Maritime Security Companies." Huffington Post. May 29. http://www.huffingtonpost.com/david-isenberg/private -military-contractors_b_1548523.html.

Isin, Engin F. 2002. Being Political: Genealogies of Citizenship. Minneapolis: University of Minnesota Press.

———. 2004. "The Neurotic Citizen." Citizenship Studies 8, no. 3: 217–35.

———. 2007. "City.State: Critique of Scalar Thought." Citizenship Studies 11, no. 2: 211–28.

———. 2009. "Editorial: The Thinking Citizenship Series." Citizenship Studies 13, no. 1: 1–2.

ITF (International Transport Workers Federation). n.d. "HIV/AIDS Transport Workers Take Action: An ITF Resource Book for Trade Unionists in the Transport Sector." http://www.itfglobal.org/files/extranet/-1/995/HIVMANUAL.pdf.

Jabri, Vivienne. 2007. "Michel Foucault's Analytics of War: The Social, the International, and the Racial." International Political Sociology 1, no. 1: 67–81.

Jacobs, Wouter, and Peter V. Hall. 2007. "What Conditions Supply Chain Strategies of Ports? The Case of Dubai." GeoJournal 68, no. 4: 327–42.

Jaffer, Kamar, ed. 2013. *Investing in Emerging and Frontier Markets*. London: Euromoney.

JAPCC (Joint Air Power Competence Centre). 2011. "NATO Air Transport Capability: An Assessment." http://www.japcc.org/publications/report/Report/20110928_-_NATO_Air_Transport_Capability-An_Assessment.pdf.

Jeffries, Robert S., Jr. 1974. "Distribution Management—Failures and Solutions." *Business Horizons*. April, 58.

Johnson, James, and Donald L. Borger. 1977. "Physical Distribution: Has It Reached Maturity?" *International Journal of Physical Distribution & Logistics Management* 7, no. 5: 283–93.

Johnson, Richard A., Fremont E. Kast, and James E. Rosenzweig. 1964. "Systems Theory and Management." *Management Science* 10, no. 2: 367–84.

Jomini, Antoine-Henri. (1836) 2009. *The Art of War*. Kingston, Ontario: Legacy Books Press Classics.

Kaluza, Pablo, Andrea Kölzsch, Michael T. Gastner, and Bernd Blasius. 2010. "The Complex Network of Global Cargo Ship Movements." *Journal of the Royal Society Interface* 7:1093–103.

Kanngieser, Anja. 2013. "Tracking and Tracing: New Technologies of Governance and the Logistics Industries." *Environment and Planning D: Society and Space* 31, no. 4: 594–610.

Kapiszewski, Andrzej. 2006. "Arab versus Migrant Workers in the GCC Countries." United Nations Expert Group Meeting on International Migration and Development in the Arab Region. Population Division, Department of Economic and Social Affairs. http://www.un.org/esa/population/meetings/EGM_Ittmig_Arab/P02_Kapiszewski.pdf.

Kelty, Christopher M. 2008. *Two Bits: The Cultural Significance of Free Software*. Durham, N.C.: Duke University Press.

Kempe, Michael. 2009. "'Even in the Remotest Corners of the World': Globalized Piracy and International Law, 1500–1900." *Journal of Global History* 5:353–72.

Keyuan, Zou. 2000. "Piracy at Sea and China's Response." *Lloyd's Maritime and Commercial Law Quarterly* 2000:364–82.

———. 2005. *Law of the Sea in East Asia: Issues and Prospects*. Oxon, UK: Routledge.

Khanna, Parag. 2011. "A New World Order." *Vision: Fresh Perspectives from Dubai*. March. http://vision.ae/en/views/opinion/a_new_new_world_order.

Kilcullen, David. 2010. *Counterinsurgency*. New York: Oxford University Press.

———. 2012. "The City as a System: Future Conflict and Urban Resistance." *Fletcher Forum of World Affairs* 36, no. 2: 19–39.

Kim, Miyoung, and Clare Jim. 2011. "Japan Quake Tests Supply Chain from Chips to Ships." *Reuters*. March 14. http://www.reuters.com/article/2011/03/14/us-japan-quake-supplychain-idUSTRE72D1FQ20110314.

Kinsey, Christopher. 2006. *Private Contractors and the Reconstruction of Iraq: Transforming Military Logistics.* New York: Routledge.

Kipfer, Stefan, and Kanishka Goonewardena. 2007. "Colonization and the New Imperialism: On the Meaning of Urbicide Today." *Theory and Event* 10, no. 2: 1–39.

Kirchgaessner, Stephanie. 2006. "U.S. Coast Guard Warned on Dubai Ports Deal." *Financial Times.* February 28. http://www.ft.com/cms/s/0/6defdda2-a7ee-11 da-85bc-0000779e2340.html.

Kirk, Mark. 2011. "Kirk Report: Ending Somali Piracy against American and Allied Shipping." Somalia Report. http://www.somaliareport.com/downloads/kirk.senate.gov_pdfs_KirkReportfinal2.pdf.

Kitchen, Rob, and Martin Dodge. 2007. "Rethinking Maps." *Progress in Human Geography* 31, no. 3: 331–44.

Konstam, Angus. 2008. *Piracy: The Complete History.* Oxford, UK: Osprey.

Kontorovich, Eugene. 2009. "'A Guantanamo on the Sea': The Difficulties of Prosecuting Pirates and Terrorists." *California Law Review* 98:234.

Korzybski, Alfred. 1973. *Science and Sanity: An Introduction to Non-Aristotelian Systems and an Introduction to Non-Aristotelian Systems and General Semantics.* Forest Hills, NY: Institute of General Semantics.

Kostyal, Karen M. 2010. *Great Migrations.* Washington, D.C.: National Geographic.

Krygier, John, and Denis Woods. 2011. *Making Maps, Second Edition.* New York: Guilford.

Lakoff, Andrew. 2007. "From Population to Vital System: National Security and the Changing Object of Public Health." ARC Working Paper, No. 7.

LaLonde, Bernard J. 1994. "Perspectives on Logistics Management." In *The Logistics Handbook,* edited by James F. Robeson and William C. Copacino. New York: Free Press.

LaLonde, Bernard J., John R. Grabner, and James F. Robeson. 1970. "Integrated Distribution Systems: A Management Perspective." *International Journal of Physical Distribution and Logistics Management* 1:43–49.

Lamble, Sarah. 2013. "Queer Necropolitics and the Expanding Carceral State: Interrogating Sexual Investments in Punishment." *Law and Critique* 24, no. 3: 229–53.

Lancaster, Jane B., Hillard S. Kaplan, Kim Hill, and A. Magdalena Hurtado. 2000. "The Evolution of Life History, Intelligence, and Diet among Chimpanzees and Human Foragers." In *Perspectives in Ethology: Evolution, Culture, and Behavior,* vol. 13, edited by François Tonneau and Nicholas S. Thompson, 47–72. New York: Plenum.

Landman, Stephen I. 2009. "Funding for Bin Laden's Avatar: A Proposal for the Regulation of Virtual Hawalas." *William Mitchell Law Review* 25, no. 5: 5159–84.

Larner, Wendy, and David Craig. 2005. "After Neoliberalism? Community Activism and Local Partnerships in Aotearoa New Zealand." *Antipode* 37, no. 3: 402–24.

Layer, Brian. 1994. *Contingency Operation Logistics: USTRANSCOM's Role When Less Must Be More; A Monograph.* Fort Leavenworth, Kans.: Transportation Corps School of Advanced Military Studies, United States Army Command and General Staff College.

Leander, Anna. 2010. "The Paradoxical Impunity of Private Military Companies: Authority and the Limits to Legal Accountability." *Security Dialogue* 41, no. 5: 467–90.

Lecavalier, J. 2010. "All Those Numbers: Logistics, Territory, and Walmart." *Design Observer.* http://places.designobserver.com/feature/walmart-logistics/13598.

Lefebvre, Henri. 1984. *Everyday Life in the Modern World.* Piscataway, N.J.: Transaction.

———. 1991. *The Production of Space.* Oxford, UK: Blackwell.

LeKashman, Richard, and John F. Stolle. 1965. "The Total Cost Approach to Distribution." *Business Horizons* (Winter): 33–46.

Lemke, Thomas. 2001. "The Birth of Bio-Politics—Michel Foucault's Lecture at the College de France on Neo-Liberal Governmentality." *Economy and Society* 30, no. 2: 190–207.

Levinson, Marc. 2006. *The Box: How the Shipping Container Made the World Smaller and the World Economy Bigger.* Princeton, N.J.: Princeton University Press.

Lewin, Kurt. 1947. "Frontiers and Group Dynamics: Concept, Method, and Reality in Social Science: Social Equilbria and Social Change." *Human Relations* (June): 5–41.

Lewis, H. T., J. W. Culliton, and J. D. Steel. 1956. *The Role of Air Freight in Physical Distribution.* Boston: Harvard University Press.

Lim, Louisa. 2011. "In Greek Port, Storm Brews over Chinese-Run Labor." *National Public Radio.* June 8. http://www.npr.org/2011/06/08/137035251/in-greek-port-storm-brews-over-chinese-run-labor.

Limbrick, Peter. 2012. "From the Interior: Space, Time, and Queer Discursivity in Kamal Aljafari's *The Roof.*" In *The Cinema of Me: The Self and Subjectivity in First Person Documentary Film,* edited by Alisa Lebow, 96–115. London: Wallflower.

Linebaugh, Peter, and Marcus Rediker. 2001. *The Many-Headed Hydra: Sailors, Slaves, Commoners, and the Hidden History of the Revolutionary Atlantic.* Boston: Beacon.

LMI (Logistics Management Institute). n.d. "LMI History." Accessed September 21, 2012. http://www.lmi.org/About-LMI/History.aspx.

Logan, John R., and Harvey Molotch. 1987. *Urban Fortunes: The Political Economy of Place.* Los Angeles: University of California Press.

"Logistics and Support." 2005. *Joint Force Quarterly,* no. 39, 4th quarter.

Lutz, Catherine A. 2001. *Homefront: A Military City and the American Twentieth Century.* Boston: Beacon.

Lutz, Catherine A., and Jane L. Collins. 1993. *Reading National Geographic.* Chicago: University of Chicago Press.

Lydersen, Kari. 2011. "From Racism to Lung Cancer, Workers Cope with Life in the Logistics Industry." *In These Times.* May 2. http://www.inthesetimes.com/working/entry/7252/from_racism_to_lung_cancer_the_risks_of_the_logistics_industry.

Lynch, Clifford F. 1998. "Leadership in Logistics." *Journal of Business Logistics* 19, no. 2: 342–46.

Lynch, Gary S. 2009. *Single Point of Failure: The 10 Essential Laws of Supply Chain Risk Management.* Hoboken, N.J.: John Wiley and Sons.

Mabert, Vincent A., Ashok Soni, and M. A. Venkataramanan. 2001. "Enterprise Resource Planning: Common Myths versus Evolving Reality." *Business Horizons.* May–June. http://mis.postech.ac.kr/class/MEIE680_AdvMIS/Advanced-Papers/Pack3/Enterprise%20resource%20planning-common%20myths%20versus%20evolving%20reality.pdf.

Maccagnan, Victor, Jr. 2004. *Logistics Transformation: Restarting a Stalled Process.* Darby, Penn.: Diane.

MacDonald, James M., and Linda C. Cavalluzzo. 1996. "Railroad Deregulation: Pricing Reforms, Shipper Responses, and the Effects on Labor." *Industrial and Labor Relations Review* 50:80–91.

MacDonald, John R. 2008. "Supply Chain Disruption Management: A Conceptual Framework and Theoretical Model." PhD diss., University of Maryland.

Mackey, Robert. 2011. "Updates on Day 15 of Egypt Protests." *New York Times.* February 8. http://thelede.blogs.nytimes.com/2011/02/08/latest-updates-on-day-15-of-egypt-protests/?src=twt&twt=thelede#strikes-reported-at-suez-canal-and-across-egypt.

MacNeil, Rachel. 2008. "Tsawwassen Land Treaty." *Canadian Geographic.* April. http://www.canadiangeographic.ca/magazine/apr08/feature_tsawwassen2.asp.

Makillie, Paul. 2006. "The Physical Internet." *Economist.* June 15. http://www.economist.com/node/7032165.

Mangan, John, Chandra Lalwani, and Tim Butcher. 2008. *Global Logistics and Supply Chain Management.* London: John Wiley and Sons.

Mann, Michael. 1988. *States, War, and Capitalism: Studies in Political Sociology.* Oxford, UK: Basil Blackwell.

Manthorpe, Jonathan. 2012. "Manthorpe: Armed Guards on Merchant Ships Deter Pirates, but Raise Legal Concerns." *The Vancouver Sun.* July 17.

http://www.vancouversun.com/news/Manthorpe+Armed+guards+merchant+ships+deter+pirates+raise/6949256/story.html.

Maritime Union of Australia. 2005. "Inquiry into the Maritime Transport Security Amendment Act 2005 and Regulations." Union submission to Senate Rural and Regional Affairs and Transport Legislation Committee.

Markusen, Ann, Peter Hall, Scott Campbell, and Sabina Deitrick. 1991. *The Rise of the Gunbelt: The Military Remapping of Industrial America*. New York: Oxford University Press.

Marmon, William. 2011. "Merchant Ships Starting to Carry Armed Guards against Somali Pirates." *European Institute*. November. http://www.european institute.org/November-2011/merchant-ships-start-to-carry-armed-guards-against-somali-pirates-1122.html.

Martin, Mary. 2011. "Longshore Workers Prepare for Long Fight: Battle Union Busting at Washington Port." *The Militant* 75, no. 44. http://www.themilitant.com/2011/7544/754402.html.

Marx, Karl. 1867. *Capital, Volume I*. Translated by Ben Fowkes. London: Penguin Classics.

———. (1887) 1993. *Capital, Volume II: A Critique of Political Economy*. Translated by David Ferbach. London: Penguin Classics.

———. (1939) 2005. *Grundisse: Foundations of the Critique of Political Economy*. London: Penguin Classics.

Massey, Doreen. 1977. "A Global Sense of Place." In *Reading Human Geography: The Poetics and Politics of Inquiry*, edited by Trevor Barnes and Derek Gregory, 315–23. London: Arnold.

———. 2005. *For Space*. London: Sage.

Mbembe, Achille. 2003. "Necropolitics." *Public Culture* 15, no. 1: 11–40.

McBride, Sarah. 2012. "Oakland Leaders Urge Broad Battle with Goldman Sachs." *Reuters*. July 31. http://www.reuters.com/article/2012/08/01/us-gold man-swaps-oakland-idUSBRE86U1Q920120801.

McClintock, Anne. 1993. "Maid to Order: Commercial Fetishism and Gender Power." *Social Text* 37:87–116.

McConnell, Daniel, Richard A. Hardemon, and Larry C. Ransburgh. 2010. "The Logistics Constant throughout the Ages." *Air Force Journal of Logistics* 34, no. 3: 82–88.

McCune, Joseph T., Richard W. Beatty, and Raymond V. Montagno. 2006. "Downsizing: Practices in Manufacturing Firms." *Human Resource Management* 27, no. 2: 145–61.

McDowell, Linda. 1999. *Gender, Identity, and Place: Understanding Feminist Geographies*. Minneapolis: University of Minnesota Press.

McEllrath, Robert. 2011. "TWIC Fails to Protect Our Port, and Workers Pay the Price." ILWU.org. June 1. http://www.ilwu.org/?p=2535.

———. 2012. "Prepare to Take Action When EGT Vessel Arrives." ILWU.org. January 3. http://www.ilwu.org/?p=3378.

McNeil, Maureen. 2010. "Post-Millennial Feminist Theory: Encounters with Humanism, Materialism, Critique, Nature, Biology, and Darwin." *Journal for Cultural Research* 14, no. 4: 427–39.

McWhorter, Ladelle. 2010. *Racism and Sexual Oppression in Anglo-America: A Genealogy.* Bloomington: Indiana University Press.

Melman, Seymour. 1974. *The Permanent War Economy: American Capitalism in Decline.* New York: Simon and Schuster.

Meyer, J. R. 1959. *The Economics of Competition in the Transportation Industries.* Cambridge, Mass.: Harvard University Press.

Mignolo, Walter D., and Madina V. Tlostanova. 2006. "Theorizing from the Borders: Shifting to Geo- and Body-Politics of Knowledge." *European Journal of Social Theory* 9:205–21.

Miller, Matt. 2012. "The Logic of Logistics." *Deal Pipeline.* November 30. http://www.thedeal.com/content/industrials/the-logic-of-logistics.php#ixzz2Ij96sGYJ.

Miller Davis, Grant. 1974. *Logistics Management.* Lexington, Mass.: D. C. Heath.

Mitchell, Don. 1996. *The Lie of the Land: Migrant Workers and the California Landscape.* Minneapolis: University of Minnesota Press.

Mitchell, Timothy. 2002. *Rule of Experts: Egypt, Techno-politics, Modernity.* Los Angeles: University of California Press.

———. 2005. "The Work of Economics: How a Discipline Makes Its World." *European Journal of Sociology* 46:297–320.

Mitman, Gregg. 1999. *Reel Nature: America's Romance with Wildlife on Film.* Boston: Harvard University Press.

Mohanty, Chandra Talpade. 2011. "Imperial Democracies, Militarised Zones, Feminist Engagements." *Economic and Political Weekly* 46, no. 13. http://www.epw.in/reflections-empire/imperial-democracies-militarised-zones-feminist-engagements.html.

Mollenkopf, John H., and Manuel Castells, eds. 1991. *Dual City: Restructuring New York.* New York: Russell Sage Foundation.

Mongelluzzo, Bill. 2012. "CBP Official: Security Partnerships Help Protect International Supply Chains." *Journal of Commerce.* May 14. http://www.joc.com/regulation-policy/transportation-regulations/cbp-official-security-partnerships-help-protect-international-supply-chains_20120514.html.

Moore, Donald S., Jake Kosek, and Anand Pandian. 2003. *Race, Nature, and the Politics of Difference.* Durham, N.C.: Duke University Press.

Moore, James. 2008. "Update on Canada's Asia-Pacific Gateway and Corridor Initiative." Transport Canada. http://www.tc.gc.ca/canadasgateways/apgci/update-august-2008.html.

Morris, Chris. 2011. "Could Chinese Investment Rescue Ailing Greece?" *BBC News.* June 25. http://news.bbc.co.uk/2/hi/programmes/from_our_own _correspondent/9520732.stm.

"A Moving Story: Companies Are Outsourcing Huge Chunks of What They Do to Logistics Companies." 2002. *Economist.* December 5. http://www.economist .com/node/1477544.

MSCHOA (Maritime Security Centre Horn of Africa). n.d. "About Us." http:// www.mschoa.org/on-shore/about-us.

Muñoz, Carlo. 2012. "The Philippines Re-opens Military Bases to US Forces." *DEFCON Hill: The Hill's Defense Blog.* June 6. http://thehill.com/blogs/def con-hill/operations/231257-philippines-re-opens-military-bases-to-us-forces-.

Muñoz, Jose Esteban. 2009. *Cruising Utopia: The Then and There of Queer Futurity.* New York: New York University Press.

Mustain, Andrea. 2010. "Great Migrations Thrill, Shock at NYC Premiere." *Live Science.* http://www.livescience.com/8882-great-migrations-thrill-shock-nyc -premiere.html.

Naim, Mohamed, M. Holweg, and Denis Royston Towill. 2003. "On Systems Thinking, Engineering, and Dynamics—Their Influence on Modern Logistics Management." Logistics and Networked Organisations' Proceedings of the 8th International Symposium on Logistics, Sevilla, July 6–8.

National Geographic. 2010. "Witness Spectacle of Magnificent Animal Journeys around Globe in National Geographic's Epic 'Great Migrations.'" http://press .nationalgeographic.com/2010/11/02/great-migrations-available-dvd-blu-ray.

"NCPDM Meets CLM in St. Louis." 1985. *Handling and Shipping Management* 28. http://business.highbeam.com/438314/article-1G1-4044370/ncpdm-meets -clm-st-louis.

Negrey, Cynthia, Jeffrey L. Osgood, and Frank Goetzke. 2011. "One Package at a Time: The Distributive World City." *International Journal of Urban and Regional Research* 35:812–31.

Neilson, Brett, and Ned Rossiter. 2010. "Still Waiting, Still Moving: On Labour, Logistics, and Maritime Industries." In *Stillness in a Mobile World,* edited by David Bissell and Gillian Fuller, 51–68. New York: Routledge.

Neocleus, Mark. 2000. *The Fabrication of Social Order: A Critical Theory of Police Power.* London: Pluto.

Neuschel, Robert P. 1967. "Physical Distribution—Forgotten Frontier." *Harvard Business Review.* March–April, 125–34.

Newman, David. 2006. "Borders and Bordering: Towards an Interdisciplinary Dialogue." *European Journal of Social Theory* 9:171–86.

Noble, David F. 1977. *America by Design: Science, Technology, and the Rise of Corporate Capitalism.* New York: Knopf.

Nyers, Peter. 2008. "No One Is Illegal between City and Nation." In *Acts of Citizenship*, edited by Engin F. Isin and Greg M. Nielsen, 160–81. London: Zed.

Oberg, Winston. 1972. "Charisma, Commitment, and Contemporary Organization Theory." *ISU Business Topics* (Spring): 18–32.

Odell, Mark. 2011. "Naval Chiefs Warn of Rise in Somali Piracy." *Financial Times*. September 11. http://www.ft.com/intl/cms/s/0/a5c5b6ae-dc84-11e0 -8654-00144feabdc0.html#axzz22sj20Dyt.

Ogilvy & Mather. 2012. "We ♥ Logistics." Effie Awards Showcase. http://current .effie.org/winners/showcase/2012/6520.

Omissi, David E. 1990. *Air Power and Colonial Control: The Royal Air Force, 1919–1939*. New York: Manchester University Press.

Organisation for Economic Co-operation and Development (OECD). 2003. "Security in Maritime Transport: Risk Factors and Economic Impact." http:// www.oecd.org/sti/transport/maritimetransport/18521672.pdf.

Ortega, Bob. 1998. *In Sam We Trust: The Untold Story of Sam Walton and How Walmart Is Devouring America*. New York: Random House.

Oswin, Natalie. 2008. "Critical Geographies and the Uses of Sexuality: Deconstructing Queer Space." *Progress in Human Geography* 32, no. 1: 89–103.

Overby, Peter. 2006. "Lobbyist's Last Minute Bid Set Off Ports Controversy." *National Public Radio*. March 8. http://www.npr.org/templates/story/story .php?storyId=5252263.

OWCW (Open World Conference of Workers). 2002. "ILWU Denounces Taft-Hartley as Anti-union Employer-Government Coalition." http://www.owcinfo .org/campaign/ILWU/ilwu_denounces_taft.htm.

Papayanis, Nicholas. 2004. *Planning Paris before Haussman*. Baltimore: Johns Hopkins University Press.

Parlette, Vanessa, and Deborah Cowen. 2011. "Dead Malls: Suburban Activism, Local Spaces, Global Logistics." *International Journal of Urban and Regional Research* 35, no. 4: 794–811.

Partridge, Damani James. 2011. "Activist Capitalism and Supply-Chain Citizenship: Producing Ethical Regimes and Ready-to-Wear Clothes." *Current Anthropology* 52, no. 3: S97–S111.

Peck, Jamie, and Adam Tickell. 2002. "Neoliberalizing Space." *Antipode* 34, no. 3: 380–404.

Peoples, James. 1998. "Deregulation and the Labor Market." *Journal of Economic Perspectives* 12, no. 3: 111–30.

Peoples, James, and Lisa Saunders. 1993. "Trucking Deregulation and the Black/ White Wage Gap." *Industrial and Labor Relations Review* 47, no. 1: 23–35.

Perotin-Dumon, Anne. 1991. "The Pirate and the Emperor: Power and the Law on the Seas, 1450–1850." In *The Political Economy of Merchant Empires*, edited by James D. Tracy. Cambridge, UK: Cambridge University Press.

"Peter King: Dubai Ports Company in 'al-Qaida Heartland.'" 2006. *Newsmax.com*. February 20. http://archive.newsmax.com/archives/ic/2006/2/20/120409.shtml.

Peters, Ralph. 1995. "After the Revolution." *Parameters* 25:11–14.

Petraeus, David. 2006. "Learning Counterinsurgency: Observations from Soldiering in Iraq." *Military Review*. January–February. http://www.army.mil/ professionalWriting/volumes/volume4/april_2006/4_06_2.html.

Pettit, Timothy J., Joseph Fiskel, and Keely L. Croxton. 2010. "Ensuring Supply Chain Resilience: Development of a Conceptual Framework." *Journal of Business Logistics* 31, no. 1: 1–21.

Pickles, John. 2004. *A History of Spaces: Cartographic Reason, Mapping, and the Geo-coded World*. London: Routledge.

Plant, Jeremy F. 2002. "Railroad Policy and Intermodalism: Policy Choices after Deregulation." *Review of Policy Research* 19, no. 2:13–32.

Plehwe, Dieter, Bernhard J. A. Walpen, and Gisela Neunhöffer. 2006. *Neoliberal Hegemony: A Global Critique*. New York: Routledge.

PMAESA (Port Management Association of Eastern and Southern Africa). 2008a. *e-PMAESA Newsletter: A Publication of the PMAESA Secretariat*. October 16. http://www.pmaesa.org/media/newsletter/2008/newsletter16_october_08.pdf.

———. 2008b. *Our Ports: Official Publication of the Port Management Association of Eastern and Southern Africa* 1, no. 4. http://www.pmaesa.org/media/ magazine/pmaesa_our_ports4.pdf.

———. 2008c. "IMO Talks Action on Piracy." *Our Ports* 5, no. 2: 6–7.

Poier, Salvatore. 2009. "Hostis Humani Generis: History of a Multi-faceted Word." *Darkmatter: In the Ruins of Imperial Culture*. December 20. http:// www.darkmatter101.org/site/2009/12/20/hostis-humani-generis-history-of-a-multi-faceted-word.

Poist, Richard F. 1986. "Evolution of Conceptual Approaches to Designing Business Logistics Systems." *Transportation Journal* 26, no. 1: 55–64.

Poist, Richard F., and Peter M. Lynagh. 1976. "Job Satisfaction and the P. D. Manager: An Empirical Assessment." *Transportation Journal* 16, no. 1: 45–50.

Pollard, Jane S., and James D. Sidaway. 2002. "Nostalgia for the Future: The Geoeconomics and Geopolitics of the Euro." *Transactions of the Institute of British Geographers* 27, no. 4: 518–21.

P&O Nedlloyd Logistics. 2004. "Knowing and Managing Your Supply Chain." Business Briefing: Global Purchasing and Supply Chain Strategies, 1–17.

Port of Oakland. 2011. "Oakland's Working Waterfront: TIGER III Funding Application Project Narrative." http://www.portofoakland.com/pdf/TIGER _application.PDF.

———. 2012. "City and Port of Oakland Achieve Significant Milestone in Former Oakland Army Base Redevelopment." http://www.portofoakland.com/news room/pressrel/view.asp?id=279.

Potter, Brian. 2007. "Constricting Contestation, Coalitions, and Purpose: The Causes of Neoliberal Restructuring and Its Failures." *Latin American Perspectives* 34, no. 3: 3–24.

Povinelli, Elizabeth. 2007. "Disturbing Sexuality." *South Atlantic Quarterly* 106, no. 3: 565–76.

Province of British Columbia. 2013. Tsawwassen First Nation Final Agreement Act. SBC 2007, Chapter 39.

Pryer, Douglas A. 2009. *The Fight for Higher Ground: The U.S. Army and Interrogation during Operation Iraqi Freedom May 2003–April 2004.* Fort Leavenworth, Kans.: Command and General Staff College Foundation.

Puar, Jasbir K. 2005. "Queer Times, Queer Assemblages." *Social Text* 23, nos. 3–4, 85–84 (Fall–Winter): 121–40.

———. 2007. *Terrorist Assemblages: Homonationalism in Queer Times.* Durham, N.C.: Duke University Press.

PwC (PricewaterhouseCoopers). 2011. "Securing the Supply Chain: Transportation and Logistics 2030, Volume 4." http://download.pwc.com/ie/pubs/2011_transportation_and_logistics_2030_volume4_securing_the_supply_chain.pdf.

Radicella, Lucas. 2012. "Panama: Canal Workers Declare Strike after Colleague's Death." *Argentina Independent.* November 23. http://www.argentina independent.com/currentaffairs/newsfromlatinamerica/panama-canal-workers -declare-strike-after-colleagues-death.

Rainey, James C., Cindy Young, and Roger D. Golden, eds. 2009. "Selected Readings: Thinking about Logistics." *Air Force Journal of Logistics* 33 (July): 50–79.

Ramadan, Adam. 2009. "Destroying Nahr el-Bared: Sovereignty and Urbicide in the Space of Exception." *Political Geography* 28:153–63.

RAND. 2004. "Evaluating the Security of the Global Containerized Supply Chain: Infrastructure, Safety, and Environment Series." http://www.rand.org/pubs/technical_reports/TR214.

———. 2009. "Film Piracy, Organized Crime, and Terrorism." http://www.rand .org/content/dam/rand/pubs/monographs/2009/RAND_MG742.pdf.

Rasmussen, Claire, and Michael Brown. 2002. "Radical Democracy: Amidst Political Theory and Geography." In *Handbook of Citizenship Studies,* edited by Engin F. Isin and Bryan S. Turner, 294–327. London: Sage.

———. 2005. "Reviving a Dead Metaphor: The Body of Politics and Citizenship." *Citizenship Studies* 9, no. 5: 469–84.

Razack, Sherene H. 2004. *Dark Threats and White Knights: The Somalia Affair, Peacekeeping, and the New Imperialism.* Toronto: University of Toronto Press.

Rediker, Marcus. 2004. *Villains of All Nations: Atlantic Pirates in the Golden Age.* Boston: Beacon.

Reid, Julian. 2006. "This Is Your Logistical Life." Metamute. http://www.meta mute.org/editorial/articles/your-logistical-life.

Reifer, Thomas. 2004. "Labor, Race, and Empire: Transport Workers and Transnational Empires of Trade, Production, and Finance." In *Labor versus Empire: Race, Gender, and Migration*, edited by Gilbert G. Gonzalez, Raul A. Fernandez, Vivian Price, David Smith, and Linda Trinh Võ, 17–36. London: Routledge.

———. 2011. "Unlocking the Black Box of Globalization." Unpublished paper, available from author.

Rice, James B., Jr., and Federico Caniato. 2003. "Supply Chain Response to Terrorism: Creating Resilient and Secure Supply Chains." Supply Chain Response to Terrorism Project, Interim Report of Progress and Learnings, MIT Center for Transportation and Logistics. August 8. http://web.mit.edu/scresponse/repository/SC_Resp_Report_Interim_Final_8803.pdf.

Rice, James B., Jr., and Yossi Sheffi. 2005. "A Supply Chain View of the Resilient Enterprise." *MIT Sloan Management Review* 47, no. 1: 41–48.

Robins, Martin E., and Anne Strauss-Wieder. 2006. "Principles for a U.S. Public Freight Agenda in the Global Economy." The Brookings Institution Series on Transportation Reform. http://www.brookings.edu/research/reports/2006/01/01transportation-robins.

Rodrigue, Jean-Paul, Claude Comtois, and Brian Slack. 2009. *The Geography of Transport Systems*. New York: Routledge.

Rodrigue, Jean-Paul, and Laetitia Dablanc. 2013. "City Logistics." In *UN-Habitat, 2013 Global Report on Human Settlements: Sustainable Urban Transport*, edited by the United Nations Human Settlements Programme, 2–15. London: Earthscan. http://unhabitat.org/planning-and-design-for-sustainable-urban-mobility-global-report-on-human-settlements-2013.

Rodrigue, Jean-Paul, and Theo Notteboom. 2009. "The Geography of Containerization: Half a Century of Revolution, Adaptation, and Diffusion." *GeoJournal* 74, no. 1: 1–5.

Rohar, Evan. 2011a. "Suez Canal Strike Could Rattle Egypt's Regime." *LINKS: International Journal of Socialist Renewal*. February 10. http://links.org.au/node/2155.

———. 2011b. "Longshore Workers Thresh Grain Shipper, Block Train." *Labor Notes*. July 21. http://labornotes.org/blogs/2011/07/longshore-workers-thresh-grain-shipper-block-train.

Roloff, James. 2003. "Lessons Learned from Operation Enduring Freedom: CCO Handbook. Year in Review: Generating Solutions Today, Shaping Tomorrow's Logistics." Air Force Logistics Management Agency (AFLMA).

Rose, Nikolas. 1989. *Governing the Soul: The Shaping of the Private Self*. London: Routledge.

———. 1996. "The Death of the Social? Refiguring the Territory of Government." *Economy and Society* 25, no. 3: 327–56.

Ross, Kristin. 1988. *The Emergence of Social Space*. Minneapolis: University of Minnesota Press.

Roth, Jonathan P. 1999. *The Logistics of the Roman Army at War (264 B.C.–A.D. 235)*. Boston: Brill.

Rothenberg, Tamar Y. 2007. *Presenting America's World: Strategies of Innocence in National Geographic Magazine, 1988–1945*. Burlington: Ashgate.

Russell, Bertrand. 1938. "On the Importance of Logical Form." In *International Encyclopedia of Unified Science*. Chicago: University of Chicago Press.

Said, Edward W. 1979. *Orientalism*. New York: Knopf Doubleday.

Salopek, Paul. 2008. "Off the Lawless Coast of Somalia, Questions of Who Is Pirating Who." *Chicago Tribune*. October 10. http://articles.chicagotribune.com/2008-10-10/news/0810090770_1_somalia-ground-for-industrial-waste-pirates.

Salter, Mark. 2004. "Passports, Mobility, and Security: How Smart Can the Border Be?" *International Studies Perspectives* 5:71–91.

Sandilands, Catriona, and Bruce Erickson, eds. 2010. *Queer Ecologies: Sex, Nature, Politics, and Desire*. Bloomington: Indiana University Press.

Sanger, David F., and Eric Lipton. 2006. "Bush Threatens to Veto Any Bill to Stop Port Takeover." *New York Times*. February 21. http://www.nytimes.com/2006/02/21/politics/21cnd-port.html?_r=0.

Sarni, V. A. 1973a. "A Management Perspective: The Next Decade." *Transportation and Distribution Management*. December, 24.

———. 1973b. "PD in the Near Future." *Proceedings of the National Council of Physical Distribution*: 47.

Sassen, Saskia. 1991. *The Global City: New York, London, Tokyo*. Princeton, N.J.: Princeton University Press.

———. 2006. *Territory, Authority, Rights: From Medieval to Global Assemblages*. Princeton, N.J.: Princeton University Press.

———. 2008. "Neither Global nor National: Novel Assemblages of Territory, Authority and Rights." *Ethics & Global Politics* 1, no. 1: 61–79.

———. 2013. "When Territory Deborders Territoriality." *Territory, Politics, Governance* 1, no. 1: 21–45.

Schary, Philip B., and Boris W. Becker. 1973. "The Marketing/Logistics Interface." *International Journal of Physical Distribution and Logistics Management* 3, no. 4: 246–88.

Sekula, Alan, and Noël Burch. 2011. "The Forgotten Space." *New Left Review* 69. http://newleftreview.org/II/69/allan-sekula-noel-burch-the-forgotten-space.

Sharman, Graham. 1991. "Good Logistics Is Combat Power (Interview with Lt. Gen. William Pagonis; Role of Logistics in the 1991 Persian Gulf War)." *The McKinsey Quarterly*. June 22, 3.

Shaw, Martin. 2004. "New Wars of the City: Relationships of 'Urbicide' and 'Genocide.'" In *Cities, War, and Terrorism: Towards an Urban Geopolitics*, edited by Stephen Graham, 141–53. Oxford, UK: Blackwell.

Sheffi, Yossi. 2006. "Resilience Reduces Risk." *Logistics Quarterly* 12, no. 1: 12–15.

———. 2007. *The Resilient Enterprise: Overcoming Vulnerability for Competitive Advantage.* Cambridge, Mass.: MIT Press.

Sheller, Mimi. 2011. "Mobilities." *Sociopedia.isa.* http://www.sagepub.net/isa/resources/pdf/Mobility.pdf.

Sheller, Mimi, and John Urry. 2006. "The New Mobilities Paradigm." *Environment and Planning A* 38, no. 2: 207–26.

Sheppard, Eric. 2002. "The Spaces and Times of Globalization: Place, Scale, Networks, and Positionality." *Economic Geography* 78, no. 3: 307–30.

Shirley, R. C. 1974. "A Model for Analysis of Organizational Change." *MSU Business Topics* (Spring): 60–68.

Shoenberger, Erica. 2008. "The Origins of the Market Economy: State Power, Territorial Control, and Modes of War Fighting." *Comparative Studies in Society and History* 50, no. 3: 663–91.

SIGIR (Special Inspector General for Iraq Reconstruction). 2010. "Applying Iraq's Hard Lessons to the Reform of Stabilization and Reconstruction Operations." http://www.sigir.mil/applyinghardlessons/index.html.

Skipper, Joseph B., Christopher W. Craighead, Terry Anthony Byrd, and R. Kelly Rainer. 2008. "Towards a Theoretical Foundation of Supply Network Interdependence and Technology-Enabled Coordination Strategies." *International Journal of Physical Distribution and Logistics Management* 38, no. 1: 39–56.

Smith, David. 2009. "World Cup Rapper K'Naan Defends Somali Pirates." *Guardian.* December 6. http://www.guardian.co.uk/world/2009/dec/06/world-cup-rapper-defends-somali-pirates.

Smith, Neil. 1980. "Symptomatic Silence in Althusser: The Concept of Nature and the Unity of Science." *Science and Society* 44, no. 1: 58–81.

———. 1984. *Uneven Development: Nature, Capital, and the Production of Space.* Oxford, UK: Basil Blackwell.

———. 2004. *American Empire: Roosevelt's Geographer and the Prelude to Globalization.* Berkeley: University of California Press.

———. 2005. *The Endgame of Globalization.* London: Routledge.

Smith, Neil, and C. Katz. 1993. "Grounding Metaphor." In *Place and the Politics of Identity,* edited by Michael Keith and Steve Pile, 67–84. London: Routledge.

Smith, Richard G. 2005. "Networking the City." *Geography* 90, no. 2: 172–76.

Smykay, Edward W. 1961. *Physical Distribution Management: Logistics Problems of the Firm.* London: Macmillan.

Smykay, Edward W., and Bernard LaLonde. 1967. *Physical Distribution: The New and Profitable Science of Business Logistics.* Chicago: Dartnell.

Soja, Edward. 1989. *Postmodern Geographies: The Reassertion of Space in Critical Social Theory.* London: Verso.

"Somali Piracy: Armed Guards to Protect UK Ships." 2011. *BBC News.* October 30. http://www.bbc.co.uk/news/uk-15510467.

Sparke, Matthew. 1998. "From Geopolitics to Geoeconomics: Transnational State Effects in the Borderlands." *Geopolitics* 3, no. 2: 61–97.

———. 2000. "Excavating the Future in Cascadia: Geoeconomics and the Imagined Geographies of a Cross-Border Region." *BC Studies* 127:5–44.

———. 2004. "Belonging in the PACE Lane: Fast Border Crossing and Citizenship in the Age of Neoliberalism." In *Boundaries and Belonging: States and Societies in the Struggle to Shape Identities and Local Practices*, edited by Joel S. Migdal, 251–83. Cambridge, UK: Cambridge University Press.

———. 2006. "A Neoliberal Nexus: Citizenship, Security and the Future of the Border." *Political Geography* 25, no. 2: 151–80.

Sparke, Matthew, Sue Roberts, and Anna Secor. 2003. "Neoliberal Geopolitics." *Antipode* 35, no. 5: 886–97.

Sparr, Pamela, ed. 1994. *Mortgaging Women's Lives: Feminist Critiques of Structural Adjustment Programs*. London: Zed.

Spector, Robert. 2005. *Category Killers: The Retail Revolution and Its Impact on Consumer Culture*. Boston: Harvard Business School Press.

Spencer, Frank. 1967. "The United States and Germany in the Aftermath of War I: 1918–1929." *International Affairs* 43, no. 4: 693–703.

Starr, Randy, Jim Newfrock, and Michael Delurey. 2003. "Enterprise Resilience: Managing Risk in the Networked Economy." *Strategy and Business* 30:1–12.

Stasiulis, Daiva, and Darryl Ross. 2006. "Security, Flexible Sovereignty, and the Perils of Multiple Citizenship." *Citizenship Studies* 10, no. 3: 329–48.

Steins, Chris. 2006. "Coming Soon: The World's Largest Airport and Logistics City." *Planetizen*. May 9. http://www.planetizen.com/node/19718.

Stenger, Alan J. 1986. "Information Systems in Logistics Management: Past, Present, and Future." *Transportation Journal (American Society of Transportation and Logistics Inc.)* 26, no. 1: 65–82.

Stockbruegger, Jan. 2010. "Somali Piracy and the International Response: Trends in 2009 and Prospects for 2010." *Piracy Studies*. March 6. http://piracy-studies .org/2010/somali-piracy-and-the-international-response-trends-in-2009-and -prospects-for-2010.

Stolle, John F. 1967. "How to Manage Physical Distribution." *Harvard Business Review*. July–August, 93–100.

Strathern, Marilyn. 2002. "Externalities in Comparative Guise." *Economy and Society* 31:250–67.

Su Seol, Kap. 2011a. "Woman Welder Sits in atop Crane to Protest Job Cuts." *Labour Notes*. July 14. http://labornotes.org/blogs/2011/07/video-woman-welder -sits-atop-crane-protest-job-cuts.

———. 2011b. "Korean Sit-In atop Crane Defeats Job Cuts." *Labour Notes*. November 10. http://labornotes.org/blogs/2011/11/korean-sit-atop-crane-defeats -job-cuts.

Sutton, Angela. 2009. "Atlantic Orientalism: How Language in Jefferson's America Defeated the Barbary Pirates." *Darkmatter: In the Ruins of Imperial Culture*. December 20. http://www.darkmatter101.org/site/2009/12/20/atlantic-orientalism-how-language-in-jefferson%E2%80%99s-america-defeated-the-barbary-pirates.

Taniguchi, Eiichi. 2012. "The Future of City Logistics." *Delivering Tomorrow: Dialogue on Future Trends*. October 29. http://www.delivering-tomorrow.com/the-future-of-city-logistics.

Taylor, Frederick. 1911. *Principles of Scientific Management*. New York: Harper and Brothers.

———. 1985. "Scientific Management." In *Organization Theory: Selected Readings*, edited by Derek S. Pugh, 11–27. London: Penguin.

———. 1995. "Report of a Lecture by and Questions Put to Mr F. W. Taylor, a Transcript." *Journal of Management History* 1, no. 1: 8–32.

Thomas, Andrew R., ed. 2010. *Supply Chain Security: International Practices and Innovations in Moving Goods Safely and Efficiently*. Santa Barbara, Calif.: Praeger.

Thomas, Christopher. 2004. "Logistical Limitations of Roman Imperialism in the West." PhD diss., University of Auckland.

Thomson, Janice E. 1994. *Mercenaries, Pirates, and Sovereigns: State-Building and Extraterritorial Violence in Early Modern Europe*. Princeton, N.J.: Princeton University Press.

Thorpe, George C. 1917. *Pure Logistics: The Science of War Preparation*. Kansas City: Franklin Hudson.

Thrift, Nigel. 1996. *Spatial Formations*. Thousand Oaks, Calif.: Sage.

———. 2000. "Performing Cultures in the New Economy." *Annals of the Association of American Geographers* 90:674–92.

———. 2006. "Space." *Theory, Culture, and Society* 23:139–46.

———. 2007. *Non-representational Theory: Space, Politics, Affect*. New York: Routledge.

Tilghman, Andrew. 2008. "Camp Bucca Detainee Abuse Hearing Begins." *Navy Times*. November 11. http://www.navytimes.com/news/2008/11/navy_detainee_abuse_111108w.

Tilly, Charles. 1990. *Coercion, Capital, and European States, AD 990–1990*. Oxford, UK: Basil Blackwell.

Titmuss, Richard. 1958. *Essays on "The Welfare State."* London: Allen and Unwin.

Transport Canada. 2011. *Transportation in Canada 2011: A Comprehensive Review*. Gatineau, Quebec: Minister of Public Works and Government Services.

Trebilcock, Bob. 2012. "Big Picture: 'The State of Automation.'" *Logistics Management*. May. http://www.logisticsmgmt.com/view/big_picture_the_state_of_automation/automation/D2.

Tsing, Anna. 2009. "Beyond Economic and Ecological Standardisation." *Australian Journal of Anthropology* 20, no. 3: 347–68.

Tuan, Yi-Fu. 1977. *Space and Place: The Perspectives of Experience.* Minneapolis: University of Minnesota Press.

Tufts, Steven. 2004. "Building the 'Competitive City': Labour and Toronto's Bid to Host the Olympic Games." *Geoforum* 35:47–58.

Turnbull, David. 1993. *Maps Are Territories: Science Is an Atlas; A Portfolio of Exhibits.* Chicago: University of Chicago Press.

Turse, Nick. 2012. "Tomgram: Nick Turse, America's Shadow Wars in Africa." *TomDispatch.* July 12. http://www.tomdispatch.com/blog/175567/tomgram %3A_nick_turse,_america%27s_shadow_wars_in_africa_.

"TWIC Rules and Regulations." 2007. *Federal Register* 72, no. 16 (January 25): 3492–604.

Tzu, Sun. 1980. *The Art of War.* Translated by S. B. Griffith. Oxford, UK: Oxford University Press.

UAE Interact. 2007. "UAE Yearbook 2007." http://www.uaeinteract.com/uaeint _misc/pdf_2007/English_2007/eyb5.pdf.

UAE Ministry of Labour. 2001. "U.A.E. Labour Law: Federal Law No.(8) of 1980, Labour Law, and Its Amendments." http://www.mol.gov.ae/newcontrol panel2010/Attachments/21062012/labour%20law%20no.8%20year%20 1980.pdf.

UEPI (Urban and Environmental Policy Institute). 2011. "Global Trade Impacts: Addressing the Health, Social, and Environmental Consequences of Moving International Freight through Our Communities." Occidental College/University of Southern California. http://kresge.org/sites/default/files/Global%20 Trade%20Executive%20Summary%203-21.pdf.

U.K. Parliamentary Foreign Affairs Committee. 2011. "Piracy off the Coast of Somalia." http://www.publications.parliament.uk/pa/cm201012/cmselect/cmfaff/ 1318/131806.htm#a4.

UN (United Nations). 1958. "Geneva Conventions on the Law of the Sea." http:// legal.un.org/avl/ha/gclos/gclos.html.

———. 1982. "United Nations Convention on the Law of the Sea." http://www .un.org/depts/los/convention_agreements/convention_overview_convention .htm.

UNCTAD (United Nations Conference on Trade and Development). 2010. "Review of Maritime Transport." http://unctad.org/en/pages/PublicationArchive .aspx?publicationid=1708.

UNECE (United Nations Economic Commission for Europe). 2003. "Sharing the Gains of Globalization in the New Security Environment: The Challenges to Trade Facilitation." http://www.unece.org/forums/forum04/forum_bk_doc4 .html.

UNEP/GRID-Arendal. 2009. "The Boom in Shipping Trade." http://www.grida.no/graphicslib/detail/the-boom-in-shipping-trade_1667.

UN Food and Agricultural Organization. 2005. "FAO Fishery Country Profile—The Somali Republic." http://www.fao.org/fi/oldsite/FCP/en/SOM/profile.htm.

UN Industrial Development Organization. 2009. "Industrial Development Report 2009: Breaking In and Moving Up; New Industrial Challenges for the Bottom Billion and the Middle-Income Countries." http://www.unido.org/fileadmin/user_media/Publications/IDR_2009_print.PDF.

UN Security Council. 2008. "Security Council Authorizes States to Use Land-Based Operations in Somalia, as Part of Fight against Piracy off Coast, Unanimously Adopting 1851." Security Council 6046th Meeting. http://www.un.org/News/Press/docs/2008/sc9541.doc.htm.

———. 2011a. "Report of the Secretary-General on the Protection of Somali Resources and Waters." http://daccess-dds-ny.un.org/doc/UNDOC/GEN/N11/540/51/PDF/N1154051.pdf?OpenElement.

———. 2011b. "Report of the Monitoring Group on Somalia and Eritrea Pursuant to Security Council Resolution 1916 (2010)." http://www.un.org/ga/search/view_doc.asp?symbol=S/2011/433.

———. 2012a. "Human Costs of Piracy off Somalia Coast 'Incalculable,' Full Range of Legal, Preventative Measures Needed to Thwart Attacks, Security Council Told." Security Council 6719th Meeting (AM). http://www.un.org/News/Press/docs/2012/sc10551.doc.htm.

———. 2012b. "Unremitting Piracy off Somalia's Coast Prompts Security Council to Renew 'Authorizations' for International Action for Another Year." Security Council 6867th Meeting (AM). http://www.un.org/News/Press/docs/2012/sc10824.doc.htm.

U.S.-China Business Council. n.d. https://www.uschina.org/reports/us-exports/national-2013.

U.S. Congress (Joint Economic Committee). 1957. *Instrumentation and Automation: Hearings before the Subcommittee on Economic Stabilization of the Joint Economic Committee, Congress of the United States, Eighty-fourth Congress, second session, pursuant to sec. 5 (a) of Public law 304, 79th Congress.* Washington, D.C.: Government Printing Office.

U.S. Department of the Army. 2012. "Army Regulation 700–137: Logistics Civil Augmentation Program." http://www.apd.army.mil/pdffiles/r700_137.pdf.

"US Jail Guards in Iraq Abuse Case." 2008. *BBC News.* August 14. http://news.bbc.co.uk/2/hi/americas/7561952.stm.

USOPM (U.S. Office of Personnel Management). 2009. "Workforce Reshaping Operations Handbook: A Guide for Agency Management and Human Resources Offices." http://www.opm.gov/policy-data-oversight/workforce-restructuring/reductions-in-force/workforce_reshaping.pdf.

U.S. Senate. 2002. "Securing Our Trade Routes: Possible Solutions; Field Hearing before the Subcommittee on Surface Transportation and Merchant Marine." Committee on Commerce, Science, and Transportation. July 1. http://www .gpo.gov/fdsys/pkg/CHRG-107shrg93216/html/CHRG-107shrg93216.htm.

Valencia, Czeriza. 2012. "$3-B Logistics Hub in Clark Operational in 5 Years." *Philippine Star.* March 29. http://www.philstar.com/Article.aspx?publication SubCategoryId=66&articleId=791633.

Valverde, Mariana. 2009. "Jurisdiction and Scale: Legal 'Technicalities' as Resources for Theory." *Social and Legal Studies* 18, no. 2: 139–57.

Van Creveld, Martin. 2004. *Supplying War: Logistics from Wallerstein to Patton.* Cambridge, UK: Cambridge University Press.

Varnelis, Kazys. 2005. "The Centripetal City: Telecommunications, the Internet, and the Shaping of the Modern Urban Environment." *Cabinet Magazine* 17: 27–28.

Vidal, John. 2008. "Shipping Boom Fuels Rising Tide of Global CO2 Emissions." *Guardian.* February 13. http://www.theguardian.com/environment/2008/feb/ 13/climatechange.pollution1.

Villarejo, Amy. 2005. "Tarrying with the Normative: Queer Theory and Black History." *Social Text* 23, nos. 3–4 (Fall–Winter): 69–84.

Viswanadham, N. 2002. "The Past, Present, and Future of Supply-Chain Automation." *Robotics and Automation Magazine, IEEE* 9, no. 2: 48–56.

Von Bertalanfy, Ludwig. 1973. *General System Theory: Foundations, Development, Applications.* New York: Penguin.

Waddell, Steve. 2010. "Canadian Counter Piracy and Counter Terrorism Naval Operations in East Africa and the Indian Ocean." Lecture at York Center for International and Security Studies, Toronto, May 26.

Walker, Charles. 2002a. "Bush Employs Taft-Hartley Act to Intervene in Dock Workers' Struggle." *Socialist Action.* October. http://www.socialistaction.org/ news/200210/taft.html.

———. 2002b. "Union Says Bush Has Dropped Threats, but Dockworkers' Fight Heats Up." *Labor Standard.* October 1. http://www.laborstandard.org/New _Postings/Labor_Tues_Oct1_02.htm.

Walker, Jeremy, and Melinda Cooper. 2011. "Genealogies of Resilience: From Systems Ecology to the Political Economy of Crisis Adaptation." *Security Dialogue* 42, no. 2: 143–60.

Wallach, Evan J. 2005. "The Logical Nexus between the Decision to Deny Application of the Third Geneva Convention to the Taliban and al Qaeda, and the Mistreatment of Prisoners in Abu Ghraib." International Law of War Association. http://lawofwar.org/logical_nexus_between_the_decisi.htm.

Walters, William. 2004. "Secure Borders, Safe Haven, Domopolitics." *Citizenship Studies* 8, no. 3: 237–60.

Wang, Eric T. G., Cathy Chia-Lin Lin, James J. Jiang, and Gary Klein. 2007. "Improving Enterprise Resource Planning (ERP) Fit to Organizational Process through Knowledge Transfer." *International Journal of Information Management* 27, no. 3: 200–212.

Warf, Barney, and Santa Arias. 2008. *The Spatial Turn: Interdisciplinary Perspectives*. New York: Taylor and Francis.

Waters, Donald. 2007. *Supply Chain Risk Management: Vulnerability and Resilience in Logistics*. London: Kogan Page Series.

Weber, Max. 1978. *Economy and Society, Volume 1*. Los Angeles: University of California Press.

Weizman, Eyal. 2006. "The War of Streets and Houses." *Cabinet Magazine*. http://cabinetmagazine.org/issues/22/bugeaud.php.

Whebell, C. F. F. 1969. "Corridors: A Theory of Urban Systems." *Annals of the Association of American Geographers* 59, no. 1: 1–26.

Whiteman, Gail, Bruce C. Forbes, Jari Niemelä, and F. Stuart Chapin III. 2004. "Bringing Feedback and Resilience into the Corporate Boardroom." *Ambio: A Journal of the Human Environment* 33, no. 6: 371–76.

Wildavsky, Aaron. 1966. "The Political Economy of Efficiency: Cost-Benefit Analysis, Systems Analysis, and Program Budgeting." *Public Administration Review* 26, no. 4: 292–310.

Williams, Bertha. 2007. "Letter to Dr. Rodolfo Stavenhagen, Special Rapporteur on the Human Rights and Fundamental Freedoms of Indigenous People of the United Nations: Tsawwassen Traditional Territory." Bill Tieleman (blog). July 24. http://billtieleman.blogspot.ca/2007/07/tsawwassen-first-nations-treaty.html.

Williams, Raymond. 1973. "Base and Superstructure in Marxist Cultural Theory." In *Culture and Materialism*, 31–49. London: Verso.

———. 1977. *Marxism and Literature*. Oxford, UK: Oxford University Press.

———. 2013. *Keywords: A Vocabulary of Culture and Society*. New York: Routledge.

Wilson, Andrew R. 2008. "War and the East." *Orbis* 32, no. 2: 358–71.

Wilson, Patricia A. 1992. *Exports and Local Development: Mexico's New Maquiladoras*. Austin: University of Texas Press.

Woo, Yuen Pau. 2011. "A Leap-Frog Strategy for Relations with Asia." In *The Canada We Want in 2020: Toward a Strategic Policy Roadmap for the Federal Government*, edited by Canada 2020, 42–48. http://www.canada2020.ca/files/canada-we-want-2020-e.pdf.

Wood, Denis. 1992. *The Power of Maps*. New York: Guilford.

———. 2010. *Rethinking the Power of Maps*. New York: Guilford.

WorkSafeBC. 2011. "Statistics 2011." http://www.worksafebc.com/publications/reports/statistics_reports/assets/pdf/stats2011.pdf.

World Shipping Council. n.d. "Trade Statistics." http://www.worldshipping.org/about-the-industry/global-trade/trade-statistics.

Wouters, Patrick. 2008. "The Good, the Bad, and the Ugly of Outsourcing Security to Private Military Companies (PMC)." Royal Higher Institute for Defence. http://www.irsd.be/website/media/Files/these/these01.pdf.

Wright, Richard. 2002. "Transnational Corporations and Global Divisions of Labor." In *Geographies of Global Change: Remapping the World,* edited by Ron Johnston, Peter J. Taylor, and Michael Watts, 68–78. Malden, Mass.: Blackwell.

Wrigley, Neil, and Michelle Lowe. 2002. *Reading Retail: A Geographical Perspective on Retailing and Consumption Spaces.* London: Hodder Arnold.

WSWS (World Socialist Website). 2012. "Workers Struggles: The Americas, Latin America." April 17. http://www.wsws.org/articles/2012/apr2012/wkrs-a17.shtml.

Zhang, Jianlong, Petros Ioannou, and Anastasios Chassiakos. 2006. "Automated Container Transport System between Inland Port and Terminals." *ACM Transactions on Modeling and Computer Simulation (TOMACS)* 16, no. 2: 95–118.

corridors and gateways of, 19,
68; making of, 11; movements
and, 227, 229; natural and sexual
selection and, 16; production of,
4; queer method and, 226; supply chains and, 8–9, 19; territory
and, 10
logistics systems: as biopolitical, 14;
Canadian, 73; infrastructural components, 60; Internet and, 229;
national, 59; process mapping and,
110; security of, 75, 215; social
Darwinism and, 15; speed and reliability of, 55–56; of supply chain
security, 93, 126
Lynch, Clifford, 42

MacDonald, James, 42–43
management science, 5, 6, 25, 204, 218
Manthorpe, Jonathan, 156
mapping: corridors and gateways,
62–65; the IRTC, 153; Paris, 189,
190–91; process, 109–10, 117; purpose of, 18; of spaces, 4, 18–19
Maputo Corridor Logistics Initiative
(MCLI), 65–66
Marine Transport Security Clearance
Program (MTSCP), 119–21
maritime sector: borders, 82–83, 93,
134; labor and unions, 46–47;
policing, 79, 130, 140, 159; security, 119–20, 126, 150–51, 154–57,
159; shipping containers, 44; space,
138, 151, 160, 176. See also piracy
Maritime Union of Australia, 120
Marmon, William, 155, 157
Marx, Karl: on circulation of capital,
11, 93, 100–102; critique of Darwin, 15, 216; on technology and
labor, 113; on value and transportation, 100, 104
materiality, 101, 193, 224

materials management, 24, 104–5
Maurice of Nassau, 106
Mbembe, Achille, 16
McClintock, Anne, 226
McCormick, Lynde, 30
McEllrath, Robert, 119
McKinlay, Alan, 91
McNamara, Robert S., 32–33
McWhorter, Ladelle, 221
Mekong corridor, 67
Melman, Seymour, 6
metaphors, colonial, 50–51
military (U.S.): in Africa, 134; bases,
3, 163, 165, 167–70; container
technologies, 30–31, 40–41, 112;
corporate interest in, 51–52, 185;
intervention in labor conflicts, 115–
16; logistic facilities, 177
military logistics: campaigns and
strategies, 26–30; conceptions of
systems, 217; corporations and, 3,
51–52, 185–86; privatization in,
167, 170, 185; scholarship on, 25–
26; standardization of production
in, 106; urbanism, 186–87. See also
civilian–military relations
Miller Davis, Grant, 31, 35
Mitchell, Don, 195
Mitchell, Timothy, 18
mobility/mobilities: capital, 100, 206;
mapping, 191; physical, 101, 211;
securitization of, 217; study of, 10–
11; urban space and, 184
Moss, Donald, 46
Motor Carrier Act (1980), 43
Murad, Zahra, 129, 145

Naim, Mohamed, 49
Napoleonic wars, 27
national borders: Canada–U.S., 73–75,
78, 86–87; flow of goods across,
53–55; programs, 85–87;

Deborah Cowen is associate professor in the Department of Geography at the University of Toronto. She is the author of *Military Workfare: The Soldier and Social Citizenship in Canada* and coeditor, with Emily Gilbert, of *War, Citizenship, Territory.*